WHY SECRET
INTELLIGENCE FAILS

Other Intelligence Titles from Potomac Books

Who's Watching the Spies? Establishing Intelligence Service Accountability
by Hans Born, Loch K. Johnson, and Ian Leigh

Flawed Patriot: The Rise and Fall of CIA Legend Bill Harvey
by Bayard Stockton

Hide and Seek: Intelligence, Law Enforcement, and the Stalled War on Terrorist Finance
by John A. Cassara

Silent Warfare: Understanding the World of Intelligence, Third Edition
by Abram N. Shulsky and Gary J. Schmitt

Spymaster: My Life in the CIA
by Ted Shackley with Richard A. Finney

The Castro Obsession: U.S. Covert Operations Against Cuba, 1959–1965
by Don Bohning

CIA Inc: Espionage and the Craft of Business Intelligence
by F. W. Rustmann, Jr.

WHY SECRET INTELLIGENCE FAILS

REVISED EDITION

MICHAEL A. TURNER

Potomac Books, Inc.
Washington, D.C.

The author, a former CIA employee, submitted this manuscript to CIA's Publication Review Board, which reviewed it to assist the author in eliminating classified information. The Board poses no security objection to the book's publication. This review, however, should not be construed as official release of information, confirmation of accuracy, or an endorsement of the author's views.

Library of Congress Cataloging-in-Publication Data
Library of Congress CIP Data is available under LCCN : 200612896.

ISBN-10 1-57488-891-9
ISBN-13 978-1-57488-891-1

Printed in Canada on acid-free paper that meets the American National Standards Institute Z39-48 Standard.

Potomac Books, Inc.
22841 Quicksilver Drive
Dulles, Virginia 20166

First Edition

10 9 8 7 6 5 4 3 2 1

Exerpts from the following sources were used throughout the book: Copyright 1990. From "Understanding CIA's Role in Intelligence" by Michael Turner, *International Journal of Intelligence and CounterIntelligence* 4 (1990), 295–305. Reproduced by permission of Taylor & Francis Group, Inc., http://www.routledge-ny.com. Copyright 1996. From "Setting Analytical Priorities in US Intelligence" by Michael Turner, *International Journal of Intelligence and CounterIntelligence* 9 (1996), 313–27. Reproduced by permission of Taylor & Francis Group, Inc., http://www.routledge-ny.com. Copyright 2004. From "A Distinctive U.S. Intelligence Identity" by Michael A. Turner, *International Journal of Intelligence and CounterIntelligence* 17 (2004), 42–61. Reproduced by permission of Taylor & Francis Group, Inc., http://www.routledge-ny.com. Copyright 1991. From "The Role of Intelligence in Crisis Management" in *Avoiding War, Problems of Crisis Management* by Alexander George, ed. Reprinted by permission of Alexander George.

To my son, Fred, for all the love.

Contents

Preface   ix

Acknowledgments   xiii

List of Abbreviations   xv

1   The Uncertainty Principle   1

2   Intelligence, American Style   17

3   Pitfalls of American-Style Intelligence   43

4   The Foreign Experience   59

5   Requirements and Priorities   72

6   Perils of Intelligence Collection   88

7   Analytic Snafus   107

8   Getting Intelligence to the Right People   124

9   Contributing Factors   132

10   Intelligence Priorities and Their Challenges   152

11   Toward Smarter Intelligence   172

Notes   189

Glossary   220

Bibliography   229

Index   245

About the Author   254

Preface

Why did I write this book? I wrote it because it was the right time to do so. Unfortunately, intelligence officials and policymakers often ignore, or at least downplay, intelligence failures. Yet, intelligence that goes awry affects national decision making and, ultimately, American national security.

Little is known about the causes of intelligence failures, in part because intelligence officials and their policy consumers are reluctant to talk about them. There is a saying in the U.S. intelligence community that the media and the public trumpet intelligence failures while ignoring intelligence successes. This would be true if the public knew as much about intelligence successes as it does about intelligence failures. However, the public does not know, largely because intelligence officials are reluctant to talk about intelligence successes—often claiming, "the secret of our success is the secret of our success." These people also shy away from talking about failures because doing so would expose the failings of American intelligence and have an impact on policy consumers, who may become more reluctant to accept and act on the intelligence they receive. This, in turn, has consequences for the U.S. intelligence community, the legitimacy and funding of which depends, at least, on the appearance of making a difference in national decision making. There is no doubt that intelligence provides benefits to national policy making, and doing so efficiently requires coping with the problems associated with intelligence failures. Dealing with the phenomenon of intelligence failures, in turn, requires an understanding of their causes. This book is a modest try at filling this gap.

I also have several basic motives for writing this book. One is that I had long wanted to write about the inner workings of

American intelligence, a subject that historically has been shrouded in secrecy and given short shrift in books about American government and national security. I joined the Central Intelligence Agency (CIA) in the 1970s as a political analyst, focusing on the countries bordering the Aegean Sea. Analytic work is important to the task of intelligence, but analysts often are mired in the minutiae of their specific accounts—regions, countries, or issues—and frequently pay little or no attention to the broader context in which their analytic work takes place. As I moved up the career ladder, however, I had the opportunity to serve as a public affairs officer for the CIA, during which I had occasion to study intelligence in general and the CIA in particular, and to expound my views publicly about them. In the process, I discovered that the root causes of American intelligence failures were to be found in the intelligence process. This stark conclusion meant having to take stock of the intelligence cycle itself, and I figured that writing a book like this would serve the dual purposes of providing a primer on U.S. intelligence while identifying those areas within the intelligence process that served to instigate failures.

I thought that this was a story worth telling, but the early 1990s were not the right time to tell it. At the time, global politics were undergoing dramatic change, and U.S. intelligence agencies were again on the defensive, trying to explain the Iran-Contra debacle and the failure to forecast the end of the Cold War. Intelligence leaders were also nervous about whether and how American intelligence would survive in the wake of the disappearance of the principal threat to the United States—the Soviet Union and its allies—and the ensuing "peace dividend." Pundits and the public probably would have perceived any book coming out about intelligence failures during this time as decidedly self-serving, smacking of chicanery.

The decade of the 1990s was an interesting time for American intelligence. The euphoria over the end of the Cold War soon gave way to the realization that the world had become more, not less, complex and that U.S. intelligence would be at the forefront of a new national security agenda comprising rogue states, failed states, ethnic cleansing, international terrorism, transnational crimes, environmental degradation, and a host of other issues. The decade witnessed intelligence debacles in Somalia, Bosnia, and Kosovo, and over the Indian nuclear tests and the various terrorist attacks on American interests in Africa and the Middle East.

In short, the 1990s provided more fodder for reflection on and study of intelligence failures. It was the terrorist attacks of 11 September 2001, however, that galvanized me into action, convincing me that this was a propitious time to put pen to paper and write about intelligence failures. I realized soon after the attacks that there would be a great public outcry against intelligence debacles, accompanied by official and nonofficial investigations. The lack of success in finding weapons of mass destruction in Iraq—the George W. Bush administration had justified the 2003 war on the grounds that intelligence clearly indicated that Saddam Hussein possessed and intended to use them—suggested that the topic would be in the public spotlight for some time to come. I thought I would enter the fray with a book about the general phenomenon, without focusing on any specific and identifiable instance of intelligence failure.

Another reason why I wrote the book was to explain my own successes and failures in the intelligence business. As a political analyst in the CIA, I spent many years trying to identify threats to the country and forecast developments in foreign nations with foreign policy consequences for the U.S. government. I believe I was good at political analysis, and I earned many plaudits and awards for doing my job well. Along with my many successes, however, came several notable failures, a situation that baffled me, because, try as I might, I could discern little difference between what made for success and what sparked failure. This conundrum got me thinking about studying the causes of failures in American intelligence—hence the book.

I am fortunate to have been a practitioner of the craft of intelligence. I spent a big chunk of my adult life in intelligence, and I learned much about the intricacies of intelligence collection, analysis, production, and dissemination, to which the public is rarely, if ever, exposed. I also have had the privilege of studying the complexities of American intelligence as a scholar, an outsider. The two perspectives—of the insider and the outsider—have given me a complete picture of the workings of U.S. intelligence.

What follows, then, is a distillation of many years of work and study. American intelligence is a vast, complex, and expensive enterprise, with tremendous strengths and distinctive flaws. This book focuses mainly on the flaws, in large measure because they are the harbingers of failure. Identifying the root causes, however, does not guarantee remedial actions or future success. The frustrating part in writing a book like this is having to conclude that there is really little that can be done about intelligence failures, because their root causes are firmly embedded in the intelligence process itself. Corrective actions can only serve to streamline the process. The best one can hope for is to minimize the chances of intelligence failures by employing America's considerable intelligence resources to collect timely and relevant intelligence information, and for national leaders to employ that intelligence in the making of wise and sound policy.

Acknowledgments

I would like to thank the many people who supported my decision to write this book. I am grateful to Margaret Billy, whose encouragement sustained me through the difficult drafting process and who read and commented on the manuscripts. Many thanks also to Dr. William Perry, whose incisive and cogent remarks greatly improved the drafts. My gratitude goes to Richard R. Valcourt, the editor in chief of the *International Journal of Intelligence and CounterIntelligence*, for his advice on the publishing process.

Many officials of the U.S. government talked to me over the years about the intelligence process and intelligence failures in particular. Some prefer to remain anonymous; others have consented to the use of their names. Regardless, they all helped me enormously in coming to grips with this difficult issue, and I would like to express my heartfelt thanks to all of them.

In addition, many nonofficial and official published sources made enormous contributions to the content of this book. The reports of the Congressional Joint Intelligence Inquiry into what the U.S. government knew about the events of 9/ 11 and the many committee prints of the two congressional intelligence oversight committees were particularly useful. Furthermore, I made heavy use of the publications of the Central Intelligence Agency, a pioneer in the study of intelligence failures, including the superb articles in *Studies in Intelligence* and the occasional papers of the Sherman Kent Center. I also adapted portions of the glossary from the CIA's *A Consumer's Guide to Intelligence*, a publication the agency distributes to intelligence consumers in the U.S. government.

This book would have been incalculably more difficult to write without these excellent sources.

Although I have used information imparted to me by many individuals and numerous documentary sources in the preparation of this book, only I am responsible for its contents, including any errors, misinterpretations, and misjudgments.

Abbreviations

ACIS	Arms Control Intelligence Staff
Aman	Israel's military intelligence
BNDD	Bureau of Narcotics and Dangerous Drugs
BRGE	Intelligence and Electronic Warfare Brigade (France)
CA	covert action
CI	counterintelligence
CIA	Central Intelligence Agency
CIC	Counterintelligence Center
COI	Coordinator of Information
COINTELPRO	program to collect information and conduct surveillance against antiwar protestors during the Vietnam War
COMINT	communications intelligence
COMSEC	communications security
CRS	Companies for Republican Security (France)
CSE	Center for Security Evaluation
CT	counterterrorism
CTC	Counterterrorism Center
DARPA	Defense Advanced Research Projects Agency
DCI	director of central intelligence
DCID	Director of Central Intelligence Directive
DCPJ	Central Directorate Judicial Police (France)
DEA	Drug Enforcement Administration
DGSE	General Directorate for External Security (France)
DI	Directorate of Intelligence

DIA	Defense Intelligence Agency
DNI	director of national intelligence
DO	Directorate of Operations
DoD	Department of Defense
DPSD	Directorate of Defense Protection and Security (France)
DRM	Directorate of Military Intelligence (France)
DS&T	Directorate of Science and Technology
DST	Directorate of Territorial Security (France)
ELINT	electronic intelligence
EO	executive order
EXDIS	exclusive distribution
FBI	Federal Bureau of Investigation
FISC	Foreign Intelligence Surveillance Court
GCHQ	Government Communications Headquarters (United Kingdom)
GEOINT	geospatial intelligence
HPSCI	House Permanent Select Committee on Intelligence
HUMINT	human intelligence
IC	intelligence community
ICSIS	Intelligence Community-Wide System for Information Sharing
IMINT	imagery intelligence
INFOSEC	information security
INR	Bureau of Intelligence and Research
INT	intelligence
INTELINK	intelligence community-wide intranet
IOB	Intelligence Oversight Board
JDISS	Joint Deployable Intelligence Support System
JIC	Joint Intelligence Committee (United Kingdom)
JITF-CT	Joint Intelligence Task Force–Counterterrorism
JMIP	Joint Military Intelligence Program
KGB	Committee on State Security, former Soviet intelligence organization

KIQ	key intelligence question
LIMDIS	limited distribution
MAGIC	codeword for intercepts of Japanese communications prior to and during World War II
MASINT	measurement and signature intelligence
MI-5	Security Service (United Kingdom)
MI-6	Secret Intelligence Service (United Kingdom)
MID	Military Intelligence Division
Mossad	Institute for Intelligence and Special Tasks (Israel)
NCC	National Crime and Narcotics Center
NCIC	National Counterintelligence Center
NCIX	National Counterintelligence Executive
NCPC	National Counter Proliferation Center
NCS	National Clandestine Service
NCTC	National Counterterrorism Center
NDF	National Defense Force (South Africa)
NFIB	National Foreign Intelligence Board
NFIP	National Foreign Intelligence Program
NGA	National Geospatial-Intelligence Agency
NIC	National Intelligence Council
NIE	national intelligence estimate
NIMA	National Imagery and Mapping Agency
NIO	national intelligence officer
NIT	National Intelligence Topic
NOC	nonofficial cover
NOCONTRACT	Not Releasable to Contractors
NODIS	No Distribution
NOFORN	Not Releasable to Foreign Governments
NPC	Nonproliferation Center
NPIC	National Photographic Interpretation Center
NRO	National Reconnaissance Office
NSA	National Security Agency
NSC	National Security Council

NSDD	National Security Decision Directive
ONI	Office of Naval Intelligence
OPEC	Organization of Petroleum Exporting States
ORCON	originator controlled
OSINT	open-source intelligence
OSS	Office of Strategic Services
PDB	*President's Daily Brief*
PDD	presidential decision directive
PHOTINT	photographic intelligence
RG	Central Directorate of General Information (France)
SCIF	secure compartmented intelligence facility
SCSSI	Central Service for Information Systems Security (France)
SEIR	*Senior Executive Intelligence Review*
Shabak	Israeli security service
Shin Bet	Israeli security service
SIGINT	signals intelligence
SIS	Secret Intelligence Service (United Kingdom)
SNIE	special national intelligence estimate
SSCI	Senate Select Committee on Intelligence
Stasi	East German state security service
TELINT	telemetry intelligence
TIA	total information awareness
TIARA	Tactical Intelligence and Related Activities (Program)
TTIC	Terrorist Threat Integration Center
UK ONLY	Releasable only to the Government of the United Kingdom
US	United States
USA	United States of America
USC	United States Code
USSR	Union of Soviet Socialist Republics
VEIL	codeword for disinformation campaign against Libya
WMD	weapons of mass destruction
WWII	World War II

1

The Uncertainty Principle

There is no such thing as absolute certainty, but there is assurance sufficient for purposes of human life.
—John Stuart Mill, philosopher

The terrorist attacks on 11 September 2001 killed many innocent people, traumatized the country, pushed the U.S. government into a new and uncharted national security direction, and sparked a national debate over whether the attacks represented an intelligence failure. The debate probably will continue for quite a long time and may not be resolved to anyone's satisfaction. Like many intelligence failures before it, 9/11[1] will go down in history as an event for which the United States should have been prepared but was not. The important question is whether America's intelligence agencies had anything to do with that unpreparedness.

Those who say that the terrorist attacks were an intelligence failure base their argument on the premise that America's intelligence agencies failed to warn political leaders about them, even though these agencies had been issuing warnings about the terrorist threat level against the United States for quite a long time.[2] Those who reject the accusation, including former Director of Central Intelligence George Tenet, do so by arguing that the role of U.S. intelligence is to provide warnings about changes in the character of the threats well in advance of a specific incident, not predict the specific incident itself.[3] Tenet long argued that American intelligence has a good record of strategic warning, including the possibilities of terrorism on American soil.[4] This distinction between strategic warning (warning of changes in the character of the threat) and tactical warning (warning of a specific event) is essential to an understanding of the nature of intelligence failures. It is also key to the defense against accusations of failure that the U.S. intelligence community mounted soon after the terrorist attacks.

The tragedy is that both sides are right. Those who charge U.S. intelligence with failing to do its job of identifying specific threats and foiling attacks associate the events of 11 September 2001 with the example of the Japanese surprise attack on Pearl Harbor in December 1941, another intelligence failure of epic proportions. Those who defend the performance of the U.S. intelligence community consider the tactical warning standard to be impossibly high, setting up American intelligence for continual failure.

In actuality, the causes of intelligence failures do not revolve around the issue of whether U.S. intelligence is doing its job right. Rather, they can be found in all aspects of intelligence, from how the public perceives intelligence to how intelligence agencies perform their specialized tasks, all the way to the specific steps in the intelligence process and how the policymakers use intelligence information.

What Is Intelligence?

Secret intelligence conjures up different images in people's minds. Some see it as a source of wonder, a world of secrets and intrigue that animates bedtime or summer reading and provides grist for the entertainment industry. Looked at this way, secret intelligence occupies the world of fantasy, a world of spy novels and sitcoms from which most Americans get their information about intelligence. Unfortunately, this popular culture also helps shape public attitudes toward the intelligence world. Others look at intelligence as a source of evil, a dark world of secrecy and deception, useful only for nefarious acts like overthrowing governments and conducting political assassinations. Sometimes, the two perspectives converge into another one to form an image of intelligence as a titillating, foreboding, and exciting thing that is beyond the law and, therefore, uncontrolled and uncontrollable.

Intelligence professionals have a different view. To them, intelligence is a particular kind of information that helps to inform, instruct, and educate the policy world. To consumers of intelligence—the policymakers—intelligence is that and more. To political leaders, secret intelligence may also be a political asset or a political liability, depending on whether intelligence information helps or hinders the fulfillment of political goals. Most times, secret intelligence is a political football that exists to serve political objectives, whether they are the discrediting of a political opponent or buttressing a politician's credentials as a "hawk" or a "dove."

However perceived, secret intelligence evokes strong passions in proponents and opponents alike. These passions arise in large part because secret intelligence is the manifestation of controversial aspects of administration foreign policy. Intelligence, as a governmental activity, exists to illuminate and support the foreign policy objectives of whichever administration is in office, and so it logically comes to be associated with that administration's foreign policy. Opponents of the particular foreign policy line usually perceive the involvement of intelligence as sinister and its activities as illegal.

However, implementing foreign policy has little to do with intelligence. There is a part of secret intelligence, covert action, that is designed to execute specific aspects of American foreign policy, but the bulk of intelligence activities have more to do with collecting, processing, analyzing, and disseminating intelligence information to decision makers—relatively dull activities, compared to the more publicly accepted image of adventurism and mayhem.

The problem centers on the lack of a satisfactory definition of intelligence. Some emphasize specific attributes, such as secrecy, and associate intelligence with those attributes. In this formulation, anything that is secret would naturally fall within the realm of intelligence, so long as government performs it. That this is too simplistic a view of secret intelligence would probably make little difference to those who espouse this perspective. Others define intelligence as an input to the policy process. For example, Mark Lowenthal, a former congressional staffer who has worked on oversight of intelligence, says that intelligence is information that meets the stated or understood needs of policymakers and has been collected, refined, and narrowed to meet those needs.[5] This is a proper role for intelligence, but it does not tell us everything about it. Still others define intelligence as an output of the intelligence process. For example, Jeffrey Richelson, who covers intelligence matters at the National Security Archive in Washington, D.C., employs the definition used by the Joint Chiefs of Staff: intelligence is the product resulting from the collection, processing, integration, analysis, evaluation, and interpretation of available information concerning foreign countries and areas.[6] For the purposes of this book, we need to combine the two perspectives mentioned earlier and define intelligence as policy-relevant information, collected through open and clandestine means and subjected to analysis, for the purposes of educating, enlightening, or helping American decision makers in formulating and implementing national security and foreign policy. This definition reflects the myriad approaches to understanding intelligence as a governmental activity.

First, the definition rightly focuses on the main mission of intelligence, which is the gathering of information based on "requirements" identified by political leaders. True, it is not easy to know what political leaders want or need, mostly because they themselves do not know. All too often, the policymakers' motivations in asking for secret intelligence are also suspect. However, this uncertainty does not take away from the central proposition that intelligence works to fulfill demands made by decision makers and engages in a variety of activities designed to address those demands. Second, the definition incorporates the specific objectives of intelligence. The intelligence process is designed to fulfill intelligence objectives. The process is usually depicted as an "intelligence cycle"—identifying needs; collecting information based on those needs; subjecting the information to analysis; producing finished intelligence based on such analysis; and disseminating the analysis to political leaders, who may then identify additional needs that start the cycle all over again. Finally, the definition used in this book includes the provision of helping political leaders implement foreign and national security policy. This is the province of "covert action," which occupies an odd place in U.S. intelligence. Covert action is not really intelligence but employs intelligence resources to give American presidents and senior government officials a capability to secretly implement aspects of U.S. foreign policy.

In a 1999 statement, George Tenet, the former director of central intelligence, provided an erudite statement about the missions of U.S. intelligence that highlights all these tasks:

- We will call it as we see it. We will deliver intelligence that is objective, pulls no punches, and is free from political taint.
- We will not only tell policymakers about what is important on their minds—we will also alert them to things that have not yet reached their in-boxes.
- We will respond to the President's and other decision makers' needs on demand—juggling our intelligence priorities and capabilities as necessary to meet the most urgent missions.
- We will innovatively develop cutting-edge technologies and apply them to our collection and analysis work.
- We will uphold our country's laws always.
- We will take risks. Analytical risks—making tough calls when it would be easier to waffle. Operational risks to secure vital information or to take some necessary action.[7]

Although there is a good deal of wishful thinking in the list, this statement encapsulates both the reality of what U.S. intelligence does and how it wants to be perceived as doing what it does.

Utility of Intelligence

There is purpose behind secret intelligence. We are all familiar with the popular images of spying on, and doing away with, the bad guys, but we are less familiar with the purposes for which intelligence agencies do what they do. Yet nearly all governments around the globe engage in intelligence in one way or another. They do so because they want to know what other governments are up to, and because they want to be able to be in a position to influence the behavior of other governments toward them.

In international politics, governments interact with one another—through foreign policy and diplomacy—as a way of keeping the international system stable and preventing conflict and war. If there were complete transparency and full exchange of information about capabilities and intentions during these interactions, then there would be little need for secret intelligence. However, because governments deliberate in secrecy and keep their capabilities and intentions to themselves, intelligence becomes a necessary governmental activity, itself subjected to a high degree of secrecy. Of course, there are different gradations of protection, of secrecy, and government authorities seek to protect their information based on criteria that they find useful at any given time. The irony is that the very activity that governments employ to reduce uncertainty and their anxieties—secret intelligence—creates conditions for uncertainty and anxiety among its targets.

Secret intelligence information provides grist for the mission-critical tasks that U.S. intelligence must effectively perform: reporting on foreign developments, forecasting important events, and warning about imminent threats to the country.[8] Intelligence theory says that when intelligence agencies perform these tasks in an effective way, policy officials' uncertainties about the adversary and their anxieties about the country's vulnerabilities should lessen.

Uncertainty derives from not knowing what other governments will do and whether they have the capability to do what they plan. Governments establish intelligence capabilities to acquire this hidden information. American intelligence employs a variety of techniques for gathering intelligence, including espionage, which tends to be illegal everywhere. The world of espionage gets much of the attention in the media and the entertainment industry. However, diplomats, as part of their daily contacts with their foreign counterparts, also acquire information of intelligence value, and this information routinely finds its way to intelligence agencies. In addition, a lot of information can be gleaned from public sources like the media and academic circles. Sometimes, friendly governments exchange or share intelligence information.

However governments get their intelligence information, they try to assess the nature and level of threat against them and then make judgments about the intentions of foreign leaders and their capabilities to follow through on those intentions. In doing so, intelligence agencies serve as safety valves that help reduce uncertainty about potential threats as well as a source for identifying opportunities to promote the national interests.

Collecting information is the principal task of intelligence agencies, although each goes about it differently. Collecting intelligence information on capabilities is easier than collecting information on intentions. A nation's capabilities may include military forces and their equipment, economic potential, industrial output, and the like. These are areas that can be subjected to numerical counting and measurement, and so constitute the main targets for most collection efforts. Intentions, on the other hand, involve the will and plans of political leaders to carry out specific actions. Since this kind of information involves intellectual processes and private deliberation among government leaders, it is often subject to repeated change, concealment, and manipulation. Collecting information about intentions requires unusual intelligence capabilities that rely less on quantification and measurement, and more on contacts, intuition, speed, and the ability to ferret out deception and other types of subterfuge.

Reducing uncertainty is complicated by the fact that we often have little feel for the gaps in our knowledge about adversaries. Intelligence gaps are the constants that inevitably increase uncertainty and anxiety, and require substantial investments to undo. The United States knew, for example, that North Korea was on the verge of developing a nuclear weapons capability—the United States can gather information on equipment purchases, production schedules, industrial activity, and the like—but Washington has been uncertain about North Korea's potential in this area. The United States is definitely uncertain about the intentions of North Korean leaders regarding nuclear weapons. The North Korean leadership is a difficult target on which to collect reliable information. The United States is therefore left with the alternative of having to speculate about the intentions of North Korean leaders regarding nuclear weapons. Speculation is fine, but it falls short as a reliable predictor of what the North Koreans will do in the future.[9] For a government to be without a clue about the enemy's intentions—let alone its capabilities—is very dangerous, for a lack of such knowledge may lead to strategic surprise.

Reducing uncertainty is also costly business. The United States reportedly spends more than forty-five billion dollars specifically on intelligence activities. This figure excludes the money and effort spent by a significant portion of the policy community in activities unrelated to intelligence but that have significant intelligence value. For example, the U.S. Department of Commerce collects information on trade and global commerce, information that undoubtedly is relevant to and highly useful in intelligence analyses. However, the expenditures of the Department of Commerce in these areas are not factored into the U.S. intelligence budgets. It would not be hyperbole to say that the U.S. government spends at least double its official intelligence budget on intelligence and related activities.[10]

The United States is not alone in appropriating stupendous amounts of money on intelligence. Nearly all the governments of the developed world have significant intelligence capabilities, and they all spend large portions of their foreign-affairs moneys on reducing uncertainty. Countries of the developing world, especially those that base their authority and power on the threat and use of violence, have the added burden of trying to uncover domestic opposition and therefore spend a significantly larger share of their budgets on intelligence.

The Intelligence Cycle

The intelligence cycle is the formal means by which America's intelligence agencies attempt to do their work of reporting on developments, forecasting events, warning about threats, and thereby reducing uncertainty. The CIA uses a simple diagram to illustrate this process (see figure 1). This diagram is useful in that it provides a thumbnail sketch of the major steps in the intelligence process, although it does have its share of critics. Lowenthal, for example, says that the CIA diagram misrepresents the intelligence process in many ways. For one thing, it has a completeness that misses many of the nuances of the process. For another, it is one-dimensional, in that it does not provide for feedback. It also fails, he says, to take into account the fact that the cycle may need to be repeated more than once before completion.[11]

Despite criticism, there is little argument that there are

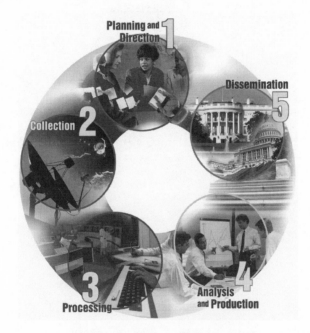

Figure 1. *CIA's Intelligence Cycle*

critical steps in the intelligence process that individually and collectively are designed to fulfill the intelligence mission. The intelligence cycle, however, includes fewer steps than CIA's chart indicates. Figure 2 is an illustration of the stages in the American intelligence cycle, which begins with the requirements and priorities process. Ideally, the decision makers should decide themselves what they want to know and relay that "tasking" to intelligence agencies. This, of course, presumes that the decision makers know the issues and are aware that there is a knowledge gap that prevents the making of effective decisions. Political leaders, however, like the rest of us, usually do not know what the issues are and often are unwilling to admit their ignorance publicly for fear of political repercussions. If they do know the issues, they may not know how to articulate what it is they need to know. Consequently, intelligence professionals must often define the issues for policymakers.

Intelligence professionals frequently find themselves in the

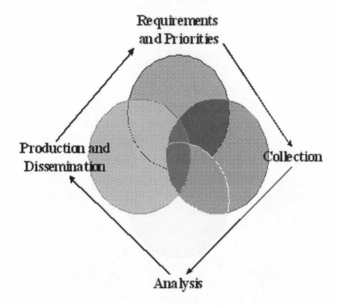

Figure 2. *Modified Intelligence Cycle*

position of having to identify gaps in intelligence for political leaders and relate that information to decision makers, a very sensitive issue, given that intelligence officers work for the politicians and are reluctant, like their bosses, to admit a lack of knowledge. There is an awkward relationship between those who make the decisions—the policymakers—and those who feed information to those who make the decisions—the intelligence folks—which can raise questions about politicization of intelligence. Intelligence professionals in the United States like to portray themselves as objective arbiters of information and as disinterested supporters of the policy process. Yet organizational arrangements, even informal ones like the policy-intelligence relationship, surely exert pressure on intelligence analysts to toe the political line in ways that may jeopardize their policy neutrality.

Reducing uncertainty also requires the completion of several mechanical processes that, in and of themselves, appear to be rather simple and straightforward but really are very complex and political. Once we define what we want to know, we must collect the information, which is the second stage of the intelligence cycle. For governments accustomed to secrecy and countermeasures, this is no easy task. Where is the needed information? Who has it? How can we get this person to give us the information? Would the information really answer the deep policy questions that were asked at the requirements stage? How valuable and perishable is this information? Would the government be embarrassed if it were to become public that it is seeking this information? These and similar questions form the intelligence requirements, which in turn spur intelligence collection. Lack of information, or wrong data, on any of these issues may provide the basis for possible intelligence failures.

Gathering intelligence spans a variety of collection disciplines and is subject to institutional and budgetary considerations. Acquisition of intelligence is also highly sensitive to political and technological constraints. Even if the information is collected, it may not be the right information and therefore may not directly address the issues formulated in the requirements process. Technological and human restraints may even prevent the gathering of information on a particular issue altogether. Worse still, there may be questions without ready answers. Former Director of Central Intelligence Robert Gates claimed during his tenure that secrets could be unveiled by intelligence information but that mysteries are so elusive that they simply defy analysis and explanation.[12]

Once intelligence agents collect the necessary information, it must be subjected to analysis, the third stage in the intelligence cycle. Without analysis, raw intelligence stands on its own, outside its context, and with little relevance. Information that has not been analyzed may also be misinterpreted and misused.

Some policymakers prefer to receive only raw intelligence,

out of the mistaken belief that they can do just as good a job at analyzing information as anyone else. There is little doubt that the policymakers are just as capable as intelligence analysts in subjecting intelligence information to analysis. But, there is a key difference—policymakers perform analysis within the context of their political world and their policy preferences, which may skew and bias their evaluations. Intelligence professionals are better placed organizationally and analytically to evaluate raw intelligence in an objective manner and provide intelligence analysis to the policy community. This certainly does not mean that intelligence analysts are free from political pressure. On the contrary, the world of the intelligence analyst is a political world, and any competent analyst has to struggle on a daily basis to balance the requirements of policy leaders and the requirements of intelligence objectivity.

The final stage of the intelligence cycle is the delivery and presentation of information to the consumer. Providing the information to the policymaker is more complicated than it appears. Significant portions of those who receive intelligence information do so in print. Some decision makers—consumers of intelligence information—prefer to hear rather than read intelligence information. Others prefer to view the information on screen or on video.

Serving the policymaking consumer requires that intelligence analysts study the consumption patterns of their consumers as well as the intelligence questions they pose. Intelligence analysts must also ensure that their intelligence product—whether written, oral, or audiovisual—is engaging enough to draw the attention of the policymaker. Above all, the intelligence product must be timely, accurate, and relevant. The policymaker may otherwise turn to other sources of information or ignore the intelligence information altogether, which may be tantamount to an intelligence failure.

Factors such as cost, time, and the availability of information certainly affect whether intelligence serves the policy consumer well. The end product, "finished intelligence," is relayed to the consumer on a "need to know" basis so as to answer the policymakers' questions as completely and accurately as possible in a timely manner. Usually this standard is too high, because, depending on the availability and quality of information, finished intelligence may answer questions only partially, or not at all. Finished intelligence may also raise new questions. The theory of the intelligence cycle suggests that these new questions should form the nucleus of new requirements, along with new foreign policy crises, national security threats, and other policy concerns. However, this is too neat a formulation for an intelligence cycle that contains, in each of its stages, the seeds of intelligence failure.

The U.S. government spends a good deal of time and money on coming to grips with the possibilities of failures and what to do about them. The CIA, for example, conducts an in-house course on "Intelligence Successes and Failures," intended to give senior managers an appreciation of the complexities of intelligence and of how to reduce the chances of failure. Implicit in the course is the proposition that so long as governments hide their activities in a shroud of secrecy, there will be intelligence activities to ferret out those secrets. The whole process of trying to keep secrets and trying to discover them carries with it the risk of failure.

The Plan

The debate over failures revolves around the degree to which intelligence is able to reduce uncertainty. Critics of intelligence tend to set the bar very high, asserting that "intelligence success" should be defined only as substantially eliminating uncertainty. Others, mostly intelligence professionals, suggest that expanding "intelligence success" into clairvoyance is a misuse of this vital resource; instead, intelligence success should reduce uncertainty only to the extent that viable options and opportunities are identified and made available to policy leaders. Clearly, these two views are at the opposite ends of the spectrum. The truth probably is somewhere in the middle.

The thesis of this book is that the roots of intelligence failures are embedded in the intelligence cycle and can only be addressed by measures that confront specific dysfunctions in the intelligence process. Other contributing factors—counterintelligence and covert action—also loom large in the making of intelligence failures. It is possible to identify inflection points[13] in the intelligence cycle and ancillary activities that invite error, misjudgment, misstatement, and misinterpretation. These inflection points correspond roughly with what Loch Johnson calls "pathologies"[14] of the cycle, which cannot be separated from factors that are intrinsic to the historical evolution of U.S. intelligence as well as to the peculiar way intelligence has come to be organized in the United States.

Chapter 2 focuses on the historical development of American intelligence and the intelligence community it has spawned. In addition, it identifies the intelligence community as a prelude to discussing, in chapter 3, the various bureaucratic dysfunctions associated with the management of intelligence. The U.S. intelligence community was designed and now functions in a way that promotes competition among the intelligence agencies over information, money, people, and access. Each of the intelligence agencies has its own dedicated intelligence capability, either operational or analytical, or both, and produces secret intelligence that each claims to be unique and relevant. Specialized collection mechanisms become the currency that intelligence agencies use to outbid or undermine each other. In the process of trying to enhance their power or protect their turf, intelligence agencies may miscommunicate or not communicate at all. Such "noncooperation" is a leading cause of intelligence failure.

Bureaucratic factors internal to the intelligence agencies are also detrimental to intelligence success. Certainly, inadequate intelligence guidance and improper or poor analyst training are among the principal culprits. Intelligence analysts, however, would add a few other factors that are important considerations in bureaucratic snafus. These factors would include such things as too many layers of management and ponderous internal procedures, clearly intended to reduce risk, that in fact delay the intelligence process.

Chapter 3 focuses on the U.S. "intelligence ethos" and the dysfunctions it creates, while chapter 4 examines, with a view to identifying critical structural variables that may be relevant for the United States, the intelligence systems of some foreign democratic nations, whose experiences may have some lessons for the U.S. intelligence community.

Chapter 5 begins the examination of the intelligence cycle by focusing on how intelligence priorities are set and policymaker requirements are determined. The interplay between intelligence priorities and "tasking" of requirements is a delicate one, because it involves the politically sensitive issue of the relationship between political leaders (intelligence consumers) and intelligence officials (intelligence producers). Inability to shape priorities, focusing on the wrong priorities, misstating and miscommunicating tasking, and misreading policymaker intentions all may help produce intelligence failures.

Chapter 6 looks at the second stage of the intelligence cycle—the collection of intelligence—and the secrecy and compartmentation that accompany it. Because each intelligence agency possesses its own specialized collection capability (commonly known as a "stovepipe"), this stage of the cycle includes the kind of turf battles and information hoarding that lead to bureaucratic competition and noncooperation among the agencies, ingredients that various investigative panels have.

Chapter 7 examines the analytic stage of the cycle, where intelligence analysts transform bits and pieces of collected raw information into national estimates and other analytic products that are intended to help policymakers shape American foreign and national security policies. This stage of the cycle probably contains the richest and the most complex sources of intelligence failures. These causes involve both cognitive dysfunctions as well as organizational and cultural impediments to successful intelligence.

Chapter 8 looks at the final stage of the cycle where finished intelligence products are produced and delivered to policy consumers. There are many opportunities for intelligence failures at this stage, including using the wrong format to deliver intelligence, disseminating intelligence to the wrong consumers, and delivering intelligence information that may not fulfill the expectations of policy consumers. Failing to satisfy consumers' intelligence needs may carry heavy penalties, for political leaders may then ignore, downplay, or even reject intelligence information.

Chapter 9 examines the roles of counterintelligence and

covert action as contributing factors to intelligence failures. The American intelligence process subsumes counterintelligence as a critical but subsidiary intelligence activity. Covert action, however, is an operational tool for implementing specific aspects of American foreign policy and as such has a detrimental effect on the intelligence process.

Chapter 10 focuses on the perennial as well as the emerging national security issues to which U.S. intelligence now devotes its resources. Each issue encompasses a role for U.S. intelligence, and this role is usually fraught with challenges that frequently contribute to intelligence failure.

Chapter 11 explores the impact of expectations and analyzes recommendations that address some of the dysfunctions of the intelligence process. One critical structural step is the concentration of authority in the person of a strong "intelligence czar." Other structural measures would be to create mechanisms for enhancing cross-fertilization among intelligence specialties in specific issue areas and melding foreign intelligence with domestic intelligence, a bane for civil libertarians. Among the suggestions in the last chapter for addressing analytic malfunctions is the use of techniques like "alternative analysis" and "deep-mining" of intelligence information.

2

Intelligence, American Style

The guy who invented the first wheel was an idiot. The guy who invented the other three, he was a genius.
—Sid Caesar, Comedian

For most Americans, the world of intelligence is remote, exotic, and arcane, carried out by shadowy spy agencies for murky reasons. The American public simply does not know, and in many respects does not want to know, what its intelligence agencies do. Many Americans associate "intelligence" with "espionage," and espionage with the Central Intelligence Agency (CIA). There are many reasons for this public ignorance about intelligence. The secrecy surrounding intelligence activities accounts for some of it; people receive little information about intelligence agencies. When they do receive some information, it is likely to be in fictional form, meant to entertain rather than inform.

The complexity of America's intelligence establishment accounts for a large part of the lack of knowledge. It is easier, and more fun, to identify spying with a single agency rather than a whole slew of them. But the United States does have many intelligence agencies, bunched together and organized under the improbable title of "the intelligence community" (IC)—improbable in that the notion of community suggests a high degree of coherence and cooperation. The distinguishing characteristics of the U.S. intelligence community are decentralization and fragmentation, with only a degree of cohesion. There are legal and political reasons for this, such as historical fears of a central secret police and a cultural preference for competition as a method of control. While decentralization makes sense in collecting specialized intelligence, fragmentation is often a kiss of death for interagency cooperation and communication. But a look at the historical evolution of American intelligence illustrates the reasons why the United States could not have developed any other intelligence structure.

Historical Reflections

Structural fragmentation and diffusion is the result of historical forces that go back to the nineteenth century. Students of intelligence like to point out that the United States does not have much of an intelligence history, but they also point out that the nation employed intelligence at the founding of the Republic and at pivotal points of history since then. Indeed, many precedents in the intelligence area were set during the early years of the United States, especially by President George Washington and his successors John Adams and Thomas Jefferson.

Washington, for example, ran his own spy ring and laid down principles governing intelligence secrecy and the provision of secret funding of intelligence. By Washington's administration, the young United States already had a hero, in the person of Nathan Hale, whose statue, with the inscription "I only regret that I have but one life to lose for my country," now stands in front of the CIA headquarters in McLean, Virginia. Benjamin Franklin also ran his own spies in London, where he was U.S. ambassador, and made arms deals with the French to ensure weapons flows to the new nation.[1] Franklin appears to have been spied on as well; a member of his staff was paid by the British to deliver information about Franklin and the Americans to the British.[2] Such double-agent operations were very common in the late 1700s, inaugurating the field of counterintelligence that would not be fully incorporated into U.S. intelligence until two hundred years later.

George Washington's successors also initiated covert-action programs about this time. In 1811, President James Madison approved a covert operation to steal Florida from the Spanish. His agent was to negotiate with the Spaniards to bring Florida into the United States peacefully. Instead, the agent tried to foment rebellion by the English-speaking inhabitants, prompting President Madison to disavow the agent and his operation. The debacle caused a rift with Spain, but the United States acquired Florida in 1819.

U.S. intelligence operations during the nineteenth century were relatively rare, mostly because the United States did not possess an intelligence service. American agents did engage in tactical military intelligence during the War of 1812 and the Mexican War of 1848, but even so, as of the Civil War U.S. intelligence capabilities were minimal.

The Civil War accelerated intelligence activities on both sides to some degree, principally because of new technologies that were incorporated into intelligence operations. The observation balloon and the telegraph were given their first major military use during the war.[3] Espionage was the most common intelligence method because circumstances—such as a common language and a common culture—made it the most convenient.[4] Moreover, the Confederate side undertook many more intelligence operations than the Union side, engaging in such covert actions as shipping arms and supplies to sympathizers, guerrilla warfare, and sabotage. According to one account, the assassination of President Abraham Lincoln was a Confederate covert action, intended to kidnap Lincoln and hold him hostage.[5]

The beginning of the modern American intelligence structure can be traced to the period immediately after the Civil War. The U.S. Navy established a permanent intelligence unit—the Office of Naval Intelligence (ONI)—in 1882 to learn about foreign ship construction methods. The army's intelligence unit—the Military Intelligence Division (MID)—came into being in 1885. However, technological developments were the main impetus for the growth of America's nascent intelligence apparatus, incorporating such techniques as collecting aerial intelligence by means of surveillance balloons and other types of craft. Moreover, new innovations in the communications industry, such as the development of the telegraph, stimulated interest in encryption and decoding capabilities.

During World War I, U.S. intelligence efforts were limited to supporting the new American foreign policy doctrine of "open diplomacy," reflecting the openness that permeated the thinking of U.S. policymakers at the time.[6] To promote this new way of doing things, the State Department assumed the responsibility of coordinating all intelligence information, an effort that lasted until 1927. Even though there is general agreement that intelligence barely made an impression on policy leaders, many precedents were set in these early years, including civilian control of the intelligence services.

In the interwar years between 1918 and 1941, code making and code breaking became important enterprises, involving the State Department, the army, and the navy, all of which began efforts to break the codes of foreign governments in order to read their secret correspondence and to make their own more secure. The State Department established the "Black Chamber," in New York City, precisely for such a purpose, and this operation managed to decode or decipher more than forty-five thousand telegrams from nineteen countries over a period of twelve years.[7] When the new secretary of state, Henry Stimson, was informed of the operation in 1929, he immediately closed down the Black Chamber, declaring, "Gentlemen don't read each others' mail."[8] Senior intelligence officials today cite Stimson's remark as an illustration of folly among policymakers, as reflecting an attitude that impedes some intelligence operations and contributes to intelligence failures. After Stimson closed the Black Chamber, its former director, Herbert O. Yardley, wrote a book revealing the secrets of American code-breaking operations.[9] When he threatened to publish another book revealing the fact that the United States had broken Japanese codes (the codeword MAGIC had been given to intercepted and deciphered Japanese messages), the U.S. government seized the book, and Congress enacted legislation to bar publication of any materials that disclosed cryptologic information.[10]

The army and the navy continued their interception programs despite the closing of the State Department's cryptologic program. In 1941, MAGIC provided information that a Japanese attack was imminent, but not where or when. Military analysts thought the attack would come in the Philippines or Southeast Asia, although they did mention Hawaii as a possible site.[11] Most senior officials were so convinced that the attack would take place in Southeast Asia that when Secretary of the Navy Frank Cox was told about the attack on Pearl Harbor, he is said to have exclaimed, "My God! This can't be true—this must mean the Philippines." The final intercepted message reached Washington in the early hours of 7 December 1941, and said that the attack would occur at 1 PM Washington time, without specifying where. This message was not sent to the Pacific in a timely fashion, because of organizational, bureaucratic, human, and even technical communications shortcomings.

The Japanese surprise attack on Pearl Harbor and the failure of U.S. intelligence to detect it ahead of time shocked the American people and provided the impetus for the establishment of a centrally organized civilian intelligence organization after the war. However, before the Japanese attack, the British had persuaded President Franklin Roosevelt to establish the Office of the Coordinator of Information (COI), which was to carry out "when requested by the President, such supplementary activities as may facilitate the securing of information important for national security not now available to the Government."[12] William Donovan, the COI, later became the head of the Office of Strategic Services (OSS) once the United States entered World War II. The COI's mandate was to gather intelligence information, but William Donovan considered analytical work only a "cover" for secret operations and focused OSS efforts principally on operations like infiltrations and sabotage.[13]

At the end of the war, President Harry Truman and his advisers followed American tradition and demobilized the armed forces, including the OSS.[14] Even with the emergence of the Soviet Union as a serious threat and the rapidly changing strategic situation, the Truman administration was slow to recognize the need for the United States to have an intelligence capability.

A good deal of public and policy opposition to establishing a central civilian organization was raised on the grounds that such an institution would be a threat to civil liberties and constitutional government. Even President Truman is said to have remarked that he wanted to be certain "that no single unit or agency of the Federal Government would have so much power that we would find ourselves, perhaps inadvertently, slipping in the direction of a police state."[15]

The military also opposed the creation of a central intelligence organization—for bureaucratic reasons, fearing some loss of turf, access, authority, and money if strategic military intelligence were to be taken away by a new intelligence-gathering agency. The FBI was opposed too, because it did not want to lose the foreign intelligence and espionage capabilities in Latin America that it had acquired in the 1920s and 1930s.

Yet Congress passed the National Security Act of 1947,[16] establishing the CIA. The creators of the CIA sought to centralize intelligence activities so that never again would the government suffer the results of too many intelligence agencies working at cross-purposes. However, it probably would have been much harder to establish the CIA if assurances had not been given that its jurisdiction would be limited. Rhodri Jeffreys-Jones asserts that the CIA may have been the politicians' easiest option, in that it was the CIA's very susceptibility to democratic debate that gave it its legitimacy and helped it to be effective politically—an agency imprisoned by democracy and subject to public debate.[17] The National Security Act went as far as to deny the CIA any police, subpoena, or law-enforcement, powers or internal security functions.

The National Security Act of 1947 accomplished many other tasks. The act created the Office of the Secretary of Defense, with little authority over the autonomous military services. A 1949 amendment to the law established the Department of Defense and incorporated the services within it. The Joint Chiefs of Staff was also created out of the loose arrangements that had existed during World War II and before. The act did not abolish the intelligence units of the army (the Military Intelligence Division) or the navy (the Office of Naval Intelligence), or other departmental intelligence services. Instead, it stipulated that each would continue to perform its own more specialized intelligence functions.

The act also created the National Security Council, a coordinating and policy-planning body consisting of the president, vice president, and the secretaries of defense and state. The act specified the CIA as an independent agency reporting to the president, through the National Security Council, to coordinate intelligence activities, provide intelligence analysis to political leaders, and engage in special activities that the National Security Council might direct. The director of central intelligence (DCI), whose position was created in 1946 to coordinate intelligence information, was designated under the act as the adviser to the president on intelligence matters. The act also gave the DCI command of the CIA.

The CIA's birthday is 18 September 1947, when the Cold War was just beginning and there was general fear that the Soviet Union would engage in subversion in pursuit of its goal of overrunning Europe. Given the bureaucratic tensions over the creation of the CIA, it surprised no one that the CIA quickly became enmeshed in bureaucratic fights to expand its authorities into areas not mentioned in the National Security Act and into covert operations designed to thwart Soviet designs in the European theater. As a matter of fact, the late 1940s and the entire decade of the 1950s were later to be known as the CIA's "Golden Age," when the agency engaged in a series of successful covert operations that built its reputation as the "quiet option" available to an American president for wielding power.

The CIA's propaganda and other psychological operations secured Italy away from the communists in 1948; overthrew Prime Minister Mohammad Mossadegh in Iran in 1953, paving the way for the return of the shah; and ousted the elected government of Jacobo Arbenz Guzmán in Guatemala in 1954.[18] U.S. intelligence also managed to get hold of Soviet premier Nikita Khrushchev's secret 1956 speech to the Communist Party Congress denouncing Stalin's abuses. Also, the CIA forecast the launching of Sputnik in 1957.

These operational successes, however, masked the CIA's many intelligence failures (see figure 3). The CIA failed to forecast the North Korean invasion of South Korea in 1950, and it failed to alert American leaders of China's entry into the Korean War on the side of the North. U.S. intelligence also failed to forecast the defeat of the French in Vietnam and

the British-French-Israeli invasion of Egypt that led to the
Suez Crisis in 1956. The CIA also failed to forecast the Soviet
invasion of Hungary in 1956.

The Sputnik launching inaugurated the space age and gave
U.S. intelligence the incentive to delve into new technological
areas. The National Security Agency was established in 1952
to consolidate three seemingly separate but related activities—cryptology (or interception of communications), code
making and code breaking (on which cryptology depends),
and communications security. Combining all these activities
in a single agency meant that the other intelligence agencies
would have to depend on the NSA for their needs in these
areas. Therefore, the NSA became a service agency for the
entire U.S. government, in and out of the intelligence community, providing services in encryption, communications
interception, and secure communications. The NSA continues to function in this capacity today.

Sputnik also forced the United States to pay closer attention
to scientific developments and to invest heavily in missile and
satellite technology. Sputnik energized U.S. intelligence in the
area of aerial and space reconnaissance, especially the satellite program already in the works within the Advanced Research Projects Agency (ARPA) of the Department of Defense.
Meanwhile, in the mid-1950s, the CIA had contracted and
built the U-2 aircraft. The CIA had also begun to develop the
CORONA satellite project, which would in the 1960s return
photographic images in film canisters. The CIA soon established the National Photographic Interpretation Center (NPIC)
to analyze the take from these new technologies.

The urgency of attaining an operational satellite program
increased with the downing of Francis Gary Powers and his
U-2 over the Soviet Union in 1960. In that year, the U.S. Air
Force established the Office of Missile and Satellite Systems
to direct, supervise, and control satellite development for the
military. To facilitate this development, the CIA and the air
force signed an agreement in 1961 to establish the National
Reconnaissance Office (NRO) to oversee and fund research
and development for reconnaissance aircraft and their sensors,
procure space systems and their associated ground stations,
determine launch vehicle requirements, operate spacecraft

after they attained orbit, and disseminate the data collected.[19] G. J. A. O'Toole says that because of satellites, overhead reconnaissance rapidly became the principal source of American intelligence.[20] The NRO remained an official state secret until 1994, when the Department of Defense and the CIA acknowledged its existence (but refused to declassify anything else about the organization).

A Joint Study Group in 1958 recommended quick compliance with the Defense Reorganization Act of 1958, which sought to consolidate military intelligence agencies within the Office of the Secretary of Defense. Secretary of Defense Robert McNamara, however, decided to allow the services to retain tactical intelligence and transfer strategic military intelligence to the Defense Intelligence Agency (DIA), which was established in 1961 as the intelligence arm of the Joint Chiefs of Staff.

The energetic use of new collection technologies enabled U.S. intelligence agencies to score some impressive successes during the 1960s. For example, U.S. intelligence forecast the Sino-Soviet split in 1962, the development of the Chinese atomic bomb in 1964, the deployment of new Soviet strategic weapons, the Arab-Israeli War in 1967, and the Soviet anti-ballistic missile system in 1968.

However, there is also an equally impressive list of intelligence failures during the 1960s. The Bay of Pigs invasion in 1961 was intended to oust Fidel Castro from power in Cuba but instead turned into a total disaster, ending the CIA's so-called Golden Age of operational successes. In quick succession thereafter, U.S. intelligence failed to forecast developments in Vietnam, although intelligence officials were split on various issues, with the CIA assessing the war as unwinnable and the military holding the view that sufficient force could bring the war to a successful conclusion.[21]

American intelligence also failed to foresee the toughness of the Vietnamese guerrillas—the Viet Cong—and the Tet Offensive of 1968, which is generally considered the watershed event that turned the American public against the U.S. political leadership and the conduct of the Vietnam War. U.S. intelligence failed in 1968 to forecast the Soviet invasion of Czechoslovakia.

The decade of the 1970s ushered in an era that weakened U.S. intelligence. Soon after the decade began, American intelligence was mired in defending itself against a public outcry about its illegal activities. Revelations came in quick succession—assassination attempts against Castro, an assassination program in Vietnam (the Phoenix Program), spying on antiwar activists in the United States, "dirty tricks" against civil rights leaders and liberal politicians, and the overthrow of democratically elected governments. The public as well as political leaders demanded curbs on U.S. intelligence, and curbs were quickly set in place.

In 1974, the Hughes-Ryan Amendment, an amendment to the Intelligence Authorization Act, prohibited the CIA from engaging in assassinations. Executive orders during the Ford and Carter administrations put additional restrictions on intelligence agencies. In addition, the U.S. Congress initiated a series of hearings in the late 1970s on U.S. intelligence activities, culminating in the establishment of formal congressional oversight, a situation that had hardly existed in the 1950s and 1960s.

The Senate Select Committee on Intelligence (SSCI) was established in 1977, and the House Permanent Select Committee on Intelligence (HPSCI) was formed in 1978. Both committees considered and rejected the notion of an intelligence charter for the CIA, but Congress nonetheless passed the Intelligence Oversight Act of 1980, which put in place, for the first time, a process for the approval of covert action by the U.S. Congress.

Despite preoccupation with survival, intelligence agencies forecast several events in the 1970s, such as the India-Pakistan War of 1971, the Turkish invasion of Cyprus in 1974, and the Chinese invasion of Vietnam in 1978. However, they failed to foresee the Arab-Israeli War of 1973, the Soviet invasion of Afghanistan in 1979, and the fall of the Iranian shah in 1979.[22]

In 1981, President Ronald Reagan issued Executive Order 12333, which continues as the governing legal instrument for U.S. intelligence activities. President Reagan's order described the agencies of the U.S. intelligence community and their activities, set in place oversight mechanisms in both the executive and legislative branches, and extended the prohibition of assassination to the rest of the U.S. government.

Congressional and executive-branch oversight did not inhibit U.S. intelligence from becoming embroiled in the Contra War in Nicaragua and the Iran-Contra Affair in the mid-1980s. These developments gave further credence to those who believed that U.S. intelligence could not refrain from illegal activities despite statutory safeguards.

U.S. intelligence was in no position in the late 1980s to forecast accurately the breakup of the Soviet Union and the dissolution of communism. The debate continues over whether U.S. intelligence agencies did a good job covering developments in the final years of the Soviet Union. On the one hand, there is substantial evidence that agencies like DIA and CIA did produce finished intelligence that marked the slow but steady deterioration of the Soviet system.[23] On the other hand, the proof is in the pudding, and the public and the media have long claimed that U.S. intelligence agencies failed to call the Soviet breakup. Preoccupation with Soviet developments probably accounted for the failure of the U.S. intelligence community to anticipate Iraq's invasion of Kuwait in 1990.

The end of the Cold War in the early 1990s brought a call to downsize the national security apparatus in the U.S. government, including the intelligence agencies. Anticipating the "peace dividend," each of the agencies began a program of reducing staff and activities, to the extent that by the mid-1990s staffing numbers were at low levels not seen since the early 1970s. At the same time, a process of "openness" ushered in a period of public debate and discussion about intelligence and its role in the American society.

Rapid technological advancements also contributed to organizational innovations in order to cope with the intelligence requirements of the post–Cold War world. Yet the American intelligence establishment did not forecast the intertribal conflict in Somalia that led to the killing of American peacekeepers in 1993, and it performed poorly in Bosnia and Kosovo. It even missed the Indian nuclear tests in 1998. Nevertheless, because of new and intractable national security threats the administration of President Bill Clinton made substantial investments in reinforcing U.S. intelligence.

By the end of the 1990s, U.S. intelligence was making a comeback from the sloth into which it had sunk in the early parts of the decade. The 11 September 2001 terrorist attacks propelled U.S. intelligence into the forefront of the national fight against terrorists and thrust the intelligence community into the center of American national security policy.

Yet, the intelligence community suffered considerable criticism for a series of failures, such as the 9/11 attacks themselves and the faulty intelligence on Iraq's weapons of mass destruction capabilities that the White House used to justify the 2003 Iraq invasion. In the fall of 2001, Congress passed the USA PATRIOT Act, which mandated for intelligence coordination between the intelligence agencies and all levels of American law enforcement. In addition, Congress in 2002 established the Department of Homeland Security, with responsibility for generating and using intelligence to protect America's borders and infrastructure. Moreover, congressional, executive, and independent investigations made serious recommendations that in December 2004 culminated in the passage of the Intelligence Reform and Terrorism Prevention Act, which established the position of the director of national intelligence (DNI), created a National Counterterrorism Center (NCTC), and provided mechanisms for greater cooperation and coordination among the intelligence agencies.

The Intelligence Community

History has endowed the United States with an intelligence community of sixteen departments, bureaus, and agencies. The IC today, even as reorganized under the 2004 act, is an informal confederation of independent agencies and possesses a structure intended to divide authority among them. Indeed, the organization of American intelligence reflects the dominant political cultural assumption, that it is desirable to "divide and rule" an establishment that potentially could affect freedoms and civil liberties. Thomas Troy, a prolific writer on intelligence matters, says that the intelligence "community" lacks that sense of oneness, of wholeness, and togetherness that constitutes a community. He asserts that if there is any sense of community in the intelligence structure, it is in the

Successes

Manipulating the Italian Elections	1948
Overthrowing Mossadegh in Iran	1953
Ousting Arbenz in Guatemala	1954
Securing Khrushchev's Secret Speech	1956
Forecasting the Sputnik	1958
Forecasting the Sino-Soviet Split	1962
Forecasting the Chinese Atomic Bomb	1964
Forecasting new Soviet Strategic Weapons	1960s
Forecasting the Arab-Israeli War	1967
Forecasting the Soviet Anti-Ballistic Missile System	1968
Forecasting the India-Pakistan War	1971
Forecasting the Turkish Invasion of Cyprus	1974
Forecasting the Chinese Invasion of Vietnam	1978

Failures

North Korean Invasion of South Korea	1950
China's Entry into the Korean Conflict	1950
The Defeat of the French in Vietnam	1954
British-French-Israeli Invasion of Egypt	1956
Bay of Pigs Invasion	1961
Developments in Vietnam	1960s
Toughness of Vietnamese Guerrillas	1960s
Tet Offensive	1967
Soviet Invasion of Afghanistan	1979
Fall of the Iranian Shah	1979
Support of the Contras	1980s
Breakup of the Soviet Union	1989-91
Somalia Developments	1993
Ethnic Cleansing in Bosnia	1990s
Genocide in Rwanda	1990s
Indian Nuclear Tests	1998
Serbian Actions in Kosovo	1999
Terrorist Attacks on September 11	2001
Iraq's Lack of Weapons of Mass Destruction	2003

Figure 3. *Some Notable Intelligence Successes and Failures*

individual agencies where people have their careers and place their loyalties.[24]

The IC today comprises sixteen separate entities (see figure 4):

- The Defense Intelligence Agency (DIA)
- The National Security Agency (NSA)
- The intelligence units of the army, navy, air force, and the Marine Corps
- The National Geospatial-Intelligence Agency (NGA)
- The National Reconnaissance Office (NRO)
- The Department of Homeland Security (DHS) and, separately, the Coast Guard, part of the Department of

Homeland Security
- The counterintelligence unit of the Federal Bureau of Investigation (FBI)
- The Drug Enforcement Administration
- The intelligence division of the Department of the Treasury
- The intelligence division of the Department of Energy
- The Bureau of Intelligence and Research (INR) in the Department of State
- The Central Intelligence Agency (CIA).

These agencies are organizationally scattered throughout the executive branch, further fragmenting the community. In addition, their disparate and specialized missions, structures, and institutional affiliations guarantee that they all compete against each other to secure benefits for themselves. For example, DIA, NSA, Army, Navy, Air Force, and Marine Corps Intelligence, NGA, and the NRO all fall under the Department of Defense (DoD) and therefore reflect the missions and priorities of the military establishment. The other intelligence units—with the exception of the CIA—either are or belong to cabinet-level, policy departments in the executive branch and so reflect the bureaucratic imperatives of their cabinet secretaries. The CIA, on the other hand, is an independent U.S. government agency, much like the Federal Reserve Bank, the Interstate Commerce Commission, and hundreds of others. The CIA, under the terms of the National Security Act of 1947, reports directly to the president of the United States through the National Security Council.

Each IC agency contributes to the broader intelligence mission in discrete and specialized ways, while simultaneously participating in the larger effort of providing policy leaders with the comprehensive and collective judgment of the intelligence community—neither an easy nor an inexpensive task. A brief overview of each agency's contributions to this complicated business would provide substance to this assertion.

Defense Intelligence Agency (DIA)
DIA, along with the CIA and the State Department's Bureau of Intelligence and Research, is an all-source intelligence

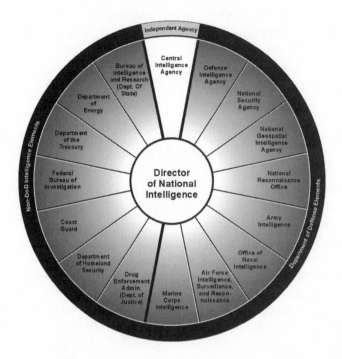

Figure 4. *The U.S. Intelligence Community*

agency located both in the Pentagon in Arlington, Virginia, and at Bolling Air Force Base in Washington, D.C. The "all-source" designation means that DIA receives raw intelligence from other intelligence collectors in the U.S. government as well as from its own sources. As pointed out earlier in this chapter, DIA was established in 1961 as the intelligence arm of the Joint Chiefs of Staff. Its mission is to engage in strategic military intelligence, which deals with issues that affect national defense policy (whereas tactical intelligence focuses on battlefield or more local situations).

DIA runs the defense attaché program and has jurisdiction over the Joint Military Intelligence College. As military officers posted to U.S. embassies abroad, defense attachés have the responsibility of observing foreign military developments and reporting that information. As such, defense attachés are collectors of intelligence information. In fact, they are generally known as "open spies" and are an integral part of the Defense HUMINT Service, created in 1993, to consolidate military espionage activities. Defense attachés also represent the Department of Defense and the military services abroad, administer military assistance programs and foreign military sales, and advise U.S. ambassadors on military and political-military issues.[25]

National Security Agency (NSA)

NSA is located in Fort Meade, Maryland, and is probably the most secretive of America's intelligence organizations. While it nominally belongs to the Department of Defense, it functions as a service organization for the intelligence community and other U.S. government agencies.

NSA performs three tasks. The first is to engage in signals intelligence (SIGINT), a collection discipline that focuses on intercepting the diplomatic, military, and intelligence communications of foreign nations and other international actors, and on making translations available to those who have a "need to know" in the U.S. government. Engaging in SIGINT collection, however, requires NSA to perform its second function, which is to break the codes and ciphers of foreign governments, while ensuring the security of U.S. communications codes. NSA's third responsibility is establishing, operating, and maintaining all secure communications within the U.S. government, in and out of the intelligence community—an activity known as "communications security," or COMSEC. According to Jeffrey Richelson, NSA creates, reviews, and authorizes the communications procedures and codes of a variety of government agencies—including the State Department, the DoD, the CIA, and the FBI.[26] COMSEC is now within the larger rubric of "information security," or INFOSEC.

The Military Intelligence Agencies

Each of the intelligence units of the army, navy, air force, and Marine Corps performs tactical military intelligence for its specific command. Each has a clandestine collection capability supervised by the Defense HUMINT Service. Since the early 1990s, there has been significant consolidation of activities within each of the service intelligence units, largely in response to the downsizing of the military at the end of the Cold War. Because of long-standing rivalries among the services, the events of 11 September 2001 reinforced the need for consolidation and greater cooperation among the service units. Joint intelligence task forces are now the norm rather than the exception.

National Geospatial-Intelligence Agency (NGA)

Established in November 2003, NGA replaced the former National Imagery and Mapping Agency (NIMA) by incorporating geospatial intelligence (GEOINT) into its imagery and mapping capabilities. NIMA had been established only in 1996 by consolidating the Defense Mapping Agency, DoD's Central Imagery Office, CIA's National Photographic Interpretation Center, the imagery exploitation unit of the DIA, and other similar agencies. However, the need to employ geospatial information—complete visualization of geographically referenced areas on the earth—induced DoD managers to expand NIMA's original jurisdiction. In addition to providing geospatial intelligence, NGA now manages imagery intelligence, or IMINT, in the U.S. government by setting imagery priorities, levying imagery requirements, and analyzing imagery for national customers. Even though it is part of the Defense Department, NGA serves the entire intelligence community and provides combat support to the military. The secretary of defense and the DNI share the management of NGA, although the DCI, as head of the CIA, also has authority regarding national imagery systems and has a large say over the appointment of the NGA director.

National Reconnaissance Office (NRO)

NRO is the manager of America's space reconnaissance programs.[27] It contracts for, builds, controls, and uses the hardware that goes into airborne and space reconnaissance. NRO also constructs and uses sensors for the exploitation of intelligence information from emissions of factories, nuclear power plants, nuclear explosions, and the like, and from foreign military equipment (materiel exploitation). In addition, NRO manages satellite systems designed to intercept communications from space, a field known as "space SIGINT." As the agency that contracts for and operates vastly expensive satellite and other hardware systems, the NRO probably spends the bulk of the intelligence community's financial resources.

Congress established the NRO soon after the beginning of the space race in the late 1950s and early 1960s, and its existence was a closely held secret for much of its lifetime. The NRO is actually a federation of intelligence and military organizations that maintain their separate identities and loosely cooperate in the common task of exploiting imagery and other information derived from its collection systems. In 1994, the White House made public the existence of the NRO, but the organization remains, along with the NSA, one of the least known of the intelligence community agencies.

Department of Homeland Security and the Coast Guard

The Department of Homeland Security (DHS) and the U.S. Coast Guard are among the newest additions to the intelligence community. The Department of Homeland Security was established in 2002 to identify and reduce America's vulnerabilities to attack and provide official assistance and recovery aid after such attacks. Many of its agencies possess intelligence capabilities, but they participate in the intelligence community by virtue of the fact that the department is a member of the IC—except for the Coast Guard, which is a separate member of the intelligence community.

Previously within the Department of Transportation, the U.S. Coast Guard was one of the over twenty-five agencies incorporated into DHS in 2002. Previously a poor cousin to the military services, the Coast Guard's inclusion into the formal intelligence community structure has elevated its stature and funding levels. Its mission, however, remains pretty much the same as in the past, focusing on perimeter security, interdiction, and search and rescue. Although not within the Defense Department, the Coast Guard continues to be regarded as an armed service.

Federal Bureau of Investigation (FBI)

The FBI is the premier federal law enforcement agency of the U.S. government and, as such, is legally prohibited from engaging in foreign intelligence activities. However, its counterintelligence unit, and only this part, is a formal member of the intelligence community. Congress in 2001 relaxed the sharp separation of law enforcement and foreign intelligence. Legislation like the USA PATRIOT Act,[28] enacted as an antiterror tool in the aftermath of 9/11, now blurs the distinction between the two by promoting cooperation between foreign intelligence agencies and the law enforcement community, including the state and local levels.

The FBI finds itself in an anomalous position within the intelligence community. As a law enforcement arm of the Department of Justice, it stays away from strategic intelligence, but its counterintelligence responsibilities, along with its myriad liaison relationships with foreign law enforcement agencies, thrust the FBI into the center of foreign intelligence activities. The bureau's counterintelligence role further inhibits coordination with criminal investigations within the Department of Justice, to the detriment of both counterintelligence and criminal justice.[29]

The FBI successfully straddled this uncomfortable fence as long as its powerful former director, J. Edgar Hoover, managed to fend off attacks on FBI turf from within and outside the intelligence community. After 9/11, the Congress responded to the FBI's less than stellar performance—the agency is accused of having botched several antiterrorism investigations and not cooperating with the CIA in counterterrorism efforts—by giving it a greater role in strategic intelligence, a move that is likely to protect the FBI for the time being from those who seek to prey on the FBI's statutory roles. Whether the putative fusion of law enforcement and intelligence will affect America's cherished freedoms and civil liberties is too soon to tell, but civil libertarians have begun a concerted push to roll back the effects of the PATRIOT Act and other similar legislation.

Drug Enforcement Administration (DEA)

Established in 1973 from disparate federal antidrug agencies, including the Bureau of Narcotics and Dangerous Drugs (BNDD), DEA now coordinates U.S. law enforcement efforts in regulating the production, importation, and use of controlled substances as well as in enforcing laws against narcotics trafficking and the laundering of money derived from such trafficking. DEA runs the National Narcotics Intelligence System (NADDIS), a centralized computer database incorporating all intelligence and investigative data available to state and local law enforcement agencies. DEA also is responsible for the El Paso Intelligence Center, which is staffed by DEA agents and representatives from fifteen other federal agencies and state and local public safety officials. The activities of the El Paso Intelligence Center include the coordination and analysis of intelligence information on the movement of drugs and people into the United States. Although involved in intelligence activities since its inception in 1973, DEA became an official member of the U.S. intelligence community (IC) in 2006 as part of the administration's efforts to provide greater credence to strategic intelligence collection in all national security priority areas and to streamline intelligence sharing among national intelligence authorities and state and local officials.

Treasury Department
The intelligence unit of the Treasury Department openly collects financial and monetary data from around the globe and subjects this information to analysis for government and business consumers. Treasury also seeks intelligence information about technology transfers and the spread of weapons technology. As such, the Treasury Department is an important element in identifying money flows, collecting trade information, ferreting out money-laundering schemes, and distributing licensing information.

Energy Department
The Energy Department maintains an intelligence capability for two reasons. First, it collects intelligence information from around the globe about nuclear-energy matters, which dovetail into other issues like nuclear nonproliferation and specific regional and country energy requirements. Second, as the guardian of the nation's nuclear weapons and manager of America's nuclear weapons laboratories, the Energy Department engages both in security and counterintelligence activities over the development, production, testing, and maintenance of nuclear weapons and associated technologies.

Bureau of Intelligence and Research (INR)
The State Department's INR is an all-source agency that engages in political, economic, and military intelligence analysis. INR does not have a collection capability of its own but is a consumer of raw intelligence from other U.S. intelligence agencies as well as of diplomatic reports from U.S. embassies abroad. The principal customer is the secretary of state, for whom it produces a variety of current and long-term intelligence products. The *Morning Summary* is the medium used to keep the secretary abreast of current developments around the globe.

Central Intelligence Agency (CIA)
The CIA's principal work focuses on its least controversial and probably most vital task—warning American leaders of strategic threats to the nation. The CIA, the only independent U.S. government agency in the intelligence community, is an all-source intelligence organization charged with engaging in three types of activities—intelligence collection and analysis, counterintelligence, and covert action. The first two activities are pretty straightforward, while the third—covert action—has been controversial, contributing to the image that the CIA is an agency that engages in "dirty tricks," such as attempting assassinations of political leaders and overthrowing governments. The public developed its perceptions of the agency's activities during its heyday, the 1950s and 1960s.

The CIA's principal task is to collect intelligence information, subject it to rigorous analysis, produce intelligence products emanating from that analysis, and disseminate these products to decision makers who have a "need to know." The intelligence cycle is a simplified depiction of this process.

In addition to receiving intelligence information from other collection agencies, the CIA receives useful information from its own collectors. In fact, the CIA is the manager of human intelligence, HUMINT, in the government, including espionage that falls within the Department of Defense, a responsibility reaffirmed by the White House in October 2005. Intelligence information collected by means of the various "collection disciplines" arrives at the CIA on a continual basis and is dispersed to analysts for evaluation and analysis.

Intelligence analysts must know not only the priorities of the policymakers but the relevance, reliability, and validity of the information. After making these determinations and setting the data in context, the analysts compose finished intelligence for a number of intelligence publications, such as national intelligence estimates (NIEs).

NIEs are coordinated IC projections about particular countries, regions, or issues of interest to decision makers. CIA analysts, like analysts in other all-source intelligence agencies, such as DIA and INR, also produce a plethora of other finished intelligence products that contribute to informed and rational decision making by policymakers.

The CIA produces a number of current intelligence products, the most important of which is the *President's Daily Brief* (*PDB*), a product so sensitive that, by presidential direction, its recipients may not retain the document but must return it to the agency for storage or destruction. Nearly every morning, senior CIA intelligence analysts take the *PDB* to their various principals (the president determines who in his administration is allowed to see the *PDB*), like the president and the secretary of defense, and brief them on the contents of the document. After the briefings, the *PDB* is brought back to the CIA for storage. The DNI has the final say on the *PDB* and often attends the *PDB* briefings at the White House and so is at hand to advise the president on intelligence matters.

In addition to intelligence analysis, the CIA engages in counterintelligence, which is the activity dedicated to undermining the effectiveness of hostile intelligence services and to guard the nation against espionage and sabotage. Counterintelligence also includes the protection of national secrets, because hostile intelligence agencies are looking not only for classified information but also for technological information that affects competitiveness and ultimately military capabilities.

The conduct of counterintelligence is a shared activity, principally between the FBI—a law enforcement agency—and the CIA, a non–law enforcement foreign-intelligence organization. Military commands have counterintelligence responsibilities on military bases and installations abroad. Because counterintelligence transcends national boundaries, its effectiveness requires a good deal of coordination and cooperation among the agencies charged with counterintelligence duties. Such cooperation between the FBI and the CIA has been spotty at best, as illustrated by the postmortem investigations of the Rick Ames and the Robert Hanssen espionage cases.

The CIA has domestic counterintelligence responsibilities only in regard to its employees. As a way of ensuring the integrity of its security, CIA, like the other intelligence agencies, subjects its employees to extensive background investigations and to the polygraph. Such efforts, though useful in protecting sources and methods, have not been wholly successful in preventing the penetration of U.S. intelligence agencies.

CIA's third function—covert action—is the most controversial. Covert action, or special activities, technically is not intelligence but employs secret intelligence resources in support of American foreign policy objectives in such a way that government sponsorship is not apparent or acknowledged. Most proposals for covert action originate outside the CIA, either within the policy frameworks of the State Department and the Defense Department or with the National Security Council. Presidential orders require the CIA to manage and implement covert actions, unless the president deems another agency more suitable. The designated agencies, usually with the CIA in the lead, employ a variety of secret techniques to conduct covert actions, which in essence depart from the traditional definition of intelligence and introduce peculiar but significant sources of failure into secret intelligence.

The CIA's myriad activities complement those of the other IC agencies to produce an intelligence program with a global reach. One would think that such a diverse but extensive effort naturally would have strong, central management, but that is not the case. The director of the Central Intelligence Agency (DCIA) now heads the CIA and, in contrast to his roles prior to 2005, has few community responsibilities.

The Ineffectual DNI

Until 2005, the DCI was the nominal head of the IC as well. He lost that job to the DNI as a result of the Intelligence Reform and Terrorism Prevention Act, which was lauded for establishing an office with substantial community management responsibilities. However, the act did little more than transfer the DCI's meager community roles to the DNI, who now engages in three functions. First, he puts together, submits, and controls the National Foreign Intelligence Program (NFIP) budget, which is the intelligence community budget, integrating intelligence requirements that policymakers feel are necessary during any given budgetary cycle. As the IC budget document, the NFIP seeks to avoid duplication and overlap, but as a management tool it often fails to compel the IC agencies to cooperate.

Compounding the problem, there are two other intelligence budgets in the U.S. government over which the DNI exercises little control. The Joint Military Intelligence Program (JMIP) budget and the Tactical Intelligence and Related Activities (TIARA) budget fall under the jurisdiction of the secretary of defense, who uses his policy clout to keep the DNI from encroaching on his intelligence domains. The DNI was supposed to get firm budgetary and personnel authorities, but Congress, buckling under pressure from the senior leadership of the Defense Department, diluted his prerogatives in this area.

Second, the DNI manages the country's counterintelligence programs, a responsibility shared by some IC agencies. The FBI continues to conduct counterintelligence domestically in the United States. The CIA conducts counterintelligence to protect its own operations abroad. Each of the military services is responsible for counterintelligence within its own ranks. While a good deal of coordination exists in this area, there is still much fragmentation, which concerns those who want a more comprehensive CI effort.[30] The establishment of the Counterintelligence Center (CIC) in the late 1980s and the National Counterintelligence Executive (NCIX) in the 1990s were the right moves in the right direction, but the lack of a unified counterintelligence strategy remains a concern.

Third, the DNI as community chief is responsible for protecting sources and methods. Most of what is secret about the intelligence process is the way it is done—the sources from which information is obtained and the methods used to obtain it. This secrecy is mainly for the protection of these sources and methods; otherwise, U.S. intelligence would be unable to gather and analyze the information necessary to understanding adversaries and issues relevant to national security. "Protecting sources and methods" forms the basis for all classification and compartmentation schemes in the government, an area over which the DNI retains complete control.

These three responsibilities—submitting a community budget, conducting counterintelligence, and protecting sources and methods—are the only ones the DNI exercises in his statutory role as head of the intelligence community. Even in this capacity, however, the DNI is more a coordinator, able only to exercise "soft power" techniques like persuasion and influence. To overcome this deficiency, the typical DNI must bring to his office attributes that would enable him better to manage the community—a personal relationship and access to the president, the skills of an excellent negotiator, and the patience of a mediator. In the past, some directors have brought such qualities to their job, to great effect. Most, however, have lacked in these qualities and therefore have been less successful in wielding their community role. Because the heads of IC agencies—except the CIA—report directly to their policy principals, the DNI's relative position in the White House pecking order also comes into play in the bureaucratic politics of the intelligence community. This is especially so regarding the Pentagon's intelligence units, over which the secretary of defense looms like an eight-hundred-pound gorilla.[31] From time to time, a particular secretary of defense may give lip service to allowing the director greater authority over the defense-related intelligence organizations, but no defense secretary relinquished any significant amount of power to the DCI in the past and he does not do so now to the DNI.

The New Counterterrorism Focus

The terrorist attacks on 11 September 2001 cast intelligence into a central national security role, a role that had eluded it in the past. American intelligence had previously focused on the terrorist threat as early as the 1970s, but counterterrorism did not become central to the intelligence mission until DCI William Casey established the Counterterrorism Center in

1986. Even so, antiterrorism competed with other intelligence priorities—proliferation of weapons of mass destruction, for example—and usually received short shrift in the Washington funding game so long as terrorism remained a foreign phenomenon. The terrorist attacks on the World Trade Center in 1993 and the other subsequent terrorist attacks on American soil, including those of 11 September 2001, elevated counterterrorism to priority status and made it a part of America's national security strategy. The Terrorist Threat Integration Center (TTIC), announced by President George W. Bush on 28 January 2003, was folded into the National Counterterrorism Center (NCTC) in 2005; both are evidence of this change in orientation.[32]

Yet refocusing America's intelligence effort has not translated into dramatic cooperation among America's parochial intelligence agencies. The meager, and principally cosmetic, attempts to force the agencies to talk to one another and act in concert have failed to produce significant results. The intelligence community now has substantially more money to throw at intelligence problems, especially the terrorism issue, but the management of the community remains fraught with duplication, overlap, and waste. In addition, the 9/11 and the Iraqi WMD intelligence failures appear to have strengthened, not weakened, the positions of many intelligence leaders in the IC.[33] This suggests that American intelligence operates within a fairly rigid set of cultural precepts—an intelligence ethos—that have protected it from those who might seek to alter the way it does business.

3

Pitfalls of American- Style Intelligence

It cannot be doubted that by some alchemy, out of the blending of inheritance, environment and experience, there came a distinctive American character.
—Henry Steele Commager

Historical forces and structural imperatives together have created a uniquely American "intelligence ethos," a series of cultural principles that are specific to the highly secretive and shadowy world of intelligence. Some intelligence and policy experts would consider the principles to be positive engines that empower intelligence agencies to accomplish their specialized missions, and accomplish them well. The precepts may work to smooth the workings of American intelligence, but they also contribute to intelligence failures in significant ways.

The Intelligence Ethos

An integrated cultural template distinguishes U.S. intelligence from other types of governmental activities. This intelligence ethos comprises eight principles, some of which are directly linked to mission-specific issues. The others are attitudinal in nature, providing intelligence officials with a worldview that justifies maintaining their closed and secret world as far removed as possible from the public and the policy world they are sworn to serve. These cultural principles have frequently undermined the intelligence process and formed the basis for some spectacular intelligence failures.

Mission-Specific Myopia

Like all organizations, intelligence agencies want to fulfill their missions and thereby ensure their own survival. As government entities, they seek to maximize the value of their information and increase their stature relative to the others; promote their bureaucratic interests; and enable them to survive in the political marketplace that places so much value on these attributes. Because of their specialized and secret work, intelligence agencies tend to be keenly interested in bringing on board people who are committed to agency goals, dedicated to the particular agency, and have a sense of unshakeable devotion to the agency's mission. Indeed, while American intelligence has come under substantial criticism for the way it does its work, none of this criticism has questioned the commitment and dedication of intelligence officers. On the contrary, numerous assessments have agreed that despite perceived and real institutional breakdowns, American intelligence officers are to be commended for their integrity and devotion to duty. If any criticism can be leveled against them, it would be that some officers in the past have interpreted their missions too liberally and have been too eager in carrying out their work.

A sense of mission is a good thing, and American intelligence officials have an unbounded sense of mission. Too zealous a commitment to the mission, however, may be a bad thing, for it can induce a myopic view of the task and of the specific agency's position in the intelligence process. For example, there is little doubt that CIA employees have an unshakable sense of the worth of what they do, a deep commitment to duty, and a profound loyalty to the organization. However, there is little corresponding dedication to the broader intelligence missions represented by the intelligence community. If anything, CIA employees "ape" their cousins in the other agencies and equate their agency's well-being with that of the entire intelligence enterprise. Such projection may lead to bureaucratic myopia and divert CIA employees from wider intelligence objectives.

Intelligence Exceptionalism

American intelligence officials also espouse the notion that intelligence occupies an "exceptional" position within the ranks of government activities. The idea of intelligence exceptionalism derives from a number of factors. First, intelligence is different because it employs broad-based secrecy to do its work. Second, intelligence is different because it entails, among other things, the breaking of other countries' laws. All countries impose heavy penalties on espionage, and the irony is that these countries simultaneously empower legally their intelligence services to spy on their friends and foes. Third, intelligence is different because it is subject to deception and disinformation, often casting doubt on the reliability and integrity of information—the principal product of intelligence activities. Fourth, intelligence is different because it is fungible—that is, it can be, and often is, used by leaders and politicians for a variety of purposes, ranging from furthering the public interest to promoting a partisan or private agenda.

A "Can Do" Attitude

Intelligence officials reinforce their absolute faith in the exceptionalism of intelligence with a "can do" attitude. This view, that American intelligence can accomplish any task successfully, is a reflection of the broader American cultural principle that Americans are doers, that they can do any task set before them better than anyone else.[1] This attitude also derives from the essential optimism of Americans, based on the assumption that imagination, daring, and persistence are the attributes most likely to yield useful intelligence about national security threats.[2] Former DCI Tenet's list of intelligence objectives in chapter 1 is a clear illustration of the "can do" attitude that has dominated the intelligence community since its inception.

Such an attitude requires risk-taking, and risk-taking can lead to poorly conceived actions or illegal operations that can come back to haunt American intelligence. The modern history of U.S. intelligence is replete with examples of risk-taking gone awry. The investigations of the late 1970s were intended in part to mitigate the effects of too eager an intelligence apparatus. American intelligence agents have come under repeated criticism since then for periodically acting like "cowboys."

There are now indications that the pendulum may have swung too far the other way, that U.S. intelligence may have become too risk averse. Observers agree that since the 1970s, U.S. intelligence has avoided risk in order to forestall running afoul of domestic law or becoming subject to political fallout. According to David Ignatius, a journalist specializing in national security affairs, the low point "came during the Clinton years. The price for doing aggressive intelligence work too often was to be called on the carpet. One intrepid CIA officer sent to Iraq in the mid-1980s [Robert Baer] to try to organize opposition to Saddam Hussein was actually summoned home and briefly investigated by the FBI for allegedly conspiring to murder the Iraqi leader."[3]

Observers consistently describe similar instances of timidity. For example, Thomas Powers, a keen observer of the intelligence scene, says that there has been a slow growth of a careerist caution in the CIA and the FBI, producing what some intelligence officers describe as "risk aversion culture."[4] He goes on to illustrate this by quoting a sign that hung over the desk of a CIA officer in Rome: "Big Ops, Big Problems. Small Ops, Small Problems. No Ops, No Problems."[5] One important reason for such caution appears to be the view that a Congress that is prodding U.S. intelligence to be less risk averse today will, in a few years from now, when operations go bad, be demanding why U.S. intelligence took such foolish chances. The various commissions that investigated the 9/11 and Iraqi WMD failures emphasized the recent tendency of American intelligence to be risk averse and recommended steps to overcome this problem.[6]

Ambiguous Mandate

Augmenting, and perhaps enabling, the occasionally overeager behavior of American intelligence is the ambiguity surrounding the intelligence mandate. The structure of U.S. intelligence attests to the fact that Americans do not want a strong, centralized intelligence apparatus that could be capable of threatening civil liberties and freedoms. To assure themselves of this, politicians have gone out of their way to ensure that the intelligence community operates on a basis of competing cultures, turf battles, and divided loyalties. The confederal structure of U.S. intelligence has been, and is, consistent with this objective. While fear of a centralized intelligence apparatus has been the principal reason for keeping vague the mandate of the intelligence community, additional factors have also come into play over the years—to fudge priorities and targets and to give U.S. intelligence some flexibility.

Such ambiguity dates to the National Security Act of 1947, which set up the modern structure of U.S. intelligence. Michael Warner, of CIA's History Staff, points out that under the regime that emerged from the 1947 act and subsequent legislation, the director of central intelligence has faced contradictory mandates: the DCI could coordinate intelligence but could not entirely control it.[7] Warner further says that because of this tendency to emphasize coordination over control, the DCI

> never quite became the integrator of U.S. intelligence that its presidential and congressional parents had envisioned. The DCI never became the manager of the Intelligence Community, his Agency [the CIA] never won the power to "inspect" the departments' operational plans or to extract community-wide consensus on disputed analytical issues, and CIA never had authority over all clandestine operations of the U.S. Government.[8]

Nonetheless, there have been occasional attempts to delineate what U.S. intelligence can and cannot do. The most recent was by Eleanor Hill, the staff director of the Joint Inquiry Congressional Panel, who described the role of American intelligence in the counterterrorist effort in this way:

- Collecting, analyzing, and disseminating intelligence information
- Issuing warnings to policymakers to counter threats to the United States
- Preventing, preempting, and disrupting actions against the United States
- Supporting U.S. diplomatic, legal, and military operations.[9]

The Joint Panel's concept is typically bureaucratic and lacks clarity as well as and specificity. For example, the role of the DCI in antiterror activities is not clear; the nature and substance of prevention, preemption, and disruption is not specified; and the statement fails to say what constitutes a warning, while linking a warning with the policymakers' ability to counter threats. Furthermore, the Joint Panel's enumeration restricts policy support to operational rather than analytic situations, something that if implemented fully would decimate American intelligence altogether. So the mandate of U.S. intelligence remains vague—a state of affairs that historically has forced U.S. intelligence to focus less on what it does and more on how it does it.

Competitive Intelligence
Competition occupies a privileged position in the conduct of American intelligence. Most policymakers and some scholars give competitive intelligence a positive spin by asserting that competition among the different intelligence agencies enables "the truth to come out." This happens presumably because in the process of competition each agency seeks to maximize its position relative to the others, usually by the kind of "one-upmanship" that enables them to outdo each other in producing intelligence. The theory presumes that this creates a situation where the intelligence marketplace puts a premium in the best intelligence, giving maximum benefits to the consumer of intelligence and the American public. Competition among intelligence agencies has probably accounted for some of America's intelligence successes.

However, like institutional fragmentation, competition has corrosive effects on intelligence. Each intelligence agency uses competitive intelligence to promote its own agenda, to undermine the activities of the other intelligence agencies, and to seek more money at the expense of the others, all of which subvert cooperation. The legendary competition between the Defense Department and the State Department, for example, frequently spills over into competition between their intelligence elements, to the detriment of effective intelligence. Likewise, the Defense Department and the CIA are often at each other's throats over a variety of issues, vying for influence in national security policy, access to national leaders, and money at the other's expense, as was the case in 2002 over counterterrorism issues and U.S. Iraq policy.[10] While there is some utility to competitive intelligence as a variation of "peer review," the net result more often than not is to stymie a unified intelligence effort.

Flexible Accountability
Because of its "exceptionalism," American intelligence has had to account for its actions and performance differently from other governmental institutions. Accountability is a hallmark of the American democratic tradition, but U.S. intelligence agencies appear to have escaped serious supervision by the U.S. Congress, the courts, and even the executive branch. Loch Johnson, who has written extensively on intelligence matters, asserts that "even in the modern era with all the congressional oversight capabilities . . . the [IC agencies] have sidestepped the government's usual checks and balances."[11] While many may consider this a subversion of the American system, it probably has had the effect of giving freer rein to the agencies on mission-specific activities.

An analysis of the record indicates that U.S. intelligence agencies have been subject to what could be termed "flexible accountability," which is the practice of varying the amount and degree of accountability, depending on the inclinations of both the intelligence agencies and their political bosses. In the early years of the U.S. intelligence community, congressional oversight of intelligence was virtually nonexistent, largely because Congress insisted on deferring to the intelligence agencies. In later years, especially after the late 1970s, Congress and the executive branch put in place a system of oversight that has produced checkered results.

Loch Johnson says that two studies of the impact of oversight have essentially arrived at the same conclusion, but for different reasons. One study concluded that oversight is ineffective because the oversight entities—Congress, the media, and the executive branch—have abrogated their responsibilities and left the intelligence agencies to their own devices. The other study found that oversight is ineffective because Congress has been placed in the position of micromanaging

U.S. intelligence, which has resulted in diminishing intelligence capabilities.[12] Recently, Senator Richard C. Shelby (R-Ala) took a different tack, claiming that Congress holds senior intelligence officials responsible for what they do but not for what they do not do.[13]

Strict Separation of Intelligence from Policy

Such policy concerns arise in an intelligence ethos that likes to keep a wall of separation between the world of intelligence and the world of policy. To intelligence officials, this is an indisputable principle, on the grounds intelligence officers must maintain objectivity and keep clear of policy advocacy. Moreover, intelligence analysts are admonished to present their intelligence data to policymakers without bias or political taint. Those who report the information also must not manipulate it to drive policy or to justify intrusive intelligence collection.[14] Failing to do so threatens the objectivity of the analyses they present.[15]

Strong impulses exist for intelligence and policy to stay apart. Policymakers hate to hear bad news that might contradict or undermine strongly held views, bureaucratic interests, or established policy. In addition, policy leaders, who typically have strong political interests, have partisan agendas that frequently come into conflict with how intelligence analysts view the world and themselves—intellectuals who seek objectivity in their analysis.[16]

Yet intelligence is irrelevant without policy, while policy is blind without intelligence.[17] If intelligence is to be effective, intelligence analysts must be close enough to policy leaders to be in tune with their goals and to understand the context of the policy struggle. At the same time, policymakers cannot expect intelligence analysts to advocate policy, or be a "team player" in policy circles.[18]

Keeping the two separate is a delicate business. Arthur S. Hulnick, a retired CIA veteran, says that there is no substitute for establishing personal relationships between intelligence officers and policy consumers at all levels in order to satisfy their respective professional needs:

> Intelligence officers have to take the initiative to find their consumers, go to see them, establish a working relationship so

that each is known to the other. . . . [T]he intelligence officer [also] has to determine what material would be useful for the consumer, not only meeting what the consumer thinks are his or her needs but also providing material that may not necessarily be welcome.[19]

The special relationship between policymaker and intelligence analyst leaves open the possibility of politicizing intelligence, but then, to paraphrase an intelligence officer, an analyst who is not on the verge of being politicized is not doing his job.[20]

Intelligence analysts contribute to the policy process by providing "actionable" intelligence,[21] but nothing prevents policymakers from providing intelligence inputs of their own or rejecting intelligence analyses. Policymakers also sometimes ask the opinions of intelligence officials on U.S. policy, which puts intelligence officers in the uncomfortable position of having to delve into policy matters. More often than not, intelligence officials do give their opinions on U.S. policy when asked; in general, however, the relationship between leaders and their intelligence advisers is so full of difficulties that its problems cannot adequately be resolved.[22]

Strict Separation of Intelligence from Law Enforcement
History and tradition have also instilled a strong belief in the proposition that America's intelligence agencies ought not engage in law enforcement. Much like the prohibition against the police activities by the military—the so-called Posse Comitatus Act—U.S. intelligence is banned from law enforcement, for several reasons. A fear exists that combining the two functions in one agency or a group of agencies would give rise to a "Gestapo" or a "KGB" that would trample American freedoms and civil liberties. Another concern is that intelligence and law enforcement are completely different missions that require different standards of proof. While law enforcement seeks to gather information that can stand up in court, intelligence agencies gather information that may be useful for decision making but may not be able to meet the stricter legal standard. The discrepancies result in procedural differences, which at times cannot be bridged. For example, while federal law enforcement carries out investigations intended

to produce arrests and convictions, intelligence carries out actions intended to turn people into spies.

The separation between intelligence work and law enforcement is firmly enshrined in a series of statutes that govern intelligence activities. However, in the wake of the terrorist attacks of 11 September 2001, the Bush administration put in place modifications in the wall separating intelligence from law enforcement. One change authorizes criminal prosecutors to seek and get surveillance warrants from the Foreign Intelligence Surveillance Court, established in 1978 to issue such warrants for use in the United States against foreign agents in the absence of criminal activity.[23] Another change empowers the FBI to collect terrorism intelligence while carrying out traditional law enforcement duties. In addition, DEA is now an official member of the intelligence community; this further blurs the distinction between intelligence and law enforcement.

Still another change gives U.S. intelligence agencies expanded powers to engage in domestic intelligence gathering.[24] The independent national commission on the 9/11 terrorist attacks even proposed establishing a domestic intelligence agency that might take over many FBI responsibilities.[25] The idea has received the cold shoulder from civil libertarians. Some prominent administration officials, such as Robert Mueller, the FBI director, also came out in opposition to a domestic intelligence service.[26]

The easing of the rule separating intelligence from law enforcement is creating anxiety. A federal commission set up in 1998 and chaired by former Virginia governor James Gilmore insisted that "it is . . . important to separate the intelligence collection function from the law enforcement function to avoid the impression that the U.S. is establishing a kind of 'secret police.'"[27] Groups concerned about the civil liberties of Americans are pushing to modify existing legislation, especially the PATRIOT Act, to keep the separation intact.[28]

Bureaucratic Pathologies

The deleterious aspects of the eight principles combine with bureaucratic pathologies to account for a majority of intelligence failures. Structural pathologies permeate the entire intelligence process, making them the most significant barriers to successful intelligence. Among the most significant structural pathologies in U.S. intelligence are the setting of priorities, and resource constraints.

Because the United States has a global reach, the domain of American intelligence is so vast and resources so insufficient that priorities are never on equal footings. At any given moment, U.S. intelligence may be devoting attention to hot-button issues at the expense of issues that have not yet caught the attention of policy leaders but may become important in the future.

Requirements drive the intelligence process. Intelligence requirements are those issues upon which policymakers want intelligence to focus; however, policy leaders must be able to articulate their demands and exert some effort in tasking intelligence agencies to meet their demands. Although this sounds simple, it is in fact complicated by bureaucratic politics. The hundreds of government officials with foreign and national security policy decision-making responsibilities often have competing, if not conflicting, geographical and functional interests. Each wants immediate satisfaction of informational needs while often remaining unsure of just what it is he or she needs to know. This results in severe competition among them to place their concerns as high as possible in intelligence requirements lists. Many government offices that are outmaneuvered in the process see their requirements either ignored or given short shrift.[29] Sometimes Congress gets into the act, too. In fact, U.S. intelligence is a political football kicked about in an intramural game of one-upmanship between the executive and legislative branches of the U.S. government.

At the end of the Cold War, two issues dominated intelligence priority lists: proliferation of weapons of mass destruction and the problem of failed and rogue states. Terrorism was high on the list but could not compete with what appeared to be the more important issues. Despite occasional terrorist acts against the United States during the 1990s, it was difficult to justify the diversion of scarce intelligence resources to the issue, because it was hard to arouse the attention of policymakers, whose agendas were occupied with other issues; once the terrorist attacks on 9/11 took place, terrorism rose to the top of priority lists. A variation of this seesawing of intelligence priorities occurs when a crisis calms down and, for political or financial reasons, it becomes difficult to justify continuing the heavy diversion of intelligence resources to an issue once the crisis appears to be over.

Diversity in priorities provides incentives for the intelligence agencies to compete with one another for scarce resources. Such competition is reflected within specific agencies as well, sometimes at the expense of sound intelligence. For example, there is intense competition between the analytic and operational sides of the CIA, which often threatens to impede sound intelligence collection and responsible intelligence production. The other intelligence agencies experience similar dynamics, which often hinder the intelligence process. The fact that virtually all intelligence analysts are hierarchically and culturally separated from policy offices is another organizational impediment to the effective use of intelligence.

Internal bureaucratic procedures can also influence the quality of intelligence. Virtually all of the intelligence agencies have internal procedures that can best be described as overly bureaucratic. The analytic process, for example, sometimes produces timely intelligence products, but most of the time analysis relies on the heavily bureaucratic procedures of going through a chain of command that includes supervisors, their bosses, and a variety of different editors. Such a cumbersome review process often delays intelligence and, in a crisis, can lead to intelligence failures.

In addition, government bureaucracies tend to create temporary procedures in crises. For example, intelligence agencies routinely cope with new or ongoing tough problems by creating ad hoc task forces, which have their own rules and procedures, and which often rely on their own dedicated information sources, all of which results in the tendency to compartmentalize information. Multiple task forces can be healthy if they contribute to diversity of views and provide a broader range of options for decision makers. However, they can also result in unnecessary duplication of effort, contribute to slow decision making, and prevent a full and objective consideration of information.

The other side of the coin is that reliance on one centralized unit can weaken crisis management. A single agency or department usually dominates a task force or a single fusion center and tends to rely on its own intelligence. For example, the DCI Crime and Narcotics Center is located in the CIA headquarters, is staffed mainly by CIA officers, and relies heavily on CIA's information. Overcoming such parochialism is not cheap or easy. Recently, the intelligence community undertook several interagency communication schemes— such as INTELINK, which is a community-wide intranet—but the normal bureaucratic tendency to protect turf and insulate against possible blame for failures has tended to weaken the kind of informational exchange that the systems are created to achieve.

Bureaucratic rivalry manifests itself also in competition between different types of intelligence collection disciplines, or stovepipes. The problem stems from the public's current fascination with science and technology, which gives rise to the erroneous belief that raw intelligence is better than finished intelligence and that intelligence derived from national technical means is more valuable than human intelligence. Worse, policymakers often tend to view raw intelligence collected through technical means as more secret, more perishable, more accurate, and therefore more valuable than the same information that has gone through the process of intelligence analysis.[30]

Furthermore, policy leaders, like much of the public, make the mistake of assuming that what people say in secret has greater currency than information gathered openly. Relying on this assumption frequently results in distortions and misinterpretation of information, because people tend to exclude other relevant information that might provide a more comprehensive picture. Listening in on secret conversations provides only snippets of information, and nothing more. An interesting illustration of this is the statement of former DCI Stansfield Turner, who, responding to criticism that the CIA failed to anticipate the Iranian Revolution in 1979, asserted that even Ayatollah Khomeini himself was surprised by the developments in Iran.

Communications Problems

Bureaucratic impediments to effective intelligence lead to communications problems between intelligence officials and decision makers. In theory, communication is the glue that holds the policymaking and intelligence communities together. Good two-way communication between decision makers and intelligence providers is essential for understanding international problems and for conducting successful foreign policy. In practice, however, there are enormous communication gaps between intelligence officials and national leaders, which frequently result in missed indicators, overlooked opportunities, and poor policies.

Intelligence officers and policymakers communicate with one another formally and informally through a variety of channels, but in doing so they also transfer attitudes and biases, which can jeopardize the objectivity of intelligence analysis. This holds true also in decisions about selecting the policy audience—intelligence officers will communicate more completely and openly with decision makers whose policies they favor. When decision makers and intelligence officials disagree, the result may be the unauthorized release of information—commonly known as a "leak"—that is intended either to influence policy or stop a planned action.

In crises, informal channels of communication often prove more significant than formal ones. An intelligence analyst who has a good working relationship with a policymaker in noncrisis situations is likely to have greater access to and influence on that policymaker during times of crisis. Even so, a variety of communication impediments may derail an informal relationship. Overcompartmentation—that is, classifying intelligence into narrow categories—is one such problem. A specific intelligence consumer, even an important policy player, may not have the necessary clearances for particular compartmented information. Obviously, compartmenting information protects the fragile source, but it also creates a communication dilemma. This was a problem after the 11 September attacks, when the CIA and the FBI classified information in such a manner that they could not easily share that information with each other, let alone with state and local law enforcement officials.

Secrecy also impedes communication. U.S. intelligence has a track record of overclassifying information, which has impeded the smooth flow of information between producers of intelligence and consumers of intelligence. Senator Richard Shelby, former chairman of the Senate Select Committee on Intelligence, asserts, "perfectly secure information is perfectly useless information."[31] Information not known cannot be acted upon.

The flip side is that too much information can also clog up communication systems. U.S. intelligence sometimes finds itself in the position of having too much information to process, digest, and communicate. Since the end of the Cold War, U.S. intelligence has collected so much publicly available information on its former adversaries—Russia and China—that intelligence analysts have experienced information overload. Undoubtedly the voluminous information contains highly valuable nuggets—which, for time being, stay hidden in databases and among piles of paper. The selective use of information technology could provide answers to the information overload dilemma, but the intelligence community has been slow to utilize high-tech solutions to this problem for security reasons.

Inflection Points

History, culture, and structure have produced an ethos that ill serves the U.S. intelligence community. The eight principles of the ethos outlined in this chapter are replete with drawbacks and unintended consequences, all of which dilute the potential usefulness of U.S. intelligence. For example, the strict separation of intelligence from law enforcement—a fundamental precept that is now undergoing significant change—worked for a long time to prevent intelligence agencies from overstepping their bounds into police functions but now inhibits close cooperation against worldwide terrorism.

The eight principles also feed into bureaucratic pathologies and communication problems that further fragment the intelligence community. Fragmentation creates competition; competition creates bureaucratic glitches; and bureaucratic impediments lead to communication problems. In fact, communication difficulties are probably the most direct and important result of a culture of competition. The several investigative commissions looking into the 11 September terrorist attacks have identified both bureaucratic and communication pathologies as the main culprits in the 9/11 intelligence failure.

The next chapter examines how some foreign democratic nations structure their intelligence systems. As in the United States, the political cultures of these nations have shaped their intelligence structures in particular ways. Yet they may have some lessons for the United States as it tries to reform its intelligence apparatus in the post-9/11 world.

4

The Foreign
Experience

*Daring ideas are like chessmen moved forward; they
may be beaten but they may start a winning game.*
—Goethe

The previous two chapters noted that the enduring elements
of American political culture determined the shape and direction of U.S. intelligence long before there was such a thing
as an intelligence community. American cultural precepts
established the parameters of U.S. intelligence when Congress
established the intelligence community in 1947; American
culture guided intelligence activities in the last half century;
and American cultural values judged the actions of U.S. intelligence to be unacceptable in the 1970s, instigating reforms that redirected American intelligence toward greater
accountability. The message is clear—American political culture is the battleground on which U.S. intelligence succeeds
and fails.

While American culture imposes legal limits and restricts
freedom of action, it does not necessarily exclude innovation
and reform. To be sure, decentralization and fragmentation
are in the "American blood," but so are pragmatism and
efficiency. There is no reason to believe that a culture of de-
centralized authority that protects individual freedoms is inconsistent with a culture of greater fusion among agencies

for the purposes of efficiency and effectiveness. In the aftermath of 9/11, the American public has sent its leaders a clear message to the effect that they want better national security; they want structural reforms in their intelligence apparatus to assure that security; and if necessary, they will tolerate lessening of civil liberties to get what they want.[1]

Among the myriad recommendations, one has attracted particular attention—improving security within the United States by adopting a system of domestic intelligence similar to that of the United Kingdom.[2] Some experts scoff at the notion of importing alien ways into a uniquely American style of intelligence. Others assert that the United Kingdom, as well as other democratic nations, has much to teach the United States in confronting new threats in the post-9/11 world. To be sure, the foreign experience is predicated on certain considerations, such as the type of governmental system, specific approaches to domestic intelligence, a perceived relationship between domestic and foreign intelligence, and societal tolerance for secrecy and internal security. While the debate has focused on the British model, other foreign arrangements can be just as instructive, as long as they are from democratic nations. In addition to looking at the way the British organize their intelligence services, accordingly, the following discussion examines the Israeli, South African, and French models.

The British Model

The United Kingdom has three intelligence services—Secret Intelligence Service (SIS), Government Communications Headquarters (GCHQ), and the Security Service (MI-5)—each of which has specific authorities and separate jurisdictions. Two of these organizations, SIS and GCHQ, have their analogs in the United States, while the MI-5 has no American counterpart. It is the subject of keen interest in American policy circles as a model for domestic intelligence in the United States.

The Secret Intelligence Service, commonly known as MI-6, is Britain's foreign intelligence organization. SIS was established in 1909 as the foreign intelligence part of an umbrella organization then known as the Secret Service Bureau. SIS became a separate entity in 1922, but the organization did not receive a statutory basis until 1994.[3] The 1994 Intelligence Services Act placed SIS within the Foreign and Commonwealth Office (FCO), under the direct supervision of the foreign secretary, who is a member of the cabinet, which in Britain wields executive authority along with the prime minister. The act also established an elaborate system of control and oversight that tightly weaves MI-6 together with the other "agencies."[4]

Britain's Government Communications Headquarters (GCHQ) corresponds roughly to the National Security Agency in the United States. GCHQ's predecessor, the Government Code and Cipher School, was responsible for securing the Enigma machine and decoding German communications during World War II, which provided the wartime allies an enormous advantage over the Germans and contributed immensely to the Allied victory in 1945. Like the NSA, GCHQ conducts SIGINT in support of all British government departments. GCHQ resides within the FCO, in which it shares equal billing with SIS and therefore reports directly to the foreign secretary.

The Security Service, MI-5, is Britain's internal intelligence organization. Like SIS, it was founded in 1909 as the internal arm of the Secret Service Bureau; it received its statutory basis in 1989 with the passage of the Security Service Act, amended in 1996. The statute places the Security Service within the Ministry of Home Affairs, which has the domestic security mandate in the United Kingdom. According to the Security Service Act, the function of MI-5 is the "protection of national security and, in particular, its protection against threats from espionage, terrorism, and sabotage, from the activities of foreign powers and from actions intended to overthrow or undermine parliamentary democracy by political, industrial or violent means."[5]

Because British culture, like that of the United States, is vehemently opposed to any "secret police" that could threaten freedoms and civil liberties, the act prohibits MI-5 from acting in a law enforcement capacity and bans it from exercising powers to arrest people or detain suspects. Rather, it must turn over intelligence to, and coordinate closely with, the police in the apprehension of suspects. When it comes across information of an imminent terrorist threat, it can take action to deter or prevent the threat, but it cannot go beyond that into areas that are reserved for the criminal justice system. This feature of British law keenly interests some American legislators, like Senator John Edwards (D-N.C.), who asserted in that the United States needs "a new agency focused on gathering intelligence threats here at home. Great Britain, Canada, and many other Western democracies already have these agencies."[6] In fact, Senator Edwards introduced legislation to that effect in February 2003.[7]

In Britain, intelligence requirements and priorities fall within the purview of the Joint Intelligence Committee (JIC), which is part of the Cabinet Office and is supervised by the cabinet secretary. However, JIC has additional responsibilities in providing policymakers regular intelligence assessments on issues of urgency as well as of long-term importance; bringing together the intelligence services and the customers; and scrutinizing the performance of the intelligence services (see figure 5). In doing so, JIC combines some of the functions of the National Security Council, the National Intelligence Council, and the National Foreign Intelligence Board in the United States. The chair of the JIC is a senior cabinet official who also serves as the intelligence coordinator.[8]

The Official Secrets Act imposes heavy burdens on British citizens who disclose national security secrets, even though there has been a steady erosion of the taboos designed to protect the British intelligence apparatus.[9] Consequently, oversight assumes an important role in ensuring the accountability of British intelligence agencies. In the British system, the prime minister has overall responsibility for intelligence and security matters, and is supported in that capacity by the secretary of the cabinet. Executive oversight is provided by the Ministerial Committee on the Intelligence Services, which includes the prime minister (Chair), the home, defense, and foreign secretaries, and the chancellor of the exchequer.[10] Parliamentary oversight is provided by the Intelligence and Security Committee, which was established by the Intelligence Services Act of 1994. The committee exercises powers similar to those of the congressional oversight committees in the United States but, unlike the American committees, is a "joint"

The Committee is charged with the following responsibilities:

- Under the broad supervisory responsibility of the Permanent Secretaries' Committee on the Intelligence Services, to give direction to, and to keep under review, the organization and working of British intelligence activity as a whole at home and overseas in order to ensure efficiency, economy and prompt adaptation to changing requirements;
- To submit, at agreed intervals, for approval by Ministers, statements of the requirements and priorities for intelligence gathering and other tasks to be conducted by the intelligence Agencies;
- To coordinate, as necessary, interdepartmental plans for activity;
- To monitor and give early warning of the development of direct or indirect foreign threats to British interests, whether political, military or economic;
- On the basis of available information, to assess events and situations relating to external affairs, defense, terrorism, major international criminal activity, scientific, technical and international economic matters;
- To keep under review threats to security at home and overseas and to deal with such security problems as may be referred to it;
- To maintain and supervise liaison with Commonwealth and foreign intelligence organizations as appropriate, and to consider the extent to which its product can be made available to them.

Source: *National Intelligence Machinery* (London: The Stationary Office, 2000), p. 19.

Figure 5. *JIC's Responsibilities*

committee of the House of Commons and the House of Lords. Furthermore, two commissions exercise judicial powers over the British intelligence services. The Intelligence Services Commissioner considers and authorizes intelligence operations, while the Interception Commission, like the American Foreign Intelligence Surveillance Court (FISC), reviews applications and issues warrants for the clandestine interception of communications within the United Kingdom.[11] Finally, the Investigatory Powers Tribunal investigates public complaints against the agencies.

The Israeli Model

For Israel, the dire threat posed by its enemies plays a big role in the way it structures its intelligence services. From its inception in 1948, Israel's sovereignty and territorial integrity have been under virtually constant attack from its neighbors. In addition, the Palestinian insurgency within Israeli-controlled territories in recent years has heightened perceptions of imminent threat. As a result, Israelis have insisted on a strong intelligence capability in order to ensure Israel's independence as a Jewish state, an issue on which there is near unanimity in Israel.

This is not to say that Israel has not experienced intelligence failures. On the contrary, Israel has had its share of much-publicized failures, but a distinguishing mark of Israel's approach has been to acknowledge the failures, learn from them, and improve intelligence in ways that would minimize their recurrence. For example, overconfidence by the Israeli security services, including the intelligence agencies, led to the failure to anticipate Egypt's attack in 1973 that sparked the Yom Kippur War.[12] Postmortem assessments identified the deficiencies, and Israeli leaders took corrective measures. For example, Israeli leaders identified the lack of satellite reconnaissance as a significant deficiency and have since been taking steps to establish a satellite intelligence capability for Israel.[13] Yet Israel's intelligence services again failed to anticipate the first Palestinian *intifadah* that began in the late 1980s, a lapse that generated calls for drastic reforms in Israel's intelligence apparatus.

As a parliamentary democracy, Israel's government exhibits characteristics similar to that of the United Kingdom. Unlike Britain, however, Israeli intelligence services are under the direct policy supervision of the prime minister's office. Like Britain, Israel separates its foreign intelligence from its domestic intelligence and security services. Moreover, and again like Britain, Israel provides for both executive and parliamentary oversight; however, there is greater fusion than in Britain between executive and parliamentary oversight.[14]

The Institute for Intelligence and Special Tasks, commonly known as Mossad, is Israel's foreign intelligence agency. Established in 1951, its responsibilities include human intelligence collection, covert action, and counterterrorism, responsibilities that, according to authoritative sources, focus on Arab nations in the Middle East and around the world.[15] Mossad's mandate also includes the clandestine movement of Jewish refugees.[16]

Internal security functions in Israel are performed by Israel Security Service, commonly referred to as Shin Bet or

Shabak. Like the British Security Service, Shabak has the authority to engage in domestic intelligence collection, but, unlike MI-5, Shabak has law enforcement authorities to detain, arrest, and prosecute individuals. Shabak also is charged with counterintelligence tasks that augment its internal security functions.

Mossad is a highly effective organization, but Shabak has come under severe public criticism and judicial review for some of its excesses and failures. In April 1984, Shabak agents beat to death a Palestinian terrorist who had hijacked a bus in the Gaza Strip. In the ensuing investigation Shabak's director reportedly falsified evidence and instructed his agents to lie to investigators.[17] In 1987, Shabak agents were accused of using improper interrogation methods to extract confessions and of lying to investigators about their methods afterward. In fact, a judicial inquiry found that it was an accepted norm for Shabak agents to lie to the Israeli court about their interrogations.[18] Shabak also came under intense criticism in 1995 for failing to prevent the assassination of Prime Minister Yitzak Rabin by a right-wing extremist.

The lesser-known but equally effective military intelligence service, Aman, probably has the broadest mandate among Israel's intelligence agencies. According to its official website, Aman provides senior political leaders with comprehensive national intelligence estimates, daily intelligence reports, risk-of-war assessments, target studies of Arab neighbors, and communications intercepts. It also engages in cross-border operations.[19] Aman is an independent service and is equal in bureaucratic status to the military services. It was Aman that Israeli leaders blamed for the failure to forecast the Yom Kippur War and to apprise them of the difficulties that would be encountered in the invasion of Lebanon in 1983.[20]

Finally, the Center for Political Research, a part of the Foreign Ministry, is charged with gathering, analyzing, and evaluating political information and with engaging in political information, or propaganda. As such, the center combines features of INR in the U.S. State Department, Voice of America, and the former U.S. Information Service.

The South African Model

Decades of political and economic repression and undemo-
cratic practices preceded democracy in South Africa. For much
of its post–World War II history, the white minority government outlawed black political groups, enforced a series of
repressive social and political laws to maintain its dominance
inside the country, and formed hit squads to kill members of
South African liberation movements inside and out of the
country. South Africa's security service played a prominent
role in this repression.

Beginning in 1990, the white government and leaders of
opposition movements, like the African National Congress
(ANC), began a series of negotiations that eventually transformed the country into a democracy with black majority rule.
The Convention for a Democratic South Africa, which brought
the parties together in 1991 and under the auspices of which
negotiations took place, promulgated in 1993 a Transitional
Executive Authority Act, in which a subcouncil on intelligence
was charged with adopting a set of basic principles that were
to serve as a basis for creating a national democratic intelligence capability. The subcouncil also put together a code of
conduct focusing on respect for freedoms and civil rights that
would be binding on South Africa's intelligence services.[21]

Negotiations produced a structure in 1994 under the direct authority of the president's office. The 1994 Intelligence
Services Act[22] established the South African Secret Service,
the foreign intelligence unit, and the National Intelligence
Agency, the internal intelligence organization. An accompa-
nying act, the National Strategic Intelligence Act,[23] defined
foreign intelligence specifically as information on any real or
potential external threat to the country's national interests
and intelligence regarding opportunities relevant to the protection and promotion of the national interests, regardless of
whether it is used to formulate foreign policy. "Domestic intelligence" refers to intelligence required for the planning and
conduct of military operations within South Africa to ensure
the country's security and stability. In its present form, internal intelligence includes military intelligence, thereby compelling the National Intelligence Service to coordinate with

the country's military, the National Defense Force (NDF). In turn, the NDF can collect internal intelligence in support of South African police, so long as it receives specific authorization before it does so. The law also permits South African police to collect crime intelligence and to institute counterintelligence measures within South Africa.

A distinctive feature of the South African model that may instruct American reformers is the provision of a National Intelligence Coordinating Committee,[24] which acts as the funnel for coordinated intelligence to consumers. This coordinating committee also engages in setting intelligence requirements and priorities for the entire South African intelligence community.

Because all intelligence agencies, with the exception of military intelligence, are under the president's supervision, there is a direct line of accountability and oversight within the executive branch. To ensure this important function, the president is charged with appointing the directors and inspectors general of the specific agencies.[25] The Committee of Members of Parliament provides legislative oversight.[26]

The French Model

France has an elaborate system of foreign and domestic intelligence that exhibits some of the American penchant for duplication and complexity. However, as a country with both a strong president and a strong premier, France has a different model from those already examined, in that the French government subordinates its foreign intelligence to the Ministry of Defense, conferring on the ministry a dominant role in French intelligence. The General Directorate for External Security (DGSE) is responsible for both strategic and military intelligence, electronic intelligence, counterintelligence outside French territories, and covert operations.

However, other agencies within the Defense Ministry compete with DGSE for resources. The Directorate of Military Intelligence (DRM), established in 1992, provides tactical military intelligence, especially specific types of SIGINT and IMINT, and has responsibilities in political and strategic intelligence that overlap those of DGSE. DRM also maintains liaison with the national police.[27] In addition, the Ministry's Directorate of Defense Protection and Security (DPSD) and the Intelligence and Electronic Warfare Brigade (BRGE) provide even greater complexity to the French intelligence apparatus. DPSD is responsible for military counterintelligence operations as well as political surveillance of soldiers and sailors to ensure "the political reliability of the armed forces."[28] BRGE, on the other hand, was created in 1993 to address shortcomings observed during the Persian Gulf War in 1991. It now provides SIGINT to the military services.[29] The Central Service for Information Systems Security (SCSSI) regulates the use of cryptosystems, particularly in commercial areas.

Domestic intelligence falls within the purview of the Interior Ministry and is embedded within the various police structures. The Ministry's Central Directorate of General Information (RG) coordinates counterterrorism intelligence and provides analytic capabilities to promote French financial and commercial interests.[30] The Directorate of Territorial Security (DST), however, has both domestic intelligence and internal security responsibilities. Its counterintelligence function includes the prevention of industrial espionage and terrorism.[31] The public face of DST is the Central Directorate Judicial Police (DCPJ), which is responsible for gathering domestic intelligence on political, commercial, and criminal matters, and, as an adjunct to judicial authorities, for law enforcement activities like detention, apprehension, and arrest. Companies for Republican Security (CRS) assists the DCPJ by providing road safety, port and airport security, and protection for VIPs. CRS has no domestic intelligence responsibilities.

The Foreign Ministry's Analysis and Forecasting Center competes with the intelligence units of the Ministries of Defense and Interior by providing political, economic, and strategic analytic products to senior policymakers. However, it does serve something of a coordinating function by integrating intelligence from the other ministries and providing coordinated analytic products. As such, the Foreign Ministry's analytic center acts somewhat like the National Intelligence Council in the United States. The National Commission for the Control of Security Interceptions, which is an independent body, acts as a regulatory agency more or less akin to the Foreign Intelligence Surveillance Court in the United States by regulating domestic and foreign intercepts.

Points of Comparison

Few would argue that Britain and France are fully democratic countries with developed protections for social and political rights, despite having domestic intelligence agencies and secrecy laws that are more stringent than those of the United States. This demonstrates two fundamental truths—that central coordination of intelligence is the preferred method of conducting intelligence and that the provision of domestic intelligence is consistent with democracy and the protection of civil liberties. These truths, in turn, belie the argument by opponents of an American domestic intelligence capability to the effect that such an organization would imperil American freedoms.

Yet there are specific differences between the United States and the countries examined here that should raise cautionary flags. In the United States, the FBI performs limited domestic intelligence functions, but the distinctive characteristic of the American model is the fusion of domestic intelligence and federal law enforcement in the bureau.[32] This is a crucial point, accounted for by several factors that affect differing intelligence systems.

First, there is a clear difference between a federal presidential system like that of the United States and unitary parliamentary democracies like those of Britain and Israel. The South African system is a modified parliamentary system, with the president elected by Parliament. The French have a system that combines the presidential and parliamentary approaches and thus tends to exhibit qualities of both. American political culture imposes many constraints on American presidents, and federalism predisposes the United States toward decentralization. In parliamentary systems, where cabinet government merges executive and legislative functions, there are fewer constraints on prime ministers and virtually no fear of centralized structures that serve to coordinate disparate but complementary activities like intelligence.

Second, whereas the United States suffered a devastating

terrorist attack on 9/11, the British, French, Israelis, and the South Africans have had far more protracted and traumatic experiences with terrorism and so have a clearer notion of what it means to provide for internal security. According to one observer, "How each country structures domestic intelligence is a function of its unique experience with terrorism and the culture's acceptance of government intrusion into the daily lives in the interest of securing freedom."[33] Each of the countries examined here has had to strike, between civil liberties and security, a unique balance that favors the latter. Moreover, each of the systems separates domestic intelligence from law enforcement, some firmly and some loosely, thereby overcoming the tendency toward a secret police. Separating out the FBI's law enforcement function from its counterintelligence responsibilities may prove useful in this regard.

Third, each of the intelligence systems examined here separates domestic intelligence from foreign intelligence but provides for a great deal of fusion between the two. In the United States, the distinction is almost absolute and is a cardinal principle of the nation's intelligence ethos (see chapter 3). Now that the United States has become a terrorist battleground, there probably is need for greater integration between domestic and foreign intelligence so as to present a common front to this mortal threat.

Fourth, virtually all nations of the globe have more tolerant approaches to secrecy and stricter approaches to internal security than does the United States. For example, the European Union allows the British government to exercise prior restraint with respect to publication of any material that may be harmful to national security.[34] Americans have a different level of tolerance when it comes to government intrusion into their lives. That may change drastically in the likely event of more terrorist attacks on American soil.

In the final analysis, structural reforms along lines proposed by Senator John Edwards make sense, even if American cultural values work against them. Establishing a domestic intelligence agency in the United States would strengthen the strict separation of intelligence from law enforcement. Moreover, such an agency—with no law enforcement powers— would be an alternative way of addressing some structural deficiencies in the American intelligence community, providing that there is a concrete way to coordinate domestic and foreign intelligence. Such coordination is intrinsic in the intelligence process, but each step in the cycle contains elements that more often than not contribute to intelligence failures—beginning with the process of setting intelligence priorities.

5

Requirements and Priorities

Doctrinal emphasis on specific estimative prediction is a root cause of high-profile warning failures.
—Jack Davis, CIA veteran

Determining intelligence priorities in an environment of relative scarcity is difficult business. While all decision makers would like to know as much as they can, in detail, about virtually everything that concerns them, intelligence agencies work under budgetary and personnel restraints that hinder such open-ended intelligence gathering. Limited budgets, inadequate numbers of personnel, and bureaucratic imperatives all serve to compel intelligence agencies to set priorities based on the national security and foreign policy concerns that are uppermost in policymakers' minds. Even when intelligence priorities are clear and straightforward, they can still become mired in the politics of the day. The controversy over prewar intelligence about Iraqi weapons of mass destruction is a case in point.

Shoddy, Hyped, and False Intelligence

In mid-2003, a public debate erupted in the media and over the airwaves regarding the failures of U.S. and British troops to find any weapons of mass destruction in Iraq after overthrowing the Saddam Hussein regime in April of that year.[1] The U.S. and British governments had gone out of their way to convince their publics that the Hussein regime possessed and was willing to use chemical and biological weapons against its enemies. In fact, this argument was the principal justification for launching the war against Iraq, which much of the world, including significant portions of the American and British publics, opposed.

Proponents of the war had argued that there was indisputable intelligence information to show Saddam Hussein's weapons of mass destruction (WMD) capabilities. After the end of the war, however, coalition forces were able to find only two semitrailers that could, under the right circumstances, be used to develop biological weapons. Subsequently, there was a steady stream of questions about whether the Bush administration had exerted pressure on intelligence analysts to provide analysis that supported the administration's war aims. As evidence, the press cited Vice President Dick Cheney's "multiple" visits to the CIA, an unusual practice by a vice president, to talk about Iraqi weapons of mass destruction and Hussein's possible ties to terrorism. A senior CIA official reportedly claimed that the visits "sent signals, intended or otherwise, that a certain output was desired from here."[2] Some intelligence insiders also claimed that while intelligence had been manipulated in the past, "never before had such warping been used in such a systematic way to mislead our elected representatives into voting to authorize launching a war."[3]

There is little doubt that the White House exerted pressure on the intelligence agencies to come up with unified, "correct" assessments about Iraq. This pressure probably came partly because of uncertainty created by the long-running feud between the Pentagon and the CIA over the interpretation of intelligence information about Iraq, with the CIA the more skeptical about Saddam's intentions and his ties to terrorism. In fact, the Pentagon reportedly created a unit soon after the 11 September 2001 terrorist attacks to engage in "aggressive research,"[4] presumably for intelligence information that would support the administration's hard-line position,[5] unlike that of the CIA. Even though the administration denied the link, there was a good deal of speculation over whether there was manipulation of intelligence to justify the war. In July 2003, the public debate shifted to whether Hussein had indeed sought to buy nuclear materials from Africa, with the White House finally admitting that the allegation had been based on bogus information and DCI Tenet taking full responsibility for this error.[6]

Such intense criticism often puts government officials on the defensive. For example, on the issue of not finding Iraqi WMD, Douglas Feith, the Undersecretary of Defense for Policy, had to deny the allegations of manipulating intelligence. Former DCI Tenet also came out with a statement saying that "our role is to call it like we see it—to tell policymakers what we know, what we don't know, what we think, and what we base it on. That's the code we live by and that is what policymakers expect from us."[7]

Sometimes, criticism can become so intense that government officials try to deflect it by heaping blame on others. Intelligence agencies and officials historically have assumed the role of "scapegoats" in order to take the heat off their policy superiors. This appears to have happened in July 2003, when DCI Tenet took the blame for the erroneous reporting of intelligence information about Iraqi purchases of African nuclear materials.[8] Tenet did so even in the face of overwhelming public evidence that the CIA believed the information was based on forged documents and had reported its suspicions to the White House in 2002.[9] In an interesting political twist, many congressional leaders subsequently came to Tenet's defense, saying that White House officials had overridden Tenet's objections to using the fraudulent information and that therefore the White House was responsible for the faux pas.[10]

These controversies point to the critical role policymakers play in the intelligence-requirements process. Iraq had been a priority target since before the first Gulf War, and concerns about Saddam Hussein's intentions had fueled intense interest in information about Iraq, weapons of mass destruction, and terrorism. Such policy interest, along with standing requirements on perennial issues like WMD, provided grist for intelligence officers to undertake a program of intelligence collection and analysis, intended to slake policymakers' thirst for relevant intelligence on Hussein's activities. Yet even intelligence about issues of high interest, as in the case of Iraq, can be subject to manipulation, can be wrong, or can be used for political purposes.

How Is It Done?

Setting the intelligence agenda in U.S. intelligence is probably one of the most complex and misunderstood of the intelligence processes.[11] The issue receives scant attention because intelligence professionals and scholars find it less "sexy" than other areas of intelligence. In addition, those who pry out the secrets of the intelligence process understandably focus more on the "tail end" of the process—the point at which consumer satisfaction with the analytical product is determined—rather than the "front end," where priorities are set. This is due to the pervasive mind-set within the intelligence profession that the "critical issue is not so much the process of setting priorities as it is to devise ways of establishing firm policy-intelligence relationships and providing relevant and actionable intelligence."[12] However, the "front end" of the process is just as important because it invariably determines the vital issues and sets the tone for subsequent intelligence activities.

The conventional wisdom says that priorities in U.S. intelligence are set by policymakers and that the job of U.S. intelligence simply is to transform the policy into the appropriate intelligence question. Bruce Clarke, former director of the National Foreign Assessment Center (the predecessor of the Directorate for Intelligence), once put it this way: "The role of intelligence is to identify the policy question, not the policy, from which collection, analysis, and production could then proceed."[13]

The conventional wisdom, however, rests on several faulty, but not necessarily false, assumptions:

- Policymakers are able to focus on national security and foreign policy issues.
- Policymakers know what the issues are and what questions to ask.
- Policymakers are able to communicate their needs.
- Policymakers know what to expect from intelligence experts.[14]

A more accurate view is one that holds that there are two decision vectors embodied within the issue of setting the intelligence agenda. One vector emanates from the top and comes in the form of policy statements, guidance, and directives; the other decision vector bubbles up from below and represents the input of expert analysts who on a daily basis produce intelligence products that serve as guideposts to setting the agenda.[15]

Intelligence analysts do work based on "requirements" or "needs" set at the policy level, and their production feeds into the whole network of intelligence questions that need to be answered. Indeed, intelligence analysts more often than not are the ones who "massage" high-level needs to get at the intelligence questions.

Arthur Hulnick and others have demonstrated the important contributions of intelligence professionals in framing policy "needs" into intelligence requirements and priorities.[16] Indeed, it is axiomatic in the intelligence business that policymakers, busy with political and electoral issues, do not have the time or inclination to focus on specific national security and foreign policy matters. Political leaders often attempt to get intelligence they like or information that supports their points of view. They do so because of their strong stakes in the success of their policies; they are proportionately receptive to intelligence that "supports" their positions.[17]

The implications are that agenda setting in U.S. intelligence is not entirely policy driven and that setting intelligence requirements is a complex process wherein intelligence often has to seize the moment and perform "opportunity analysis and other kinds of agenda setting activities."[18] Former DCI Robert Gates likened the process of setting intelligence priorities to three concentric circles. The inner circle comprises those informational needs that deal specifically with the vital interests of the United States—namely, physical threats to the nation. The second circle surrounding the inner one deals with issues that are of direct threat to the interests of the United States. The outer circle deals with issues that are important but not immediately threatening to the country's security.[19] Of course, this corresponds roughly to the typologies of the national interest developed by scholars Hans Morgenthau, Charles Beard, and others.[20]

Gates's formulation probably sufficed in the simpler world of the Cold War, but it is now insufficient to explain the greater complexity of today's more violent world. One problem with Gates's formulation is that it does not answer the question of who identifies the threats or even decides what constitutes a threat. Defining the threat is clearly a political issue, one that is central to formulating policies that serve the national interest and the specific policy agendas of policy leaders.

However, even here, agenda setting really is an interactive bargaining process among three environments: the policy world, the bureaucratic dynamics of the intelligence community, and the intelligence collectors and analysts. The policy environment provides broad policy guidance and mixes with the other two environments in an unformulated, amorphous way. Organizational dynamics focus on the rules and procedures that translate policy into institutional imperatives, as well as establish priorities derived from specific mandates, mission statements, and tasking. The analyst/collector environment provides the expertise that undergirds intelligence analysis. The intensity and depth of interactions, as well as the power relationships, among these three milieus determine the salience of issues in the intelligence agenda.

The Policy Environment

The policy environment comprises policymakers, the media, and public opinion. This environment is dominated by political issues, but the defining principle has long been what Hans Heymann, an intelligence veteran, calls the "catechism of the intelligence officer, namely the thesis that intelligence is and should be strictly separated from policy."[21] Yet, in order to produce relevant analysis, intelligence must have some connection to policy. Richard Betts, a scholar of the intelligence process, once put it this way: "The significance of information—which is what good analysis should discover—depends in many ways on what our national interests on the matter are, and those interests are defined politically."[22]

The political nature of policy "needs" is at the core of the uneasy policy-intelligence relationship. While the conventional wisdom says that the relationship works in only one direction—from policy to intelligence—in actuality the relationship works both ways. Policymakers do provide broad policy guidance, through speeches, statements, electoral platforms, and the like.[23] These policy statements find expression in more concrete policy directives that outline objectives and specific requirements. For example, the Clinton White House in the fall of 1995 issued Presidential Decision Directive 35 (PDD 35), enunciating the specific intelligence issues deemed important to the administration.[24] This policy guidance served as a basis for intelligence questions that drove the intelligence process into the twenty-first century. President George W. Bush did not replace PDD 35, relying instead on obvious foreign policy developments—the 9/11 terrorist attacks, the Iraq war, North Korea, the Islamic insurgency—to serve as guides for intelligence requirements.

Intelligence for its part also provides an input to the policy process. U.S. intelligence agencies provide hundreds of briefings and analytical products annually to administration officials, congressional members and their respective staffs, and journalists. Such interactions may be the result of queries on specific foreign policy or intelligence issues derived from newspaper headlines or media attention, but the net effect is to force intelligence officials to consider these political issues as intelligence requirements. Consequently, the products that result—written assessments, oral briefings, or technical reports—feed into making policy. David Gries, a retired CIA operations officer, contends that although no one event—media attention, public interest, intelligence analysis, or policy concern—is likely to prompt a major policy change, taken together they often nudge policy in new directions or make new policy.[25]

Aside from such directives, there is no formal structure to apprise intelligence officials of policy decisions. But many informal channels—the frequent informal meetings, for example—ensure the necessary flow and exchange of information in both directions.[26]

Some policymakers clearly do not want intelligence analysis—because they are suspicious of it, do not want unwelcome news, or realize it may reduce their flexibility. For example, CIA's negative reports about Jean Bertrand Aristide during the Haiti crisis in the early 1990s sparked demands to curb such analysis.[27] In addition, during that crisis there was a general impression that the Clinton administration was "rather disengaged from the role of the [CIA] and intelligence or the problems of intelligence collection."[28]

More often than not, policymakers are not as clear about what their requirements are and often want others to define the policy agenda for them. Frequently, policymakers rely on the media to perform issue definition, and this poses a danger to the integrity of intelligence analysis, because policymakers, who typically are unfamiliar with what intelligence can or cannot do, often seek answers that will support preconceived ideas, policy stands, or political opinions.

Policymakers also try to use intelligence in ingenious ways for political purposes, ranging from acquiring information to defending policy and helping make new policy decisions.[29] Conversely, they may ignore intelligence if it contradicts their policies or preconceived notions. Pessimistic estimates about Vietnam in the 1960s, for example, constituted intelligence successes in that they "called it" right, but they were not welcomed in policy circles and failed to prevent disastrous policy choices.[30] It is at this level that the producer-consumer relationship can get quite murky, with the policymaker trying to get the "right" answers to his policy questions and the intelligence analyst trying to keep as far removed from policy influence as possible without becoming irrelevant.

In addition, the information revolution, of which the media is a part, has made it harder to set intelligence priorities. Instantaneous information and resource constraints are compelling intelligence officials to rethink how they conceive intelligence and to redefine tasks in order to contribute to supporting policy in unique ways. According to a senior intelligence official, the information revolution itself has become part of setting priorities.[31]

In other cases, policymakers want intelligence to tell them the issues on which they should focus. This happens frequently and takes the form of the policymaker asking intelligence officials to formulate specific policies or provide policy options. For example, asking the DNI during congressional testimony what the U.S. government should do about an international development is clearly an attempt to elicit policy judgments. One example occurred in 1996 at a meeting of the Senate Select Committee on Intelligence (SSCI), during which then-Senator Bob Kerrey (D-Nebr.) asked the then-DCI John M. Deutch his thoughts on the future threats to the United States. In his elaborate question, Senator Kerrey, who was more versed than some of his colleagues on the limits of intelligence, gave the clear impression that the DCI's assessment would drive his judgments about policy issues. He justified this position saying, "Nobody in 1990 had Bosnia on the screen, but now we have 20,000 troops on the ground."[32] Similar tugs-of-war between congressional leaders and intelligence officials are all too common.

The fundamental issue here is the role of intelligence in the policy process; it centers on the fact that U.S. intelligence is prohibited from assessing U.S. policy. Yet an estimate of what is likely to happen abroad cannot be separated from some consideration of what effects policy initiatives will have on the situation. This dilemma pits the intelligence official dangerously close to policy prescription.

Intelligence Community Dynamics

In addition to the policy environment, the rules, regulations, and operating procedures within the intelligence community (IC) provide a context for setting intelligence priorities. Despite the fact that different institutions tend to have different ingrained attitudes, the intelligence community as a whole strives to speak with one voice on the issue of intelligence requirements. While the record on this is mixed, the IC has had a degree of success in generating coherence in the agenda-setting process.

The intelligence community participates in determining intelligence priorities in three ways. First, the interagency process produces priorities derived from agency mission statements, mandates, and jurisdictions. Essentially, the DNI, who is responsible for advising the president on intelligence matters, reflects interagency consensus.[33] Here, the DNI's relationship with the president and his advisers plays a big role. A professional relationship probably would ensure that the president and his colleagues receive intelligence that has been vetted through the bureaucratic process. A personal relationship, on the other hand, would put the DNI close to the president's ear but poses the danger that the DNI's advice would not necessarily reflect interagency agreement, as in fact happened with DCI William Casey and President Ronald Reagan.[34]

Interagency consensus is also reflected formally in the National Intelligence Council (NIC) process of producing coordinated judgments (see chapter 7 for details on the estimative process). The NIC is composed of senior regional and issue experts (national intelligence officers, or NIOs), who are supposed to be attuned to the needs of consumers, the urgency of specific issues in their areas of expertise, and the availability or lack of information on any particular topic within their area of jurisdiction. NIOs are responsible for national intelligence estimates (NIEs) and other similar estimative products— all geared to satisfying needs either enunciated in documents like National Security Presidential Directives or perceived by senior experts as pertinent to the consumer. According to a senior intelligence official, the estimative process is now designed to put together expert teams to "figure out answers rather than stake out positions."[35] The NIC, for example, has increased its emphasis on alternative scenarios for decision makers rather than single-point predictions.[36] These advances, however, have not forestalled turf battles and bitter disagreements over interpretation of data.

Second, intelligence community dynamics transform policy guidance into key intelligence questions through documents that list issues, topics, or questions that are deemed to be of intelligence interest. In the past, formal guidance to the IC for intelligence requirements was given each year through identification of "national intelligence topics" (NITs) and "key intelligence questions" (KIQs) and through more technical directives assigning numerical priorities to specific topics.[37] Now the NIC produces a document detailing the priorities through an interagency process that includes interviews with consumers of intelligence.[38] The document contains directives to the rest of the intelligence community from the NIC, the interagency body designed to coordinate intelligence judgments.[39]

Third, individual intelligence agencies have started to set priorities that are commensurate with specific institutional missions and budgetary limits. For example, each of the CIA's directorates has adopted strategic plans. The strategic plan of the Directorate of Intelligence (DI)—the analytical arm of the agency—focuses on the analytical agenda, including such priority items as terrorism, organized crime, drug trafficking, rogue states, weapons proliferation, and politically unstable regions.[40] According to a senior CIA official, the setting of priorities is now driven more programmatically than organizationally.[41]

The Analyst/Collector Environment

Perhaps the most controversial aspect of the agenda-setting game centers on the role of the intelligence collectors and analysts. The collector typically is the case officer, the reports officer, or any other type of operations officer who collects information of intelligence interest. The analyst could be the NIO or an intelligence analyst in the bureaucratic trenches. Intelligence analysts bring area and issue expertise to bear on intelligence issues and produce the bulk of current and long-term intelligence. Analysts are the ones who draft, coordinate, and produce current intelligence items for the *Senior Executive Intelligence Review* (SEIR), the *President's Daily Brief*, the various Staff Notes that circulate at the lower echelons of the intelligence bureaucracies, and the Typescripts that address specific consumer questions about specific issues.[42] Intelligence analysts more often than not are also the ones who draft the NIEs or the SNIEs in their areas of expertise under the guidance and supervision of the NIO.

An intelligence analyst is expected to have and maintain expertise on a country, geographical region, or an issue through higher education, area familiarization trips, discussions with experts, and professional development. However, analysts are also expected to know the key intelligence concerns that pertain to their areas of expertise. Analysts keep abreast of the key issues and the pertinent questions by poring over all source materials—intelligence documents, State Department cables, intercepts, and the like—and by establishing and keeping close contacts with intelligence collectors, their operational counterparts charged with collecting intelligence, whether that intelligence be human, signals, electronic, or some other kind of method (see chapter 6 for details on intelligence collection). In short, the intelligence analysts perform the bulk of the grunt work associated with intelligence tasking.

In addition, intelligence analysts, as experts in their fields, are expected to initiate studies that address questions yet unformulated by consumers. According to a former head of the State Department's Bureau of Intelligence and Research (INR), "most of our pieces, whether focused on the short term, medium or long term, are self-initiated."[43] Such self-initiated products are designed to "make us smart enough to recognize changes in the patterns of international events that will become important to the U.S."[44]

Intelligence analysts usually produce some studies based on an annual production plan. An apt description of this process was given over twenty years ago by the former vice director for foreign intelligence at DIA:

> a production plan for all military intelligence production, called the Defense Intelligence Production Schedule, . . . is coordinated on an annual basis and seeks to assure that there is no unnecessary duplication in the products produced. The . . . production schedule provides an inventory for the customers of the types of products that are being produced and a schedule for their production which indicates when these products are going to become available.[45]

Intelligence analysts routinely append dissemination lists to their products, and these lists are tailored to a precise understanding of who in the government has operational responsibility for the problem addressed (see chapter 8). When a policy decision is under discussion, dissemination routinely includes all participants in the process. On self-initiated products, the analyst would want to ensure that all readers who are likely to need the information in fact receive it.

Despite this, and maybe because of it, the role of the intelligence analyst remains controversial. Because intelligence analysts possess detailed information and knowledge about their areas of expertise, they have the potential of greatly influencing both the priority issues and the contexts in which the issues are addressed. However, they operate within a bureaucratic milieu, with imperatives of its own, that tends to impede intelligence analysts from wielding the kind of influence their expertise would dictate. They are able to have impact only to the extent that they can muster support from their counterparts in other agencies, from the collectors, and from their immediate superiors.

When analysts do establish such coalitions, they can wield enormous influence in setting the intelligence agenda. Some recent NIOs have been known to be powerhouses in determining the issues for policy consideration. Such power comes from a strong personality as well as from having thorough knowledge of an issue, which is often absent in the policy and bureaucratic process environments. Moreover, the various current and long-range intelligence products can be and often are used as "bully pulpits" through which to focus policy and bureaucratic attention on particular issues.

Inflection Points

The process of setting intelligence priorities tends to be dynamic rather than static. The U.S. intelligence community is organized around the processes of interacting entities rather than around their particular attributes.[46] The conclusion one logically reaches is that the ideal situation is one of much free interaction among the three environments, supposedly conducive to harmony of interests in setting the right intelligence priorities. In such a situation, all three environments would overlap and correspond to produce near unanimity on the agenda.

In the ideal scheme, there would be nearly perfect communication among the three environments, nearly perfect understanding of the roles each plays, and nearly perfect response mechanisms. Such a situation logically would exist only in cases where the issue is general, identifiable, clear, and predictable. There have been only a few such cases, the most illustrative being the near total agreement among the three environments during the Cold War that the Soviet Union posed the most direct threat to the interests of the United States.

However, reality is closer to the opposite scenario, in that none of the environments would interact to set intelligence priorities. In such a situation, there is little communication between and among the three environments, virtually no understanding or acceptance of the roles of each of the environments, a great deal of resistance to penetration from the other environments, and a good deal of jockeying for position on issues. Under these circumstances, there would be no agreement on the issue whatsoever, and any requirements would probably reflect parochial interests and contain a good deal of bias; any intelligence assessment would almost certainly be rejected or disavowed by the consumers who reside in the other, antagonistic environments. This kind of situation would exist primarily when issues are unclear, ambiguous, unpredictable, and controversial.

The analytical disarray in 1978 that prevented the drafting of any estimate about the fall of the shah of Iran would fall into this category. The debate over whether or not the Soviet Union was the principal supporter of international terrorism during the 1980s would probably also fall in the same category.[47] Certainly, confusion and uncertainty over terrorist aims as well as intentions during the 1990s would fall in this scenario as well.

Most of the time, no one environment has the sufficient clout—because of disparities in political issues, outcomes of turf battles, imperfect information, and asymmetrical power relationships—to impose its own priorities. In most cases, two of the influence areas have to team up to exert the influence necessary to determine the agenda. The result is that priorities are determined by a dominant coalition, which may or may not include the policymaker.

Three possible permutations serve as models of what happens in setting priorities in U.S. intelligence. One possible combination is a situation in which the analysts/collectors and organizational dynamics together wield sufficient influence to drown out the policy environment. This happens more often than intelligence officials would admit, mostly in cases where policymakers, uninterested in or unaware of the issue, allow the community process and analyst/collector environments to call the shots. Intelligence analyses dealing with arcane and esoteric topics—such as tracking the destruction of the Brazilian Amazon rain forest—would fall in this category. In such situations, the community process and analyst/collector environments seek to impose their views by educating the policy environment of the importance of the issue and informing policymakers of its national security and foreign policy implications. For example, policymakers for a long time resisted the notion of considering the spread of AIDS as a national security matter, until IC agencies, health departments, and CIA analysts in particular—who had been tracking the spread of AIDS during the 1980s on the basis of a model developed by them—were able to launch a concerted effort to put the issue at the forefront of policymaker attention.

Another possible combination is one in which the policy and the analyst/collector environments interact but work together to exclude the community process environment. This short-circuiting of bureaucratic processes is also fairly common and occurs most frequently in crisis situations or in circumstances where timeliness is of essence. For example, President John Kennedy was not averse to calling analysts on the telephone and getting answers to his questions right on the spot. Policymakers routinely get together with analysts over lunch or seek impromptu oral briefings. In crisis situations, moreover, policymakers—in the Situation Room of the White House, for example—may ignore finished intelligence and read raw information coming through cables or intercepts, in effect acting as their own intelligence officers, thereby bypassing the interagency process altogether.

The net result of the exclusion of the community process environment is that the policymaker gets his/her questions answered quickly—producing greater customer satisfaction. But the information may be uncoordinated, may not reflect the best community judgment, and may compel the intelligence community to establish more formal and rigid procedures that would have the net effect of restricting such interactions in the future.

A final combination is one in which the policy world and community dynamics environment interact but exclude the analyst/collector environment. DCI William Casey, for example, a close confidant of President Reagan, often provided the president with detailed briefings on a variety of foreign policy issues without input from the analyst/collector environment.[48] He would consult trusted advisers and a few NIOs but would sometimes ignore or exclude analysts and collectors.

While the interaction of the policy and bureaucratic environments without input from the analysts or collectors can produce a reliable agenda, it may also substantially hurt long-term agenda setting. The analyst/collector environment may resist future direction from the policy or bureaucratic process environments, with the net result that policy questions may either not be answered or be answered in such a way that they would be meaningless or irrelevant to the consumer. The policy and process environments would have the option of dealing with the issue on their own, but doing so would establish politically charged intelligence priorities. In short, this kind of outcome would lack both the right policy questions and the appropriate analytical response.

In short, agenda setting in U.S. intelligence is an interactive process that requires a careful balance of interests among policymakers, bureaucratic mechanisms, and intelligence experts. While a balance of interests and power relationships would provide the most agreeable intelligence agenda, one environment, more often than not, tends to be excluded from wielding its share of influence in agenda setting. Excluding a specific influence area from agenda setting may be dependent on the particular issue under consideration, or it may be due to other political factors. Regardless, one thing is clear—who sets intelligence priorities does matter. The nature and substance of intelligence priorities matter even more, because they drive the rest of the intelligence process, beginning with the collection effort.

6

Perils of Intelligence Collection

If we could read the secret history of our enemies, we should find in each man's life sorrow and suffering enough to disarm all hostility.
—Henry Wadsworth Longfellow, nineteenth-century poet

Policymaker requirements initiate the intelligence process, and intelligence collection gives it substance. Collection can contribute to intelligence success if intelligence agencies know what they need to collect and then use their considerable resources to get the information in a timely enough fashion to answer the key questions of decision makers. On the other hand, intelligence collection can help create failure if the information is deficient or late, or if information is unavailable.

Information of intelligence value is the lifeblood of the intelligence process. All U.S. intelligence agencies exist to collect intelligence information of importance to the nation's security. Most community agencies—especially the NSA, NRO, NGA, and CIA—have dedicated and specialized authorities to collect information in unique ways, and these authorities enable them to manage their particular collection methodologies. Furthermore, three of the community's agencies—the Defense Intelligence Agency, the State Department's Bureau of Intelligence and Research, and the Central Intelligence Agency—are considered to have all-source capabilities, in that in addition to their own dedicated collection mechanisms, they receive intelligence information gathered by the other specialized agencies of the community. Nearly all of the community agencies employ highly esoteric methods to acquire foreign secrets, all intended to satisfy the informational needs of policy leaders.

Collection Disciplines

U.S. intelligence services employ a variety of techniques for gathering information, known collectively as "collection disciplines." These techniques range from publicly available information to highly classified data garnered from technological methods known as "national technical means." Each of these methodologies has its strengths and weaknesses, with the weaknesses often contributing to intelligence failures.

Imagery
The United States devotes a large portion of its intelligence resources to the collection of imagery intelligence, or IMINT. Imagery information is derived from airborne and space collection platforms, such as satellites and aircraft. The U-2 spy planes that were successful in photographing the construction and deployment of Soviet medium-range missiles in Cuba in the early 1960s were engaged in imagery intelligence. In the 1960s and 1970s, photographic intelligence, or PHOTINT, was the mainstay of imagery intelligence. PHOTINT was derived from spools of film carried on aircraft like the U-2 or its successor, the SR-71 Blackbird, or ejected from satellites and captured by specially designed airplanes as the spools descended to earth below small parachutes.

Today, sophisticated satellites—both orbiting and geosynchronous—can take real-time images of large swaths of the earth or peek at a specific location on the ground in detail. The intelligence community has radar, infrared, and ground-penetrating satellites that can peer through clouds at any time of a day, sense heat sources on the ground with great precision, and detect underground sources of radiation or variations in density and composition.

The United States also employs unmanned aerial vehicles, or drones, for strategic and tactical imagery collection.[1] The

National Reconnaissance Office, the existence of which was classified until 1994, manages IMINT physical assets for the entire intelligence community, while the National Geospatial-Intelligence Agency manages the requirements and analysis pertaining to imagery intelligence.

The United States is reputed to have the most technologically sophisticated collection systems, but such sophistication comes at a high cost in hardware, personnel, and money. Indeed, the bulk of the intelligence community budget is devoted to research and development in this area and to such big-ticket items as satellites and spy planes. Beginning with the onset of the space age in the late 1950s, the U.S. intelligence community shifted its collection emphasis, first to PHOTINT, and then to IMINT, such that by the late 1970s some senior intelligence officials, like then DCI Stansfield Turner, were convinced that imagery intelligence could replace spies as the principal method of collecting intelligence.

Advocates of imagery say that its advantages make the huge outlays worthwhile. One, imagery is compelling; an image is concrete evidence of an activity, and there is little arguing over its content. Such a capability is advantageous particularly for monitoring treaty compliance. Two, acquiring imagery intelligence is not politically sensitive. Obviously, governments are not fond of foreign aerial scrutiny of their territories, but they also want to retain the option for themselves. In addition, with all the gadgetry in space today—ranging from Global Positioning System satellites to infrared sensor satellites—there is little governments can do about imagery collection. International legal issues, like the rights of states over whose airspace satellites traverse, are perennial concerns, but the international community has yet to reach a consensus on those rights. Three, imagery intelligence has the advantage of producing large amounts of collateral physical evidence that can be used for intelligence purposes.

However, imagery's disadvantages may outweigh its contributions to intelligence. One, platforms for acquiring imagery intelligence are expensive to build and maintain, siphoning off important resources from other areas of the intelligence community. Since the 1980s, many in the intelligence community have complained that the United States relies too much on imagery intelligence at the expense of other collection mechanisms. Some have even suggested that downplaying other types of intelligence has inadvertently contributed to intelligence failures. As evidence, they cite such events as the Iranian hostage crisis in 1979, inability to forecast the demise of the Soviet Union in 1991, the various intelligence shortcomings in the first Iraq War in 1991, the Somalia debacle in 1993, and other recent events in Bosnia, Kosovo, and elsewhere.

Two, despite the enormous outlays in technological prowess, imagery can be defeated by deception methods. A substantial part of the reasoning for the war against Iraq in 2003 was predicated on imagery intelligence about Iraq's weapons of mass destruction. According to former DCI George Tenet, the Iraqis went to great lengths to mask their intentions across the board, including their efforts to acquire dual-use equipment with higher levels of sophistication.[2]

Three, imagery intelligence is woefully inadequate, despite its compelling nature, in explaining motivations and foretelling intentions. For example, an image of a specific military base provides only a snapshot of whatever is going on there; it cannot readily reveal how and for what purposes political leaders intend to use the assets on that base. Knowing the intentions of foreign leaders is important for making determinations about the nature and substance of national security threats against the United States. Imagery can help in this area if used right, but it fails miserably if employed as the dominant source of intelligence about enemy plans.

Signals Intelligence
U.S. intelligence services rely in part on signals intelligence (SIGINT) to overcome the deficiencies of imagery intelligence. SIGINT, pure and simple, refers to communications intercepts. The National Security Agency is the manager of SIGINT in the U.S. government, even though some of the other agencies are authorized to engage in specialized forms of SIGINT to fulfill their own missions. The CIA, for example, engages in clandestine SIGINT in support of its espionage operations. However, the NSA is the principal agency that eavesdrops on diplomatic and military communications, of hostile and friendly nations alike.

SIGINT is the collective product of a number of subsidiary collection disciplines. Communications intelligence (COMINT) is the main source of SIGINT. NSA performs most of its work through a variety of listening posts, aerial and space platforms, and classified sensors around the globe. Electronic intelligence (ELINT) also contributes to SIGINT, by gathering information from the electronic emissions of gadgets like telephones, fax machines, copiers, typewriters, and computers. Finally, telemetry intelligence (TELINT)—the interception of encrypted signals from foreign military systems like ballistic missiles and warheads—enables the intelligence community to make assessments about foreign military capabilities.

To do its job right, the NSA uses authority under the law to engage in such related activities as breaking the diplomatic and military codes of foreign governments and ensuring the security of its own communications. These activities require sophisticated equipment like sensors, radars, and satellites (the satellites, though owned by the NSA, are managed by the NRO). All this paraphernalia require substantial financial resources. According to one observer, the United States is expending "incredible amounts of money on satellite collection," which threatens to overwhelm the intelligence budget.[3] It would be safe to say that SIGINT and IMINT together account for at least half the intelligence community's resources, in terms of both money and people.[4]

SIGINT has significant advantages as well as disadvantages. The main advantage of SIGINT is that it enables intelligence analysts to make some judgments with relative certainty about the intentions of foreign leaders and foreign capabilities. Insofar as motivations, plans, and intentions are communicated through the airwaves, telecommunications cable networks, or in print, they can be intercepted and used for intelligence purposes. SIGINT can also be employed as a supplement to IMINT to give intelligence officers a good idea of what is going on in the target country. SIGINT's disadvantages, however, may dilute its effectiveness as a collection tool. First, SIGINT produces information in quantities so huge that, according to investigators, it tends to overwhelm the intelligence process. The vast "take" is the result of the "vacuum cleaner" approach that the NSA uses, whereby it intercepts everything possible with the hope of separating out the important nuggets later. Such an approach may have contributed to over-looking an important signal by terrorists the day before the attacks of 11 September, a signal translated and analyzed only after the attacks had occurred.[5]

Second, NSA has been having a difficult time maintaining its competitive advantage in the current environment of rapid technological innovations and cryptologic sophistication in the private sector. Some analysts claim that the NSA has fallen behind the private sector in its ability to make use of computer technology and other high-tech equipment.[6] Consequently, NSA has had to juggle tradeoffs between modernization and readiness.[7] Such painful choices have become particularly stark since the attacks of 11 September.

Third, SIGINT can be subject to deception and disinformation, and such deception may go undiscovered until well after the damage has been done. Fourth, SIGINT, like IMINT, is pro-hibitively expensive, using up enormous resources at the ex-pense of other, less expensive collection systems.

Measurement and Signature Intelligence
Straddling both imagery and signals intelligence is an ob-scure collection discipline called "measurement and signa-ture intelligence," or MASINT. This technique employs the resources of both IMINT and SIGINT for deriving intelligence information from predictable measurements of materiel, such as shipping containers, trace elements from smoke stacks, or the chemical composition of an object from afar.[8] MASINT also uses the analysis of unique signatures, such as the wakes left by warships, to derive useful intelligence.

MASINT, as a relatively new discipline, has the potential to contribute a great deal to effective intelligence but lacks an institutional champion—a manager—to give it the clout it needs in the shadowy world of the intelligence community. If it were to get a backer, MASINT could overcome some of the disadvantages of both IMINT and SIGINT and bridge the di-vide between the two disciplines.

Human Intelligence
One collection discipline that relies less on technology and more on human labor is human intelligence, or HUMINT. This

is the realm of espionage, or spies, and so is the central component of the intelligence game that fires up the public's imagination. The CIA is the HUMINT manager in the U.S. intelligence community, but it shares this realm with Defense HUMINT Service and some other agencies of the community. The CIA, however, accounts for the bulk of espionage on behalf of the U.S. government.

The CIA's Directorate of Operations (DO), renamed the National Clandestine Service (NCS) in October 2005, sends personnel abroad—case officers—whose job it is to recruit spies who can provide information on the capabilities, motivations, and intentions of foreign governments. The spies typically are high-level officials in foreign governments or non-state groups, such as terrorist cells or international crime syndicates, who agree to give CIA case officers information about their organizations and their activities. The spies' motivations are not always apparent, but they range anywhere from ideological reasons and opposition to their own governments or groups all the way to financial gain.

The case officers recruit their spies based upon a long period of assessment, during which they befriend the potential recruit in order to determine his or her access to relevant information and susceptibility to recruitment. The assessment period may last for years, and it may end in failure to recruit. Once the CIA decides to recruit a potential spy, the case officer makes a pitch, which immediately throws the case officer and the potential recruit into a paradoxical situation. If the person who was pitched were to decline the offer and tells his superiors, the American case officer's usefulness in all likelihood would come to an end. However, if the potential recruit were to accept the pitch, the relationship between the case officer and the "asset" may result in important information for the U.S. government.

Such a system of assessment, pitch, and recruitment has generally worked and has been instrumental in providing the U.S. government with valuable information. However, the technique works less well in penetrating and collecting information about nongovernmental groups, such as terrorists, that pose the greater threat to the United States and its allies today. HUMINT methodologies must be continually modified to produce a new type of agent who can penetrate terrorist cells or drug cartels and come out alive to tell his story. While this may be an obvious solution, bureaucratically entrenched entities like the CIA's NCS are resisting significant change in this direction.

The case officer system operates on the principle of "cover." Most American case officers who go abroad do so under official cover, either diplomatic or military, and are supported by other U.S. government agencies through a system of "backstopping" agreements, in which the agencies agree to provide all the necessary accruements—a cover employment story, work telephone numbers, normal identification cards, library cards, and other "pocket litter"—with which the case officers can live their cover stories.[9] As part of the agreement, the CIA embeds the case officer into the ranks of the diplomatic corps or the military service. In this way, CIA officers use their cover positions for access to potential spies or as protection in case a potential recruitment goes awry. This system of official cover works relatively well when recruiting agents to spy on governments but becomes essentially useless in cases involving terrorists and other non-state groups.

The CIA also provides "nonofficial cover" (NOC) for some of its case officers, who as NOCs serve in commercial or other private enterprises to recruit spies and collect national security information. Because NOCs cannot be officially associated with anyone in the CIA, servicing the NOC case officer is a much more cumbersome, intricate, and elaborate process. Chiefs of station (COSs), CIA officers who head CIA stations abroad, do not like to be in charge of NOCs, for the simple reason that they essentially have no control of them and therefore have little impact on their activities. The nonofficial character of an NOC's cover also makes the case officer highly vulnerable to discovery, intimidation, prosecution, and even death. This is also true for case officers who are under deep covers for the purpose of penetrating terrorist groups or international crime syndicates.

The case officers, either under official or nonofficial cover, collect information from their spies on the basis of requirements provided them by CIA headquarters, which itself receives its guidance from the requirements process in Washington.

The CIA's guidance to its case officers provides the impetus for specific and targeted recruitment of spies and forms the nucleus of the type of information that case officers seek.

Case-officer recruitment represents only one part of HUMINT activities. Intelligence agencies may also receive valuable information from émigrés and defectors, who choose to leave their countries or abandon their ties to non-state groups and, for a variety of reasons, decide to help the U.S. government. Emigrés and defectors probably constituted the principal sources of information about Soviet activities during the Cold War. The U.S. government receives the bulk of its information about such closed societies as Cuba and North Korea from émigrés and defectors, although such information may occasionally be suspect, as in the case of Iraqi émigrés who advised the U.S. government before the war in 2003.[10]

HUMINT's contribution to the intelligence process over the years has been uneven. HUMINT assets provided valuable information on many of America's foreign policy crises, such as the Sino-Soviet split in 1962, but it may also have contributed to some of America's foreign policy debacles, such as China's occupation of Tibet in the early 1950s.[11]

In addition, the competition between technical collection disciplines and HUMINT in the 1970s served to damage the number and quality of HUMINT assets in critical areas of the globe. For example, DCI Turner fired many of the then-DO case officers in the late 1970s as a cost-saving measure, arguing that technical collection methods would take up the slack.[12] In doing so, he probably eliminated America's eyes and ears on the ground in such places as the Middle East, possibly contributing to the Iran hostage situation and the failure to forecast the Soviet invasion of Afghanistan, both in 1979. More recently, HUMINT assets had to take second place in Bosnia, Kosovo, and Iraq to the more sophisticated and compelling techniques of imagery and signals intelligence.

HUMINT's main advantage is that it is labor intensive and therefore, compared to national technical means, cheap. HUMINT also has the advantage of being capable of providing relevant and timely information on the motivations and intentions of foreign political leaders.

On the other hand, HUMINT's disadvantages probably

outweigh its advantages. One, American case officers may not have sufficient training and know-how to perform their jobs well. According to one analyst, CIA operatives are not particularly well prepared; they seldom speak foreign languages well and almost never know a line of business or a technical field.[13] Two, the process of recruiting spies is time consuming and lengthy, which often brings into question the benefits of such an activity in relation to its cost. Three, HUMINT information is highly perishable and therefore has a low threshold of utility. Four, HUMINT is often vulnerable to deception and double-agent operations. Five, spying is illegal everywhere, and case officers who have been caught in the process of recruitment have embarrassed the U.S. government and damaged relations with both unfriendly and friendly governments. Six, espionage is risky to the lives of intelligence agents and their assets. In many cases, American operatives trying to penetrate non-state groups have been captured and killed. Seven, because HUMINT assets are often employed in covert actions, espionage operations sometimes become enmeshed in political controversies at home. Eight, many people believe that spying is ethically wrong, an activity that diminishes the moral standing of the United States around the globe.

Open-Source Information
Relying on classified sources of information makes the intelligence agencies resistant to the use of publicly available information. Paradoxically, intelligence officers have long recognized that open-source intelligence, or OSINT, has the potential to outstrip all other collection techniques in the quantity and quality of intelligence information. Once a stepchild of other collection disciplines, OSINT is now regarded by many intelligence officials as a highly valuable source, not only as a supplement to intelligence information acquired through clandestine means but also as the principal source of critical national security information. Consequently, the U.S. intelligence community is grudgingly devoting ever-larger resources to the collection of open-source materials.

OSINT encompasses several different activities. Intelligence services routinely subscribe to newspapers, scientific journals, and political magazines. Intelligence analysts read books, attend professional conferences, and exchange views with academicians. Organizations like the Foreign Broadcast Information Service, part of the CIA's Directorate of Science and Technology, listen to foreign radio and television broadcasts, translate foreign newspapers and journals, and publish them in daily and weekly reports that are circulated to intelligence analysts and government officials.

There is much debate within the intelligence community about the utility of OSINT. Proponents strenuously argue that OSINT's principal advantage is its ready availability. Advocates maintain that this publicly acquired information is, if sifted thoroughly and analyzed correctly, a potential gold mine of intelligence information that could supplement the take from other disciplines. Adherents cite statistics to illustrate OSINT's value. For example, because of greater openness and transparency around the globe, 80 percent of all intelligence information can be gleaned from open-source materials.[14] According to one source, 95 percent of all economic intelligence now comes from open sources.[15] To take greater advantage of open-source materials, the director of national intelligence in November 2005 established the Open Source Center with the CIA, absorbing the Foreign Broadcast Information Service (FBIS), which had monitored printed and electronic media around the globe since 1942.

Opponents of using OSINT argue with equal vigor that the methodology contains many pitfalls that could damage the intelligence process. One, the sheer volume of open-source materials makes it difficult to separate the wheat from the chaff. Like the large volume of information gleaned by SIGINT, huge quantities of open-source information can divert analysts from critical intelligence activities to the mundane tasks of sifting, collating, and cataloguing. Two, OSINT can be vulnerable to disinformation and therefore to faulty forecasting. Three, open-source information, contrary to popular opinion, can be quite expensive. Books, journals, magazines, and all other open-source materials cost money, resources that intelligence services probably would prefer to spend on their own unique, dedicated, and specialized forms of classified collection techniques.

Because of the community's ambivalence toward OSINT, the private sector has spawned enterprises to fill the gap. Open Source Solutions, for example, is a firm that seeks to provide government and the public with comprehensive collated open-source information.[16] Lexis-Nexis has been around a long time, providing extensive and invaluable archival material. New ventures like Infosphere appear virtually on a daily basis on the World Wide Web. So long as the intelligence community remains convinced that intelligence information gathered through clandestine means is more important than information gleaned from public sources, there will be great demand for the information products provided by private companies.

ORCON

Because most community agencies possess proprietary means of collecting intelligence, they tend to guard jealously their collection capabilities and their information. The agencies do so by manipulating the weaknesses of existing classification regulations, which generally derive from a series of executive orders giving the DCI and now the DNI legal authority to set classification policy, such as specifying "caveats," supplements to basic classification categories. (Up to 2005, the DCI, in turn, conveyed his orders by means of Director of Central Intelligence Directives [DCIDs]. As management tools, DCIDs are classified and cover the entire gamut of managerial issues concerning the intelligence community and its agencies, including policies on controlling access to intelligence information.)

The most restrictive, and therefore the most controversial, of the classification caveats is the designation ORCON, which stands for "originator controlled." This designation derives from various internal and external rules, but more specifically from Executive Order 12958, which provides that classified information originating in one U.S. department or agency shall not be disseminated beyond any recipient agency without the consent of the originating agency. The "Third Party" rule provides procedural guidelines for exceptions in order to facilitate use and dissemination within and among community agencies, but the requirement of permission remains intact.[17] Complaints within the intelligence community prompted the discontinuation of ORCON in the mid-1990s, but former DCI Tenet restored it toward the end of the decade.

The intelligence agencies, but especially the CIA, employ the ORCON designation for particularly sensitive information. By so designating a piece of information, the agencies intend, at least from an official standpoint, to "protect sources and methods," which is the standard legal mantra used to justify classifying documents and preventing their disclosure. The rationale for secrecy, again from an official point of view, is to protect the source of the information and the method by which it was gathered. Agencies have also, however, used the ORCON authority to hide embarrassing secrets or information that might cause them damage. In addition, intelligence organizations use it to protect their knowledge base; the adage "information is power" is particularly apt in this regard.

In practical terms, the use of the ORCON designation means that an analyst who wants to use ORCON information must first get the permission of the controlling agency. The intelligence agencies—the CIA uses ORCON more extensively than the others—have developed elaborate procedures for releasing ORCON information. A DIA analyst who wants to use ORCON information from the CIA must not only get the permission of CIA's NCS but also must submit his report to the NCS to ensure that sources and methods are protected. In addition, the CIA and other intelligence agencies apply similar procedures to regulate the internal use of ORCON information. For example, a CIA analyst in the Directorate of Intelligence (DI), the CIA's analytical arm, must obtain the NCS's permission to use ORCON information in reports or other intelligence products.

The reality is that ORCON endows the internal segments of the agencies, like the CIA's NCS, with significant power. For example, the NCS has exclusive say on what to release, whom to release it to, and how the information is to be used. Again, information is power, and the NCS wields a lot of power both in the CIA and in Washington.

The ORCON technique has a chilling effect on the use of relevant intelligence information in formal or written assessments.

Originator-controlled methodology serves as a further speed bump in an already heavily bureaucratic intelligence process and has a tendency frequently to frustrate timely intelligence analysis. In addition, agencies often use ORCON to hinder intelligence sharing among themselves. According to the Joint Intelligence Inquiry, which looked into the performance of intelligence agencies prior to and after the 11 September events,

> Within the Intelligence Community, agencies did not adequately share relevant counterterrorism information. . . . This breakdown in communications was the result of a number of factors, including differences in the agencies' missions, legal authorities and cultures. Information was not sufficiently shared, not only between Intelligence Community agencies, but also within individual agencies, and between the intelligence and the law enforcement agencies.[18]

Using ORCON authority to deny the use of intelligence information undoubtedly has a ripple effect on the latter stages of the intelligence cycle. It significantly affects intelligence analysis and may put the policymaker in the position of having to make critical national security decisions without the benefit of all the available information. If Senator Richard Shelby is correct in saying that "perfectly secure information is perfectly useless information,"[19] he is describing an intelligence community that tries to make its information perfectly secure.

The Classification System

ORCON is only one of the many restrictive designations employed by the intelligence agencies. The others, unlike the ORCON control, are intended to deny access to information based on the criterion of "damage to national security." The scheme in use today dates back to the 1960s and includes three different designations:

- The Confidential designation is used for any national security information the disclosure of which could reasonably be expected to cause damage to national security.

- The Secret designation is used for information that requires substantial degree of protection, when it is determined that unauthorized disclosure could reasonably be expected to cause serious damage to national security.
- The Top Secret designation is for information that requires the highest level of protection and when it is determined that unauthorized disclosure could reasonably be expected to cause exceptionally grave damage to national security.[20]

The DNI is also authorized to set additional classification parameters by issuing a variety of code-word controls intended to restrict information further by establishing specific "compartments." The compartments may denote a particular collection technique or a specific intelligence program. Individuals with a "need to know"—this determination is based on a person's position and job within the government—receive briefings on the programs designated by those code words and thereby are "cleared" for those programs. For example, the Reagan administration in the 1980s authorized a deception and disinformation program against Libya that was code-named VEIL; only individuals who were authorized, or cleared, for VEIL were allowed access to specific information on this program.[21]

There are additional caveats that, although like ORCON they are technically not part of the classification system, are meant to restrict access to information even further. The NOFORN designation denies information to foreign governments that may have an intelligence-exchange relationship with the United States. The NOCONTRACT designation denies information to individuals and businesses that have a contractual relationship with the U.S. government. Even unclassified materials may receive a restriction, through the use of the FOR OFFICIAL USE ONLY (FOUO) designation, which theoretically limits the use of such materials to government officials.

In short, intelligence work takes place in relative secrecy. Secrecy is the glue that binds the U.S. intelligence community with those whom it is supposed to serve. There undoubtedly are legitimate national security reasons for secrecy, but maintaining secrecy has often been abused in ways that has kept intelligence from getting to the very consumers who need it most.[22] Secrecy has also been used as a form of government regulation—a bureaucratic regime with recognizable and predictable patterns of self-perpetuation—to exclude the public from knowing what it is reasonably in the public's interest to know.[23] Former DCI Tenet, for example, refused to declassify some information even for use by members of Congress who, as members of the Joint Intelligence Inquiry, were investigating the 9/11 attacks.[24]

In addition, secrecy in intelligence comes into conflict with the American democratic tradition of transparency in government. The tension between the requirements of secrecy and the democratic requirement of openness has produced a series of compromises that have satisfied neither friends nor foes of secrecy in government. American officials like to point out that U.S. intelligence is the most "open" of the intelligence services around the globe. Nevertheless, this tension is a manifestation of the delicate balance that needs to be maintained between the national security requirements to protect sources and methods, and the public's "need to know." This balance is constantly evolving, with the pendulum swinging either way depending on how the president and his advisers perceive the nature of the threat and the appropriate response to it. The administration of George W. Bush has tilted the balance in favor of greater secrecy since the events of 9/11.[25]

An Ounce of Prevention

The U.S. government, like its counterparts elsewhere, has a lot of secrets to keep, and it uses the classification system and other preventive methods to ensure the integrity of its secrets. Foreign governments understandably are intensely curious about American secrets and are constantly trying to uncover them through a variety of means, most notably through espionage. Discovering those who are trying to steal American secrets and preventing them from doing any further damage falls within the rubric of counterintelligence (CI), which straddles the gulf between the necessity to maintain secrecy and the compelling interest to prevent others from getting at those secrets.[26] Chapter 9 examines counterintelligence in greater detail.

In the United States, CI is a collection as well as an analytic activity. Counterintelligence officers employ a variety of the collection methodologies noted above to gather CI information and use analytic techniques to assess vulnerabilities and opportunities (see chapter 9). As such, nearly all intelligence agencies engage in counterintelligence under the authority of the DNI.

In practical terms, counterintelligence responsibilities are divided between the CIA, empowered to conduct CI outside the borders of the United States, and the FBI, which does so within the United States. This division of labor may seem straightforward on the surface, but it is actually complicated by differing and conflicting missions. Because the CIA is considered the premier espionage agency of the government, its primary interest is to use people—spies, agents, double agents, or defectors—to ferret out the secrets of foreign governments. When it discovers spies working against the United States, it tries to turn them into double agents to spy for it. The FBI, on the other hand, being a law enforcement agency, is interested in uncovering criminal activity and, more often than not, takes measures to arrest those who may be responsible and prosecute them in a court of law. The clash of mission and cultures often results in bureaucratic battles between the FBI and the CIA.

Counterintelligence involves more than identification, surveillance, and arrest. It also involves the collection and analysis of intelligence information in order to differentiate between who is a spy and who is not; determine what the spies want; and assess weaknesses in the target country's capabilities as well as the gaps in America's defenses against foreign espionage. Even here the requirements, missions, and cultures of the FBI and the CIA diverge significantly. Whereas the CIA is looking to use people for strategic information that may give it clues about the behavior of foreign governments, the FBI is interested in information that will stand up in court to convict those who spy against the United States. The differences in approach frequently hinder cooperation between the two agencies. Even when the two organizations work together, as they sometimes do, their separate methods preclude clean-cut successes.

The case of Aldrich Ames, for example, took over eight years to solve, during which the CIA and the FBI refused to share their suspicions with one another, failed to share information during the investigation, and declined to mount joint counterintelligence operations. Pundits have dubbed this failure to cooperate the "Hanssen Effect," alluding to Robert Hanssen, a senior FBI counterintelligence officer who was able to operate with impunity as a Soviet (later Russian) spy for fifteen years until his capture in 2001.[27]

Bureaucratic competition and noncommunication between the FBI and the CIA undoubtedly has allowed foreign spies relatively free rein in the United States. Failing to unmask foreign agents is tantamount to allowing foreign governments access to the capabilities and intentions of the United States. That in turn may contribute to intelligence failures, by skewing analyses of what foreign governments know, do not know, or intend to know or do.

Inflection Points

Intelligence collection is specialized activity that feeds the parochialism among the agencies of the intelligence community. Each agency's distinctly narrow focus, in turn, is reflected in its classification policy and counterintelligence operations.

One would think that a comprehensive intelligence effort conducted with limited resources would induce intelligence agencies to cooperate in collecting intelligence and preventing others from collecting against the United States. A study prepared by the staff of the House Permanent Select Committee on Intelligence (HPSCI) in 1996, however, found that there is a widening lack of coordination among collection disciplines. This is due, according to the report, to the prevalent practice of "stovepiping" the collection systems, which inevitably result in turf and resource battles.[28] Yet the intelligence community continues in this practice, to the chagrin of many reformers who argue that the habit of operating in isolation induces each agency to develop its own idiosyncratic system of acquiring and sending information.

The agencies and their managers usually do not "talk" to one another in ways that would allow rapid cooperative targeting. To receive the needed information, they need to procure for themselves specific equipment designed to sense that information.[29] Many observers have attributed the 9/11 intelligence failure precisely to a lack of inter- and intra-agency communication and linkage. Moreover, extreme compartmentation—the intelligence community continues to insist on such isolation—produces a situation where each of the collection managers is oblivious to what the others are collecting. This happens primarily because each collection manager controls its own budget and the allocations within that budget. Such isolation inevitably produces overlap, duplication, and waste.

Establishing greater linkage and synergy among the collection disciplines would be difficult, given the entrenched cultural and legal imperatives of each of the major intelligence agencies. In addition, creating an environment for greater communication among the collection systems would probably be prohibitively expensive. Some would even argue that increased information sharing and linkage would defeat the purpose of "competitive intelligence" as it now exists in the U.S. intelligence community, whereby each of the agencies competes with the others to produce and disseminate the best available intelligence. Synergy would also make intelligence collection vulnerable to greater amounts of misinformation, disinformation, and distortion.

Nevertheless, more cross-fertilization and cooperation among collection managers would probably pay dividends over the long term. Bringing all information gathered by disparate intelligence agencies together in one place would reduce inefficiencies and enable intelligence analysts to address better the tendency toward parochialism among the collectors. However, the world of intelligence analysis has its own problems, problems that in part mirror the discontinuities of the collection disciplines.

7

Analytic Snafus

Community estimates of early 1962 and mid-1963 relating to the Chinese nuclear program represented a comedy of errors, resulting in an intelligence success.
—Report of the 1983 CIA Senior Review Panel

Collecting intelligence information is of little value unless someone corroborates and evaluates the information, sets it into context, and uses it to form a series of judgments about foreign capabilities and intentions. The intelligence community employs thousands of intelligence analysts to do just that—to transform accurate and relevant information into meaningful insights, in a form consumers can use at the time they need them. If intelligence fails to do this, it fails altogether.[1]

Analysis is the heart of the intelligence process; its success boils down to the skill and expertise of the individual analyst. While there is a specific job title "intelligence analyst," analysis takes place at different levels of intelligence hierarchies. In the CIA, for example, the reports officers in the National Clandestine Service take the first crack at analyzing raw information from agents, by subjecting it to evaluation and corroboration and transforming it into useable reports, long before the intelligence analyst in the Directorate of Intelligence (DI) even sees the information. The DI analyst, in turn, uses the sanitized information—sanitized by the reports officer to excise sources and methods, information the DI analyst has no need to know—and employs analytic techniques to derive judgments and conclusions. Requirements in the form of key intelligence questions or issues, generally in document form, guide the analyst in this task.

The World of the Analyst

The typical intelligence analyst is a regional, country, or issue specialist who is considered to have, by virtue of experience and higher education, sufficient substantive expertise to do intelligence analysis. Most U.S. intelligence agencies, including those engaging in all-source intelligence, do not provide much substantive training to new analysts beyond rudimentary orientation to the intelligence community and the particular agency, occasional familiarization tours to the region or country, and some internal training courses on intelligence writing and procedure. In the CIA, for example, the training division, as well as CIA University, periodically conduct seminars on the role and performance of intelligence analysis, but these conferences do little to hone the analysts' substantive expertise. On the other hand, seasoned analysts who have perfected their skills on the job probably are some of the better trained and able intelligence analysts in and out of the government.

The analyst's job is to gather and collate all relevant intelligence information, subject it to analysis, and draft reports for senior intelligence officials and policymakers—in short, to make sense of the secret world of intelligence and communicate those insights to senior decision makers. Analytic reports essentially come in two forms: current intelligence and long-term research. Current intelligence deals with daily issues or fast-breaking developments.

Among the important current intelligence items are the CIA's *President's Daily Brief*, the *Morning Summary* produced by the State Department's Bureau of Intelligence and Research, CIA's *Senior Executive Intelligence Review*, and a variety of daily publications produced by the Defense Intelligence Agency. Agencies that are not all-source produce their own daily products, but they are intended primarily for internal consumption or for analysts in the all-source agencies.

Long-term research reports are forward-looking assessments of what might happen, based on available information, in a region, country, or issue. Long-term research projects include various intelligence assessments, memoranda, staff reports, and the national intelligence estimates (NIEs) and their cousins, the special national intelligence estimates (SNIEs).

Providing high-quality intelligence analysis is a distinguishing feature of American intelligence. While most governments that engage in the task of intelligence possess analytical capabilities, none devotes more time, energy, and money to current and long-term intelligence analysis than the United States. The reason why relates to the mission of U.S. intelligence to provide objective assessments in support of policy decisions. Policy leaders and intelligence officials prefer current intelligence over long-term research. Political leaders naturally lean toward fast-breaking issues or current crises, compelling U.S. intelligence to become "fully absorbed in current intelligence, leaving no time for long-term research projects that look beyond the horizon."[2] This preference for current intelligence has been bolstered by the shift from the enduring targets of the Cold War to fluctuating targets in the current era and may be eroding the ability of U.S. intelligence to perform strategic analysis.[3]

For intelligence officials, current intelligence is exciting work. The daily briefings and products are an invaluable opportunity for intelligence managers to introduce special topics in order to focus the attention of senior leaders and their staffs on a particular threat or issue. In that way, intelligence officers are sometimes able to influence the policy agenda. Current intelligence is also an opportunity for intelligence to look good and to occupy center stage.[4]

Whether conducting current or long-term research, intelligence analysts must consider numerous factors when arriving at judgments. Analysts know that the product of their work is not necessary for the conduct of diplomacy or military operations but is simply a "force multiplier." That is, when dependable analysis is available, it adds value to national security and foreign policy deliberations as well as to diplomatic and military plans. George Tenet, the former director of central intelligence, characterized intelligence analysis as the ultimate opportunity cost. By this he meant that whatever investment is made today on intelligence may mean the difference tomorrow between success and disaster, life and death.[5]

There is no question about the usefulness of intelligence analysis, providing that it accomplishes its objectives. The question of what objectives analysis tries to accomplish is critical in the intelligence failure debate. If the task of intelligence analysis is to report goings-on in a foreign country, for example, then the analyst has an easy task to perform, a task that is similar to what journalists do. Covering events in a foreign country is easy, because the developments are tangible and they take place in the immediate past. Thomas C. Mahnken, who has written about intelligence in historical perspective, asserts that U.S. intelligence has been especially successful in monitoring the development of established foreign weapons systems, detecting combat-proven technology and doctrine, and identifying tactical military technologies and concepts.[6] However, if the task of intelligence analysis is to forecast and warn of impending threats, the analyst has a more difficult job, because of the intangibles involved, such as motivations and intentions.

The problem revolves around the differences between concrete, observable evidence and what David Kahn, an early pioneer in the study of intelligence, calls "verbal intelligence."[7] Physical information generally comes from inanimate objects and identifiable entities. It includes such things as natural resources, installations, the number of weapons available, and volume of commercial trade. Concrete, observable intelligence is descriptive, involving what foreign policy analysts would call "capability analysis." Sometimes, intelligence from physical objects may infer intentions, but divining them from capability analysis is so inexact that misinterpretation can occur. Verbal intelligence, on the other hand, may be useful for determining intentions because it derives from words and utterances concerning plans, orders, morale, perceptions, intentions, estimates, promises, motives, and the like.

The distinction between what is physical and what is verbal is a useful one, because war and politics—the main concerns of the consumers of intelligence and hence of intelligence producers—involve both physical attributes and mental operations. Knowing the capabilities of an adversary enables the government possessing such intelligence to adapt to the situation. But intelligence from physical entities is limited information, because it cannot provide the time necessary for making adaptations. On the other hand, the mental component, verbal intelligence, may give the state the time needed to adapt resources and use them to best advantage.

Forecasting intentions is more difficult than reporting capabilities; it is the real culprit behind failures of intelligence analysis. Intentions are a form of verbal forecasts. Such forecasts include orders, commands, plans, estimates, expectations, pure prophesies, as well as expressions of intentions. All of these are verbal statements about the future that suggest reasons for acting, assuming that the forecast were to come true.[8] Intentions, according to this formulation, are decided-upon, planned future actions, focusing on what the actor plans to do.

Intentions by themselves say little about what an adversary will do. Because intentions are formulated or unformulated plans about the future, forecasting them requires additional information. Intentions, for example, may remain purely internal, if the foreign leader fails to formulate them, does nothing, or is prevented from carrying them out. An analyst who is focusing on the question of what an adversary will do in the future, therefore, must correlate known intentions with past actions in order to arrive at a reasonable forecast or probability of the action occurring in the future.

There are several reasons why a complete reliance on capability analysis for estimating intentions is unwise. First, while the physical component, which forms the basis for an estimation of capabilities, cannot be easily disguised as can a plan or an order, it can be camouflaged and used as feints, ruses, spurious demonstrations, and displays.[9] That is, it is possible for an adversary to create and sustain bogus capabilities.

Second, estimating intentions based on capabilities generally provides less time for reaction. When the attributes of an enemy are sufficiently clear to be observed by the intelligence analyst, the action is largely in place and ready. A warning based on these profiles provides little reaction time. In contrast, intelligence on the adversary's plans may be received even before the enemy has set those plans in motion—that is, before any observable physical events take place. Verbal intelligence gives the analyst considerably more time for forecasting and warning.

Third, while physical events are observed chronologically, mental plans are ordered logically.[10] Actions, patterns, and signatures relating to a variety of future activities will be observed as occurring in a linear order through time, and there may be few criteria for knowing which profiles go with which future action. However, events rarely, if ever, occur in a linear fashion. The novelist Tom Robbins uses the term "spray" to describe how things normally happen—"spray," because "events are seldom as linearly linked as those who tout history would prefer to believe."[11] The analyst observing events is thus faced with the tasks of determining which events are relevant to the various possible sources of action the enemy may take without knowing which course of action the enemy intends to take. The analyst who has access to the enemy's plans is less dependent on the temporal order and is thus less rushed by the flow of observations over time.

The analyst requiring more information for gauging intentions has several methodologies available to him. *Indicators* are patterns of behavior that may provide clues on the identity, capabilities, or intentions of an adversary. Indicators most often come in the form of physical intelligence, in that they are activities observed by the analyst. The analyst may also note *signatures*, particular displays of equipment or facilities that may identify a military unit or future activity. For example, photos of incomplete Soviet medium-range missile bases in Cuba in the early 1960s left little to the imagination of American intelligence analysts as to Soviet intentions regarding the use of these bases once they became operational.

The combination of indicators and signatures provide the intelligence analyst with a *profile*, a picture of future activity.[12] All the segments in the profile are incomplete approximations and are subject to interpretation. The analyst's job is to employ expertise and skill to narrow the choices among possible futures and arrive at a reasonable judgment.

A competent and mature analyst can intuitively discern the aforementioned issues in his analytic work. Two additional factors come into play once the analyst arrives at a judgment. One, the analyst must be able to assert conclusions in a convincing way. Most of the intelligence agencies have multilayered editorial processes that go well beyond stylistic issues and involve substantive matters as well. The analyst must be in a position to convince his boss and his boss's boss, and so on up the chain of command. Second, the analyst must become a promoter of his argument not only with his superiors but also with counterpart analysts in other intelligence agencies. Most CIA analytic products, for example, have to go through an internal and external coordination process that seeks the concurrence of other analysts. To arrive at such agreement, there is a natural inclination to dilute the message and arrive at the most general and the least controversial conclusion. Pandering to the "lowest common denominator" tends to produce intelligence judgments of questionable quality, a phenomenon that occurs at the higher level of the estimative process as well.

Finally, the analyst must be able to market the product to policymakers, who tend to believe themselves to be excellent analysts; who may know personally the world leaders intelligence analysts only write about; and who believe they read people well.[13] Policymaker respect for analytic products is an ongoing challenge, which affects the "surge capability" of the intelligence community—that is, its ability quickly and effectively to respond to crises.[14]

Coordination requires more energy and adds substantially more time to the analytic process that begins with the intelligence question and ends with providing an answer to that question. Doing this puts considerable pressure on the analyst to play it safe and take fewer risks. Many intelligence failures, undoubtedly, have occurred because of caution and the penalties exacted by the coordination process.

The existence of multiple agencies, each competing for its own resources and trying to enhance its own organization, contributes to emphasizing worst-case scenarios in assessing possible outcomes. This "cry-wolf syndrome," the preference for the most damaging series of events that could occur, is difficult to resist, mostly because no individual analyst or agency wants to incur the risk of being wrong. Prudence then dictates erring on the pessimistic side. However, sophisticated policymakers, knowing the analysts' proclivities to "cry wolf," may discount repeated warnings, even if correct. Policymakers try to overcome this tendency toward pessimism by asking for an array of forecasts and interpretations, but intelligence analysts in all intelligence agencies are affected by this syndrome.

The Estimative Process

While most analysis occurs at lower levels of the intelligence agencies, the estimative process is the bread and butter of intelligence analysis. In the intelligence community, the National Intelligence Council (NIC) is responsible for producing all national estimates and other, similar products. The NIC, however, does a lot more than that. Because it serves as the community think-tank on strategic issues, the NIC supports the DNI in his role as head of the intelligence community, serves as the focal point of policymaker tasking, reaches out to nongovernmental experts in academia and the private sector, and contributes to resource-allocation matters.[15]

The NIC comprises more than twelve national intelligence officers (NIOs), recruited from around the intelligence community and the private sector to be substantive experts.[16] The NIOs focus either on global regions or on issues, such as counterterrorism or weapons proliferation. There is also an NIO for Warning, who specializes on indications of impending threats in order to warn appropriate officials.

The NIOs have the responsibility to ensure that intelligence analysts at the lower levels adequately cover key intelligence issues, but in keeping with the NIC's general mission, they also advise the DNI; interact with intelligence consumers; engage outside substantive experts; promote collaboration among analytic producers on strategic warning, and advanced analytic tools and methodologies; articulate issue priorities to guide intelligence collection, evaluation, and procurement; and produce estimative intelligence products.[17]

The NIOs' principal analytic product are the NIEs and SNIEs, which are considered to be the DNI's most authoritative written judgments on national security issues. The NIOs are supposed to provide policymakers with the best, unvarnished, and unbiased information—regardless of whether analytic judgments conform to U.S. policy.[18] Whether they actually succeed in doing this is an additional focus in the debate about failures of intelligence.

One essential feature of national estimates is that they draw on all of the information and wisdom available to the U.S. government on the subject at hand, whether from official sources or private ones. A second feature is that NIEs go beyond the description of the situation to project the course of events into the future. Estimates do not predict in the absolute sense, but they outline a range of possible futures and attempt to assign their relative probability of occurrence. A third feature is that while the consensus of the intelligence community is the preferred goal, estimates seek to identify areas of substantive dissent and report them to the policymaker. A final feature is that the estimate must be clearly presented, concisely written, and short enough that the policymaker will have the time to read it.[19]

Like the analytic products at lower levels, estimates go through a coordination process in order to accomplish their goal of presenting unified judgments of the intelligence community. The process of coordination takes place after an acceptable draft is available for review by the principal agencies of the intelligence community. The NIO typically calls the coordination meetings, during which the NIO goes through the draft line by line and each of the agencies presents its views by agreeing, presenting revisions, or dissenting. When there is disagreement, the NIO seeks compromise language. When the disagreements are deep and unbreachable, the dissenting agency may seek to state that fact in the text or add a "footnote" to the text explaining its dissenting opinion.

Such disagreement reportedly surfaced during the drafting of the estimate on Iraq's weapons of mass destruction program in 2002. The disagreement focused on whether some equipment procured by Iraq could have dual uses. Apparently, the DIA disagreed with the estimate's central finding that the equipment—trailers and aluminum tubes—was used in making biological weapons.[20] According to former DCI

Tenet, such coordination is an open and vigorous process that allows dissent by individual agencies in the final product.[21] The NIE then is reviewed by the National Foreign Intelligence Board (NFIB)—composed of agency principals and chaired by the DNI—which approves the final draft of the estimate for dissemination.

The analytic process has several problems. One is that despite volumes of information, there is rarely enough relevant data to arrive at unchallengeable conclusions. Two, because collected intelligence information concerns human actions, it can be manipulated to deceive the analyst.[22] Three, consumers appear to have mixed feelings about intelligence estimates, with some policy consumers apparently unaware of their existence at all. Other consumers dismiss the estimates as neither timely nor relevant. Four, the most damning criticism focuses on estimative failures, such as the demise of the Soviet Union, or on the dilution of the analysis through the interagency coordination process, which often leads to watered-down results.[23]

Homogenizing judgments has been a particularly thorny problem, one that led Gen. Norman Schwarzkopf, the commander of U.S. forces in the Persian Gulf during the Gulf War of 1991, to remark that intelligence estimates were so late and so vague as to make them virtually useless to him. To overcome the deleterious effects of coordination on terrorism analysis, the Bush administration established the Terrorism Threat Assessment Center in 2002, intended to relay threat analysis to the White House and prepare the "Daily Threat Matrix" that supposedly served as the fulcrum for antiterrorism decisions.[24] The center was incorporated into the National Counterterrorism Center (NCTC) in 2005, and the matrix was subsequently discontinued.

From a legal standpoint, the NIEs and SNIEs are the DNI's estimates. They are disseminated to policy consumers over the DNI's signature after approval by the National Foreign Intelligence Board (NFIB). Even though dissenting opinions may be included during consideration by NFIB, estimates remain the DNI's products and his responsibility. In mid-2003, for example, then-DCI Tenet had to defend the judgments of the 2002 NIE on Iraq's Continuing Program for Weapons of

Mass Destruction, which originally had been commissioned by the Senate Select Committee on Intelligence and later used by President George Bush to justify the war in Iraq.[25] In his statement, Tenet asserted that the NIEs are designed to provide the best coordinated judgment of the intelligence community, based on the best available information. Tenet concluded by saying that he stood by the assessment.[26]

Different DCIs over the years have played this role differently. In some cases, they have insisted that their own particular views be enshrined in the estimates. Former DCI William Casey, for example, was criticized in and out of the intelligence community in the early 1980s for insisting that an estimate on Mexico be revised to reflect his conclusions. Other DCIs, however, have opted to advise the president and other senior government officials outside the NIE process by separately registering their opinions.[27]

Most DCIs have put their own imprint on the estimative process. Some have been intensely interested in this function and have played active, constructive roles in the preparation of NIEs. Other DCIs have slowed and confused the estimative process. Still other DCIs have not been all that interested in the estimative process, preferring instead to downplay the NIC and use other avenues to provide intelligence estimates to policymakers. Ultimately, the success of the estimative process turns on the relationship that exists between the intelligence director and the president. The closer the personal relationship between the director and the president, the higher the chances that the director will have a lasting impact on policymaking. An illustrative case is that of DCI John McCone, who was a close friend of President John F. Kennedy and therefore had substantial influence with the president. McCone did not have a similar relationship with Lyndon Johnson, who became president after the Kennedy assassination. Consequently, President Johnson largely ignored McCone's reflections on Vietnam, which were contrary to his views.[28]

The closer the relationship between the director and the president, however, the easier it is to inject political matters into the estimative process to the detriment of unbiased intelligence. Politicization of intelligence, an issue that dogged

DCIs William Casey and Robert Gates, can be an important contributor to intelligence failure.

Politicized Intelligence

Policy leaders determine the utility of the intelligence they receive based on ideological and political factors. Because they generally want to receive information that bolsters their political views, policy leaders sometimes exert so much pressure on intelligence analysts that they alter judgments to suit the view of their customers or further their own interests. Distortions also occur when analysts exclude, withhold or disguise intelligence, or present policymakers with raw, unanalyzed, and misleading intelligence in order to curry favor with them. Furthermore, intelligence may be skewed by subtle, almost unconscious, misinterpretations of ambiguous information or by willful attempts to influence policy through intelligence judgments.

In any hierarchical organization, people are tempted to "cook the books" to fit the policymakers' recipes. Such "politicization" of intelligence injects bias into the process and affects how policymakers respond to international situations. There are a number of examples of this. One was the redrafting of a conclusion of a 1969 National Intelligence Estimate on Soviet Strategic Forces, under pressure from the White House, to paint the Soviets as more bellicose than the data indicated. Another is the NIE on Mexico in the early 1980s (mentioned above), which was redrafted to reflect White House assumptions about Mexico's ability to revamp its political system and revive its economy.

Altering intelligence judgments to suit the perceived preferences of policymakers can be subtle or blatant. In recounting the Cuban missile crisis, Robert Kennedy reported that "personalities change when the president is present, and frequently even strong men make their recommendations on the basis of what they believe the President wishes to hear." Kennedy also observed attempts by senior policymakers to "exclude certain individuals from participating in a meeting with the president because they held a different point of view."[29] Some policymakers also make known their distaste for bad news and those who bring it.

In addition, the complexities of U.S. relations with other countries may affect intelligence reporting. For example, in an effort to gain access to sites for SIGINT collection against the Soviet Union in Iran, the United States made arrangements with the shah that reduced the CIA's ability to collect intelligence on domestic developments in Iran. The arrangement stipulated that the CIA would rely on the shah for domestic information on Iran, and in return the shah would let the United States build and maintain listening posts on Iranian territory. The agreement made it difficult for the United States to gauge domestic opposition to the shah and thereby hurt its ability to respond effectively to the Iranian Revolution of 1979.[30]

Cognitive Issues

Whether at the lower levels of the analytic process or at the National Intelligence Council, intelligence analysts confront a myriad psychological issues that complicate their work and at times contribute to faulty, poor, or inaccurate analysis— ingredients for intelligence failure. For the analyst, intelligence analysis is a high-stakes business that often induces an atmosphere of immediacy and crisis behavior. Moreover, bureaucratic pressures to produce analysis in short time frames, with incomplete information, reinforce this sense of crisis. Former DCI Tenet evinced this difficulty in 2003 when he asserted that analysts "rarely have the luxury of having all the facts before [they] have to arrive at conclusions."[31] As a consequence, intelligence analysts employ cognitive processes to try making sense of a highly complex and uncertain world.

In crises—and most current intelligence tends to foster a perception of a crisis—stress plays a critical role in how analysts respond to information. Stress affects the analytic process in several important ways. One, in stressful situations individuals tend to make incremental decisions. Two, short time frames and immediacy induce analysts to deal with tidbits of information on an urgent basis, often without analyzing them. Three, in such situations, analysts tend to reinforce their preconceptions by assimilating new information within the context of existing information. Germany's failure to identify the location of the D-Day invasion in 1944 may have resulted from such a crisis-induced process. The Germans, aware of the urgency of their situation, determined that the Allied invasion would occur at Calais and incorporated all subsequent information to reinforce that assumption.[32]

Stress also reinforces the preference for current affairs, a pattern by which policymakers and intelligence analysts focus almost entirely on what is going on at any given moment and on the latest piece of information without attempting to put it into broader context. Such a narrow focus may turn some analysts into "news junkies," unable to finish analytic projects because of the constant need to update information. This probably happened in the aftermath of 9/11, with the likely consequence that important antiterrorism information probably was overlooked or totally lost.

Furthermore, crisis conditions enhance the desire for cognitive consistency. Jack Davis says that individuals cannot remake their perceptual world with every new cognitive cue, especially under crisis conditions, and so analysts tend to assimilate new information into existing images.[33] Richards Heuer, Jr., who has studied the psychology of intelligence analysis extensively, contends that the human mind is poorly designed to deal with uncertainty and so tends to seek information that confirms an already-held judgment and rejects information that is contrary to the prevailing view.[34] Robert Jervis, Jr., an astute analyst of cognitive processes, asserts that the tendency to fit new information into preexisting images is greater when the information is more ambiguous. This, in turn, makes the intelligence analyst more confident in the validity of his image, which then reinforces his commitment to the established view.[35] In short, intelligence analysts tend to see what they expect to see and sometimes what they want to see.[36] Relying on a specific mind-set to make assessments distorts how analysts perceive new information and makes the "estimative process vulnerable in anticipating unusual developments; revolutions and other political watersheds; military surprise; [and] economic turning points."[37]

Relying on the mind-set was the cause of the failures to anticipate the sharp rise in OPEC influence in the 1970s and then the sharp drop in OPEC influence in the 1980s.[38] Intelligence analysts and policy leaders also failed to anticipate the attacks on the United States on 11 September because they refused to accept evidence running counter to their existing beliefs and assumptions.[39] Both policy officials and intelligence analysts assumed (1) that terrorism against U.S. interests would continue to be conducted only outside the borders of the United States; (2) that Sunni Islamic terrorist organizations were less political and therefore less inclined to attack the United States; and (3) that such terrorist groups were too splintered and poorly equipped to mount a major attack on the United States. Government officials accepted the validity of these assumptions at face value, giving credence to the assertion that "the major causes of all types of surprise are rigid concepts and closed perceptions."[40]

Moreover, faulty and false assumptions derive from the human tendency to believe that things will remain as they are. Human beings are comfortable with what they know and balk at what they do not know. Accepting the notion that what one knows will continue to be true is far easier than acceding to new information that alters that view. Doing so would require reexamination of assumptions, which is psychologically difficult for individuals. Cord Meyer, a retired CIA official, wrote:

> In each case bits and pieces of information had been collected in advance that should have alerted the intelligence analysts and policymakers to what was coming. But to find these germs of wheat in the abundant chaff and to understand their significance in time to affect decision making was not an easy job in the face of a preponderance of evidence pointing the other way. More important, these intelligence gems usually contradicted the prevailing optimistic assumptions of the policymakers.[41]

The preference for what is known appears to have been behind the failures to anticipate the Korean crisis of 1950 and the Iranian crisis in 1979.

In addition, analysts' preconceived ideas tend to shape their analyses, in that an image of a benign enemy will generally elicit a more positive view of the target's intentions. Conversely, an image of a hostile foe will generate a more negative assessment of the target's intentions and capabilities. There are

numerous indications that the U.S. government may be doing exactly that with regard to al-Qaeda and other terrorist
groups.

Furthermore, intelligence analysts, as government employees, may reflect the political and ideological viewpoints of their
political superiors. Analysts sometimes come under pressure
directly from senior officials to conform to prevailing policy
assumptions. Most times, however, the pressure to conform
is indirect and subtle, originating from superiors or from the
analyst himself, who may want quickly to move up the hierarchy and would want to be perceived as a team player. Whatever the reasons, the tendency to seek conformity may lead
analysts to withhold, embellish, or distort intelligence information.

Inflection Points

The analytic stage of the intelligence cycle contains numerous inflection points that can sour the intelligence process
and ultimately produce intelligence failure. These inflection
points begin with collectors, who may fail to process intelligence information properly or transmit accurate and timely
data to the intelligence analyst. The analyst, in turn, may not
have the expertise or the training to make sound and relevant assessments. In addition, the analyst, whose job is
stressful to begin with, may let stress exacerbate crisis orientation to emphasize current events and existing perceptions.
The analyst then is thrust into having to assimilate new information into existing images and is likely to prefer things to
stay as they are. Bureaucratic malfunctions, such as heavily
layered review and cumbersome coordination processes, add
to the powerful vortex of discontinuity that often precludes
effective analysis.

All these trouble spots suggest the necessity for ever-
constant vigilance against conformity and mediocrity—difficult in governmental bureaucracies that punish mavericks
and reward those who play it safe. Yet analytic snafus can be
minimized, in part, by embedding a cadre of individuals
throughout all analytic functions and charging them with
thinking outside the box, considering the unthinkable and

taking reasonable risks—and by rewarding them for doing so. The intelligence community recognized the imperative for unconventional thinking soon after the terrorist attacks of 11 September and took modest steps toward its realization. However, the incremental approach is not enough; a culture of persistent creativity, innovation, and unconventional thinking is necessary for sound intelligence analysis.

Analytic malfunctions can also be lessened by recruiting the right kind of people to do analytic work, providing them training in all aspects of intelligence analysis, and giving them the bureaucratic freedom and organizational resources to do their job.

8

Getting Intelligence to the Right People

*Why get all worked up about future troubles when every-
one is feeling so good?*
—U.S. summit planner

The most fragile link in the intelligence process occurs at
the end of the intelligence cycle, after the collection, analysis,
and production stages are complete. When analysts are ready
to deliver intelligence to the right people, they confront issues about formatting and packaging of products. Once the
intelligence is delivered, policymakers encounter the problem of having to make some fundamental decisions about
how they will use the intelligence they receive. Altogether,
these decisions determine the degree to which intelligence
makes an impact on national-security decision making.

Producing Intelligence

Once the intelligence analyst concludes his analysis, the most
immediate decision he confronts is how the intelligence analysis is to be communicated to the customer. Delivering the
product in appropriate ways is an art in itself. Deliberations
for this actually begin at the analytic stage (the intelligence
community considers analysis to be a part of the intelligence
production process), and the choice of format depends on

such factors as the urgency of the issue, the nature of the information, and what is known about the preferences of customers. "Hot-button" intelligence issues are more perishable and likely to be perceived as more immediate. Such information is likely therefore to be communicated in ways that expedite its delivery, such as briefings in person, via teleconferencing, and through sophisticated electronic means.

In addition, customer preferences are critical to the success of intelligence, and so the analyst must know what kind of intelligence the customer wants and how he wants to receive it. For example, President Ronald Reagan, although a voracious reader, preferred to receive intelligence in video form, and so intelligence managers who valued their products and their contributions to the national security process had to make sure that President Reagan received his intelligence in this fashion.[1] Presidents Jimmy Carter and Bill Clinton were keen consumers of the written word and preferred receiving their intelligence in printed form.

Urgent intelligence is usually communicated in oral briefings, by a variety of intelligence officials at all levels of the hierarchy. The intelligence community delivers thousands of routine briefings to its constituents every year; the CIA, for example, gives over a thousand oral briefings to members of Congress and administration officials annually. The DNI, as the president's intelligence adviser, talks directly to the president and other members of the national security team almost on a daily basis. Senior intelligence officials brief key administration officials on the *President's Daily Brief.* Lower-level intelligence analysts provide oral briefings to their customers, such as outgoing U.S. ambassadors, midlevel officials at State and Defense, and members of Congress and their staffs.

Written products have long been the principal means of delivering intelligence to consumers. Many working intelligence products appear simply in the memorandum style. These memoranda can be in the form of talking points (brief bulleted statements) or concise but basic papers that require no additional production work beyond editing and printing. Intelligence analysts employ a variety of names to denote these reports, the most common being "intelligence assessment," "intelligence memorandum," and "typescript." Intelligence analysts also write for each other; in the CIA, for example, staff notes are a way for analysts to exchange ideas and spur discussion on specific intelligence issues. These basic products are normally distributed to working-level officials in and out of the policy community.

Most written products intended for higher-level consumers go through a production process that includes making them as appealing as possible to the customer. The adage that "presentation is half the battle" is a common refrain among intelligence managers. To make written assessments appealing, the documents may include such eye-catching add-ons as photographs, imagery, charts, and tables. The manuscripts eventually are printed on good-quality paper with slick covers—all designed to attract the attention of the reader and make the information usable to the customer. A printing and photography facility on the grounds of CIA headquarters compound in McLean, Virginia, performs the vital printing function for the intelligence community.

Disseminating Intelligence

To receive intelligence information, a customer must have a "need to know." The customer's position in the government and his or her security clearances determine the "need to know." Senior national security and foreign policy personnel have the highest clearances and, given the offices they occupy, clearly need to receive intelligence. The White House and the National Security Council are key consumers of intelligence analysis, and much intelligence is directed toward them. However, since American intelligence has a global reach and addresses nearly all global and transnational issues, intelligence finds its way into virtually all corners of the executive branch.

The Congress too is an important consumer of intelligence information—especially the members and staffs of the intelligence, foreign affairs, and armed services committees—who have the necessary clearances and are deemed to have, by virtue of their oversight responsibilities, the need to know nearly all intelligence information. Since the 11 September terrorist attacks and the consequent push for greater intelligence and law enforcement cooperation, many state and local officials also now possess clearances to receive national intelligence in order to do their jobs of thwarting terrorism. Other intelligence recipients may occupy positions in which they may have varying levels of need to know and therefore varying levels of security clearances, which naturally affect the nature and type of intelligence information they receive.

On many occasions, intelligence agencies receive raw intelligence deemed to be so sensitive that intelligence managers decide to give it no distribution (NODIS) beyond the immediate senior intelligence and political leadership. Less controversial but still sensitive information may receive limited distribution (LIMDIS), restricted to individuals identified as having an absolute need to know, or exclusive distribution (EXDIS) to a special group of senior policy recipients. Sometimes additional dissemination restrictions, such as the UK ONLY designation (meaning that the intelligence may be shared only with British officials and those of no other foreign governments), further limit the distribution of particular intelligence information.

To accommodate this need for discrimination, intelligence analysts create dissemination lists comprising individuals in the government known to have the requisite qualifications for receiving intelligence products. Analysts must therefore have a good idea of the identities and qualifications of their customers. Even though an analyst may receive help from the appropriate bureaucratic elements in creating the lists, maintaining their currency remains the analyst's responsibility. Leaving out or overlooking an important recipient in a dissemination list (DISSEM LIST) undoubtedly creates the conditions whereby key consumers may not receive the information they need, thrusting them into a position of having to make decisions based on incomplete information.

Disseminating written analytic products is further complicated by the fact that consumers are located far and wide around the globe. Some sensitive intelligence finds its way to local consumers via couriers, who require receipt signatures for each of the numbered intelligence products. Sometimes couriers wait for recipients to read the document, such as the *PDB*, right there and return it to the intelligence agency for destruction. The bulk of intelligence products intended for recipients abroad, such as those in U.S. embassies and military bases, may be dispatched electronically or via diplomatic courier or the diplomatic pouch.

The intelligence community has been slow to take advantage of new information technologies to disseminate intelligence products. Military intelligence is farther ahead than its 'civilian counterparts in employing electronic distribution, through the Joint Deployable Intelligence Support System (JDISS). The CIA's CIASOURCE and INTELINK—which connects collectors, analysts, and consumers—seek to fulfill a similar purpose to that of the military, but the CIA, citing security reasons, has resisted the expansion of electronic systems into an integrated approach to intelligence sharing. The director's computerized Intelligence Community-Wide System for Information Sharing (ICSIS) is likely to be similarly limited, because its designers have created a series of agency-specific electronic "shared spaces" accessible only to the users of the system and providing only such information as each agency sees fit to permit others to see.[2]

Using Intelligence

The intelligence process poses a paradox for both the intelligence analysts and their policy customers. On the one hand, analysts are urged to maintain objectivity and "tell it like they see it." On the other hand, the analysts' job is to provide policy support to the policy world, which operates on political principles. Even covert action, a highly controversial issue in government circles and among the American public, exhibits this schizophrenia, considering that covert operations are intended to implement foreign policy by a part of the government that is supposed to stay apart from that policy.

While intelligence officials and policymakers affirm the separation of intelligence from policy, there is a good deal of disagreement over the degree to which supporting the policymaker spills over into policy advocacy. The literature of intelligence is filled with instances of politicized national intelligence estimates (NIEs) as well as the tainting of intelligence by policymaker manipulation (see chapter 7). Policy support comes in many forms, but the essential criterion is to provide policymakers with "accurate, timely, and relevant intelligence." This phrase has become an analytical mantra within U.S. intelligence. U.S. intelligence has not done, and does not do, its job unless it can ensure that its intelligence products are accurate, that they are communicated to customers in a timely fashion, and that they address matters that are important to policymakers. Intelligence fails altogether if the standard is not met, regardless of the amounts of money, time, and energy devoted to collecting, analyzing, and producing intelligence. Timely, accurate, and relevant intelligence is necessary to reduce uncertainty, thereby enabling political and military leaders to have depth and quality in their decisions, develop more effective strategies, and conduct operations that are more successful than they would otherwise be.[3]

Once the wide array of intelligence finds its way to customers, then senior policymakers must decide which items they will read, believe, and act upon. Unfortunately, this decision is often driven by bureaucratic considerations. Every agency's special briefing team competes to get information, often drawn from different and highly compartmented sources, to senior officials. In addition, a key customer may receive simultaneous visits from representatives of two or three intelligence agencies bent on selling their intelligence products. Such diversity of intelligence products may provide policy leaders with a diversity of views, but they may also confuse and restrict the options available to the consumer, who is ultimately looking for some help in deciding what to do about specific problems.

The utility and success of intelligence information ultimately depends upon how the policymakers use it. All intelligence analysts want their products to see the light of day by reaching the intended consumer, who would then use the information to make sound and wise national security decisions. Analysts "make a difference" virtually on a daily basis, but the "successes" generally pass without fanfare or publicity.

The analyst, however, straddles a delicate balance between bureaucratic imperatives and political requirements. The bureaucracy wants him to play by the rules, toe the line, support the organization, be a team player, and impart unbiased intelligence information. The political world wants him to come as close to policy advocacy as possible. Policy officials, occupying political positions, may have their own views about developments, which may not be consistent with the intelligence they receive. In such situations, the policy consumer may disagree with the intelligence analysis, distrust its content, or ignore its message altogether—eventualities that possibly negate the entire raison d'être of intelligence.

As noted, political leaders often are loath to receive controversial information or bad news, and when they do, they may simply discard the information as unworthy or wrong for their needs. President Lyndon Johnson, for example, routinely ignored CIA assessments indicating that the Vietnam War was unwinnable. Such shortcutting of the intelligence process demeans the very idea of secret intelligence and raises the risk of intelligence failures.

Inflection Points

Producing and disseminating intelligence is a critical but mundane step in the entire process designed to serve intelligence customers. At this stage of the cycle, intelligence agencies produce their assessments and deliver them in ways intended to make the customers receptive to the intelligence. The idea is that policymakers will then use the information in making national security decisions. However, if decision makers chose, for whatever reasons, to reject or ignore, and therefore not act on, the information they receive, the risk of contributing to "policy failures"—a type of intelligence failure attributable to policy inaction—becomes real. The following inflection points constitute the key areas at this stage that can derail intelligence:

- Analyst unfamiliarity with customer preferences
- Employing the wrong medium to deliver intelligence information
- Unattractive and inadequate intelligence products
- Incomplete or inappropriate dissemination lists
- Consumer rejects, ignores, or fails to act on intelligence information.

The irony is that meticulously collected and analyzed intelligence can fail to achieve its intended result at this final and frail stage of the intelligence process. Strangely enough, the intelligence cycle comes full circle at this point, with the disseminated product inspiring new questions and instigating new requirements, which trigger the cycle all over again.

9

Contributing Factors

The more things change, the more they are the same.
—Alphonse Karr, nineteenth-century philosopher

Organizational arrangements and the stages of the intelligence cycle account for the bulk of problems associated with failures of secret intelligence. However, other intelligence activities introduce new dynamics into the mix. At a minimum, these new factors are additional unknowns, which tend to exacerbate the conditions for intelligence failures. Counterintelligence (CI) and covert action (CA) in particular act as spoilers, often skewing the intelligence process and throwing it off track.

Pundits generally make a solid argument in favor of counterintelligence as a critical supporting activity focusing on the protection of secrets and the catching of foreign spies, an effort without which American intelligence operations would be subject to foreign penetration and manipulation. According to one expert, effective counterintelligence is as vital to the national security as skillful diplomacy, military strength, and accurate foreign intelligence.[1] Therefore, there is a direct link between intelligence and counterintelligence. However, covert action elicits a more emotional response and is subject to much controversy, focusing on issues of legitimacy, ethics, and morality in foreign policy.[2] Strictly speaking, covert action is not intelligence at all but a method of implementing U.S. foreign policy objectives by using intelligence resources.

In addition, CI and CA possess certain attributes that set them apart from other intelligence functions. The 1947 National Security Act does not mention either activity, and therefore their legitimacy can only be inferred. Neither CI nor CA is necessary for the conduct of intelligence operations, although the absence of one or the other would raise questions of the adequacy of security and the appropriateness of levels of intelligence performance. If neither activity is integral to the intelligence process, both are generally considered key aspects of how the United States carries out its foreign intelligence activities. These considerations thrust both CI and CA into the center of the intelligence failures debate, but given their special status within the intelligence process, CI and CA bring different and unique problems to secret intelligence.

Counterintelligence

The public tends to associate counterintelligence with catching foreign spies, and there is a healthy dose of spy-catching in this activity. CI's counterespionage component encompasses programs intended to protect American secrets as well as to thwart those trying to steal those secrets. Counterintelligence, however, is a lot more than that. It also includes activities that people normally do not associate with counterintelligence, such as personnel security, analysis to determine what foreign governments want to know about the United States, and operations to mislead and misdirect foreign intelligence agents away from their intended targets—American secrets. According to an observer, CI is "a conglomerate of several disciplines and skills . . . [that] might include analysts, surveillance specialists, case officers, technical experts, and [administrative] specialists."[3]

Management
Counterintelligence is information necessary to protect U.S. political, economic, and military assets from espionage, sabo-

tage, and other similar activities. This deceptively simple definition suggests the kinds of traditional activities associated
with CI but is inadequate to describe the broad scope of counterintelligence. Today, U.S. counterintelligence agents
work against terrorists, drug lords, money launderers, international criminals, and a host of other threats to American
national security—as well as foreign spies. Yet the U.S. government continues to insist on defining CI in the more traditional
terms, reflecting the lack of consensus in the government about
the nature and substance of counterintelligence. Disagreements over counterintelligence are a reflection of fragmentation in the U.S. counterintelligence community.

The management of U.S. counterintelligence activities is
as convoluted as the management of the U.S. intelligence
community. Officially, the FBI and the CIA share the function, with the FBI engaging in counterintelligence within the
nation's borders and the CIA outside the United States. In
actuality, however, each agency conducts its own CI, largely
free of any guidance from above or coordination with others.
Furthermore, the DNI, who is the nominal central authority
for *coordinating* U.S. counterintelligence activities, has delegated that authority to the specific agencies. According to
one expert, the best characterization of the DNI's counterintelligence role is "central liaison," not centralized coordination.[4] The former chair of the Senate Select Committee on
Intelligence, Senator David L. Boren (D-Okla.), agrees, justi-
fying it in these terms: "Fragmentation of counterintelligence
authority is the price we pay for a free society."[5]

Fragmentation is responsible for the lack of coordination,
cooperation, and communications among the CI agencies and
directly contributes to failures in secret intelligence. Ironi-
cally, many presidents have recognized this deficiency in the
American intelligence system, and some have taken steps to
overcome it. For example, the Clinton administration's Presidential Decision Directive 24 in 1994 created the National
Counterintelligence Center (NCIC) to strengthen the coordination of informational and issue follow-up needs of the U.S.
counterintelligence community. In the late 1990s, the Clinton
administration's Presidential Decision Directive 75 also established the Office of the National Counterintelligence Executive

(NCIX) to focus specifically on economic and industrial espionage against the United States and to produce CI products and services for the government and the private sector.[6] Yet these meager attempts were unable to overcome the CI culture of bureaucratic turf battles and noncooperation and have fostered an environment in which each agency seeks to underplay its own security problems and exaggerate the problems of its competing agencies. For example, the FBI for a long time resisted establishing any internal mechanisms to identify spies in its own ranks. As a result, the U.S. House of Representatives passed legislation in 2003 to establish an FBI counterintelligence office to investigate spying within the bureau.[7]

Functions
After the events of 9/11, American intelligence agencies began incorporating activities intended to counter terrorism at home as an integral part of counterintelligence, such that counterterrorism now overlaps significantly with CI operations in the United States.[8] In fact, the FBI, in an internal reorganization following the terrorist attacks, combined the two into an Office of Counterterrorism and Counterintelligence.[9] Today, American counterintelligence includes three functions that U.S. intelligence agencies perform with varying levels of proficiency—protecting secrets, thwarting attempts by foreign intelligence services to acquire those secrets, and catching Americans who spy for those foreign intelligence services.[10]

FACILITY AND PERSONNEL SECURITY The most obvious responsibility of CI is to protect secrets, and agencies do this by focusing on facility and personnel security. The physical security of secrets includes measures intended to allow individuals with a "need to know" to have access to secrets while denying that access to all others. This category involves such mechanical measures as the use of safes, passwords, identification badges, security guards, and alarms, but much of this denial technology is available to both domestic and foreign consumers, thereby diluting its effectiveness. For example, former energy secretary Bill Richardson testified in 1999 that the U.S. government gave modern security technology to such intelligence adversaries as Russia to facilitate the safeguarding of Russian nuclear materials.[11] The counterterrorism focus has induced the federal government to tighten up its physical security procedures somewhat, but modern computers and the proliferation of technologies in the private sector to counter these procedures are making physical security an ongoing challenge.

Personnel security rests on the assumption that only those individuals who must have access to secret information indeed do have access to it, and that they possess the loyalty and the sense of responsibility to keep secret information secret. To ensure adherence to these principles, agencies engage in myriad activities, such as background investigations and reinvestigations; polygraph examinations; detection of employee lifestyle issues, like alcohol and substance abuse and irregular spending patterns; and the "need to know" principle, which has already been mentioned here and discussed, in chapter 6.

All potential intelligence employees must undergo rigorous background investigations designed to explore the veracity of personal and professional information supplied by applicants as well as to identify longer-term problem areas. Some intelligence agencies, like the CIA, also require medical checks before employment. A polygraph examination usually accompanies the background investigation and focuses on lifestyle and security issues.[12] Once employed, a new recruit stays in a probationary status for a period of usually three years. During this time, the director has the legal authority to terminate an officer's employment for any reason (and sometimes without cause). At the end of the probationary period, the employee undergoes a reinvestigation and another polygraph examination, this time focusing almost exclusively on security and counterintelligence issues. At this stage, the agencies are interested in whether the employee has adhered to agency security requirements, including whether the employee is free of any unauthorized association (with foreign intelligence officers, for example) that may compromise the officer's position as an intelligence official and the information to which he has access. Upon surmounting this hurdle, the officer is subject to periodic and regular reinvestigations and polygraph examinations, generally once every five years.

Intelligence officers also have responsibilities over the classified materials they use in their work. Most facilities of intelligence agencies are designated as "secure compartmented intelligence facilities" (SCIFs), in which highly classified and compartmented information may be stored and viewed by intelligence personnel. Even though combination locks, locked safes, alarms, and similar devices protect these facilities, employees play a big role in ensuring their security.[13] Indeed, in most agencies, the employee who is last to leave for the day must ensure that all materials are stored safely and securely away in appropriate storage areas and cannot leave the building and the premises before receiving the go-ahead from security officers. Security personnel routinely and regularly check the offices to ensure their locked-down status, and any slip-up may earn the employee a security violation report, which may become part of his personnel record. The unauthorized removal of classified materials from the building likewise may constitute a security violation. Several American spies in the past removed classified documents from their places of work and sold them to foreign governments. Even an inadvertent removal may pose the danger of leaking the information to the public. One expert notes that, while illegal, the unauthorized publication of U.S. classified intelligence materials in the press occurs almost on a daily basis.[14] Repeated security violations may become grounds for retraining, reinvestigation, and polygraph examination, or even termination of employment.

While ensuring that employees observe security procedures while at work is an important concern, personnel security also involves monitoring employee dealings with foreigners. Obviously, American intelligence officers are prime targets for recruitment by foreign intelligence services as well as non-state groups, and any unofficial relationship with a foreign official may raise questions. In addition, American intelligence officers often officially host foreign intelligence officers at their agencies for a variety of approved reasons, and controlling these visitors and their access becomes a personnel security issue. Some liaison services send intelligence officers to reside in the United States and work in American intelligence agencies, and these officers receive the clearances and badges appropriate to perform their liaison work. However, there is a saying in the CIA that "there is no such thing as a friendly service," and controlling and monitoring the access of these foreign liaison officers may pose a personnel security problem.

Addressing these issues is not an easy task, but American intelligence agencies employ a variety of techniques to confront them. One obvious and time-honored technique is the use of the "need to know" principle, with which intelligence agencies limit the number of people who can legitimately have access to classified information. Another method is the use of encryption devices, employed for all classified communications, to frustrate foreign spies and hackers. Still another technique is the provision of security countermeasures, such as sweeping for electronic listening devices (bugs) and the use of "bubbles," SCIFs, and other secure communication areas.

While these measures may appear impressive on the surface, some real and identifiable problems associated with them together may help compromise secret information and thereby skew or misdirect intelligence analysis. The principal problem is that no uniform security standards apply to all American intelligence agencies, across the board. Each intelligence agency conducts its own counterintelligence activity and hence employs common security measures differently to suit its needs or uses different security procedures entirely. For example, the State Department has long resisted the notion of employing the polygraph for its own employees, insisting that the reliability of the polygraph is at best suspect and that its use is demeaning, tantamount to saying that the agency does not trust its employees. The FBI similarly resisted employing the polygraph on its agents until after 9/11. The Defense Department employs the polygraph on some of its employees but not all. The Energy Department, which operates the nation's classified weapons laboratories, has long resisted the polygraph and is currently using only a limited program of polygraph examinations for some of its employees.[15] Such uneven application of security measures spans the entire range of physical and personnel security areas, making some intelligence agencies less secure than others. Applying security measures in varying forms dilutes the nature and meaning of clearances for classified and compartmented information, even though the DNI is empowered by law to set uniform security standards within the intelligence community. The U.S. Congress has investigated the issue several times and in all cases has arrived at similar conclusions: "The record of past espionage cases illustrates that the current [background] investigations process fails dismally [to catch spies]."[16]

THWARTING FOREIGN INTELLIGENCE OPERATIONS A major responsibility of U.S. counterintelligence is to frustrate the efforts of foreign intelligence operatives seeking to steal American secrets. This can be accomplished by identifying who they are, expelling them or denying them entry, controlling their movements and access, surveilling them by physical and electronic observation, and using "double agents" to preoccupy and mislead them.[17]

Identifying espionage agents requires record keeping, information sharing, and surveillance. Information gathered in these ways must be subjected to analysis in order to determine which foreign officials are espionage agents and which are not. American intelligence generally has a good sense of the known and suspected foreign intelligence officers in the United States. It also has a good idea of the techniques and methods of foreign intelligence services that spy on the United States. However, American intelligence agencies rarely share the information with each other; worse, they sometimes use the information they have to undermine and undercut each other—all because of the fragmentation of the U.S. intelligence and counterintelligence communities. While traditional espionage still constitutes the mainstay of counterintelligence, new targets, such as American economic and commercial secrets, tend to complicate counterintelligence efforts in this area. The FBI is reportedly now taking seriously the threat of economic espionage against the United States, by refocusing some of its efforts toward identifying and preventing espionage directed at corporations, research centers, and universities.[18]

One way of addressing espionage against the United States by known and suspected agents who are under official cover is to expel them from the country and deny them further entry. This has the obvious advantage of seriously damaging espionage operations in the short term. However, this tactic has several longer-term drawbacks. For one thing, foreign governments can retaliate and expel American agents, to the detriment of U.S. intelligence capabilities. For another, such expulsions tend to damage seriously relations with foreign governments whose agents have been expelled.[19] Foreign intelligence services can overcome the setback by resorting to other espionage methods, such as the clandestine insertion of agents into the country. Such "illegals" pose greater danger to the United States, because they are much more difficult to identify, as they are under no official cover but masquerade as ordinary Americans.

Limiting the movements and subjecting known and suspected foreign espionage agents to physical and electronic surveillance provide greater benefits than expelling them. During the Cold War, Soviet and Eastern Bloc diplomats were restricted in their movements in the United States, generally limited to within a twenty-five-mile radius of their official places of business in Washington, D.C., New York City, and elsewhere. Similar restrictions continue to be placed on diplomats of governments that are hostile to the United States, such as Cuba. Such restrictions enable American counterintelligence officers to keep up better with the movements of targeted foreigners and conduct physical surveillance on their activities, even though terrorists and other criminal elements are free of such restrictions. Surveillance has the added benefit of potentially identifying additional foreign agents and providing information about the nature and types of intelligence in which the foreign agents show interest. Telephone taps, listening devices, and other types of electronic forms of surveillance (such as intercepts) also serve to identify their contacts and subsequently either block their communications or convert them to double agents. Since the 9/11 attacks, the U.S. government has been using expanded authorities under the 2001 PATRIOT Act to use surveillance against foreign spies as well as terrorists in the United States.[20]

The disadvantages of these surveillance techniques revolve around their limitations. Physical and electronic surveillance presuppose that the foreign agents are unaware of their existence and will conduct their activities as though they are not being watched or overheard. Obviously, this is a false presumption; foreign intelligence officers routinely assume that they are being watched and listened to, and thus take appropriate actions to conceal their activities, meetings, and communications. U.S. intelligence is continually finding new and better ways to deal with the countermeasures, but new and unconventional surveillance techniques sometimes come into conflict with civil liberties; in 2003, for example, Congress killed legislation authorizing a Pentagon computer-surveillance program that would have combed private information to identify potential terrorists.[21] Worse, foreign intelligence agents sometimes use the fact that they are under observations and their communications under surveillance to spread disinformation that may prejudice American intelligence analysis.

CATCHING AMERICANS WHO SPY Espionage is illegal everywhere, and spying against one's own government is treason. However, unmasking and prosecuting Americans who spy on behalf of foreign governments is one of the toughest aspects of counterintelligence, primarily because it involves issues of trust and loyalty. Notwithstanding the seeming distrust and disloyalty inherent in such techniques as background investigations and the polygraph examinations, intelligence agencies in the end have no choice but to assume the loyalty of their employees and to confer a great deal of trust on their officers. Not doing so would bring into question the reliability of their activities as well as the reasons for their very existence.

Yet FBI sources say that over one thousand Americans have been caught and convicted of espionage since World War II.[22] Some of these cases have become notorious (see figure 6). One of the most notorious of recent cases was that of Robert Hanssen, the FBI counterintelligence chief who spied for the Soviet Union and then Russia until the mid-1990s. Before that, Aldrich Ames, a CIA officer, provided the Soviet Union critical information about CIA operations, information that reportedly caused the deaths of over ten American "assets." In the mid-1980s, American counterintelligence unearthed a vast family-run espionage business, headed by ex-navy cryptanalyst John Walker, that had given Moscow virtually all of American naval codes and other information.[23] James J. Angleton, CIA's counterintelligence chief until the early 1970s, was convinced that the agency, as well as some other parts of the U.S. government, was riddled with Americans who were working against their own government. The zeal with which he pursued what many people believe to be his obsession resulted in numerous wrecked careers and flagging morale, doing damage that finally got him fired in 1974.

The motivations of Americans spying against the United States vary widely. During the Cold War, ideology and financial gain were the principal reasons. Among the spies that

Name	Affiliation	Worked For:
Earl Pitts	FBI	Russia
Harold James Nicholson	CIA	Russia
Aldrich Ames	CIA	USSR, Russia
Robert Hanssen	FBI	USSR, Russia
Jonathan Pollard	Navy	Israel
Edward Howard	CIA	USSR
Ronald Pelton	NSA	USSR
Larry Wu-Tai Chin	CIA	China
Sharon Scranage	CIA	Ghana
Robert Kim	Navy	South Korea
John Walker	Navy	USSR
Michael Walker	Navy	USSR
Arthur Walker	Navy	USSR
Jerry Whitworth	Navy	USSR
Clyde Lee Conrad	Army	East Germany
William Bell	contractor	Poland/USSR
James Harper	contractor	Poland/USSR
James Hall	Army	East Germany
David Boone	NSA	USSR
Ronald Lipka	NSA	USSR
Glen Souther	Navy	USSR
Douglas Groat	CIA	?
Ana Belen Montes	DIA	Cuba
David Barnett	CIA	USSR
Richard William Miller	FBI	USSR
Felix Bloch	State	USSR
George Trofimoff	Army Reserve	USSR/Russia
James Clark	Army	South Africa
Theresa Squillacote	Pentagon	South Africa
Kurt Stand	?	South Africa
Jeff Martin Carney	Air Force	East Germany

Figure 6. *Some Recent Notorious Espionage Cases*

were caught, some either favored Marxism or opposed the actions of the U.S. government, thereby allowing foreign intelligence agents the chance to cultivate and recruit them. Others chose to work against the United States for pecuniary benefits, despite the fact that intelligence agencies have the worldwide reputation of being rather stingy with their money. Aldrich Ames, for example, reportedly received the princely and unheard of sum of nearly three million dollars for his espionage activities over a decade.

Unmasking Americans who are working for foreign governments poses operational and legal problems. Most information about American spies comes from defectors and double agents, who may, as part of their debriefings, either directly identify the Americans or unwittingly provide information that may lead to the Americans' identification. For example, CIA's acquisition of the East German Security Service (Stasi) files resulted in the arrest and trial of four Americans who worked for Stasi during the Cold War, as well as hundreds of Germans.[24] Vitaly Yurchenko, a top KGB defector who later redefected to the Soviet Union, identified Americans Edward Howard and Ronald Pelton as working for the Soviet Union.[25] These kinds of "gifts" are often buttressed by decoding breakthroughs that may reveal the identities of Americans working for foreign governments.[26] Often, family members, either for reasons of conscience or patriotism, turn in spies. The only reason that the United States was able to put a stop to the "Walker Ring" in 1985, for example, was that John Walker's ex-wife turned him in to the FBI. In other cases, lifestyle issues may be a spy's undoing. Aldrich Ames, for example, paid cash for a high-end house and automobile despite his relatively low government salary, took frequent foreign trips, and often engaged in drunken binges that exposed his vulnerabilities. Even then, U.S. counterintelligence experts did not focus on Ames until after American intelligence assets in the Soviet Union began disappearing in ways that could not have been coincidental. The loss of assets in the Soviet Union, supplemented by unexplained lifestyle issues, finally convinced CIA and FBI counterintelligence officers to focus on Ames. Identifying him, surveilling him, developing a solid legal case against him, and finally arresting him took nearly seven years.

Frequently Americans provide information to foreign governments, willingly or unwittingly, because of their opposition to U.S. government policies. The recent history of the United States is replete with examples of government surveillance of antiwar protesters, who may have been used as "agents of opportunity" by foreign governments hostile to U.S. policies. For example, one such U.S. government operation during the Vietnam War, COINTELPRO, involved FBI counterintelligence agents in the collection of information and surveillance of antiwar protesters, in violation of American law. In the wake of the 9/11 attacks and the subsequent revision of the law, there are reports that the FBI is keeping tabs of those opposed to the U.S. war in Iraq, a charge the FBI has denied.[27]

Other Americans unknowingly provide critical information to foreign government in order to promote their own private interests. One recent case was Gao Zhan, an American scholar of Chinese origin, who, once charged with spying for Beijing, reportedly claimed in 2003 that he dealt with Chinese business entities and research institutes, "not the Chinese Government per se."[28] According to East German Stasi files, many Americans, including businesspersons, gave away commercial and other sensitive information at industrial fairs, professional conferences, and academic seminars.[29]

Still other Americans may agree to work for a foreign government in order to further what they believe to be the right cause. Jonathan Pollard, for example, a naval intelligence analyst, agreed to provide information to Israel because he thought he was contributing to Israel's defense against its enemies.

Covert Action

Covert action is defined as activities of the U.S. government intended "to influence political, economic, or military conditions abroad, when it is intended that the role of the U.S. government will not be apparent or acknowledged publicly."[30] This definition belies the fact that many covert actions do become apparent and, even if not acknowledged, are wholly attributed to the U.S. government. There is little doubt of American sponsorship of a variety of notorious cases, including assassination attempts on foreign political leaders. Despite public knowledge, the U.S. government generally avoids public comment on specific cases unless compelled by circumstances to do so. Many American covert operations became known in the mid-1970s as a consequence of several congressional investigations into CIA activities, but the government has continued its silence as a general rule. This veil of silence has been lifted somewhat since the events of 9/11, as CIA covert operatives have often joined their military counterparts to conduct open and acknowledged operations, including assassinations, against terrorists in Afghanistan, Southeast Asia, and elsewhere.[31] Such obvious and known events are generally referred to in the intelligence business as "overt-covert operations," suggesting a dilution of the government's definition of covert action. Some observers, in fact, assert that because it has become so public, many overt government institutions, such as the National Endowment for Democracy, have assumed some covert-action responsibilities.[32]

The definition is useful, however, in pointing out the peculiar status of covert action in intelligence. The 1947 National Security Act does not mention covert action at all, only the DCI's authority as head of the CIA to engage in "special activities" as the National Security Council may from time to time direct. This provision of the law has generally been considered the legal authority for covert operations—now known as the "third option," a useful technique to be used when diplomacy has failed and military action is too drastic an alternative. Some experts assert that there is a "symbiotic" relationship between covert action and other elements of intelligence.[33] However, the symbiosis occurs only to the extent that in practice covert actions involve intelligence assets and resources in their conduct.

The CIA traditionally has been the manager of U.S. covert actions. CIA's mission statements have included this role since the early 1950s; it was subsequently codified in a series of executive mandates, including Executive Order 12333,[34] which continues as the basic regulation governing U.S. intelligence activities. On October 15, 1987, President Reagan signed National Security Directive 286, which reaffirmed the principle set forth in Executive Order 12333 that the CIA is the agency responsible for the conduct of covert actions, subject to a presidential determination that another agency, or group of agencies, is more suitable. Since 9/11, however, the Bush administration has modified the rules somewhat to allow greater coordination and cooperation between CIA covert operatives and U.S. military special operations.

Covert Action Types
Covert action takes many forms and includes propaganda, political and economic action, and paramilitary activity, or a combination of the three. Propaganda activities range from such innocuous government programs as the broadcast of radio messages around the world about U.S. political and cultural developments (e.g., the Voice of America) all the way to highly secret disinformation campaigns. In between the two extremes is an area that employs techniques from both and includes such programs as paying or manipulating foreign journalists to write favorable news items about the United States. Propaganda's ultimate intention is to manipulate foreign public and official opinion and direct it in ways more favorable to U.S. foreign policies. While such manipulation may have short-term benefits for the United States, it may also result in "blowback," the wafting back of deceptive information to American audiences, including intelligence analysts, thereby affecting American opinion and skewing intelligence analyses.

Political and economic action includes secret financial and other support of foreign political leaders, political parties, labor unions, and other groups the success of which might be favorable to the United States. Manipulating and fixing elections and overthrowing governments generally fall under this rubric.[35] The United States clearly rigged the Italian election of 1948 so that the Communists would be defeated and politicians favorable to Western interests would be elected. The CIA orchestrated the ouster of Prime Minister Mohammad Mossadegh in Iran in 1953 and the overthrow of President Jacobo Arbenz Guzmán in Guatemala in 1954. CIA covert operatives in 1973, under instructions from Dr. Henry A. Kissinger, the national security adviser at the time, supplied weapons to the Chilean military, manipulated the Chilean media, and tampered with the Chilean economy in order to create the conditions for a military coup that ousted the democratically elected socialist president, Salvador Allende.[36]

Paramilitary activity includes training foreign military and police forces as well as conducting quasi-military operations like sabotage and counterinsurgency. Historically, coups and assassinations fell within this category, although they clearly straddle the divide between political action and paramilitary activity. The CIA has a small, dedicated paramilitary force, but most of its activities in this area are conducted either in cooperation with U.S. military forces[37] or are contracted out to private concerns.[38] Such a paramilitary force was employed in Afghanistan[39] and has been an important part of U.S. military actions in Iraq.

The Controversy
Whatever its nature, covert action evokes strong passions among proponents and opponents. Proponents of covert action contend that it is an effective presidential tool in cases where military action would be too drastic or too visible. During the Cold War, American presidents were all too willing to employ covert action to achieve their foreign policy objectives, mostly because CA provided quick fixes to thorny foreign policy problems at minimal cost. Cord Meyer, a former senior CIA official, for example, asserted that the CIA acts "as an executive agent in carrying out decisions reached at the highest level of American Government."[40] However, Gregory Treverton, a veteran CIA operative, argues that the presumption of secrecy makes it tempting to ignore longer-term costs of covert operations.[41] This became apparent in the investigations of the 1970s, which revealed that CA imposed heavy political costs on American administrations and Congress.

Consequently, Congress passed a series of prohibitions that tied the hands of American covert operatives. The restrictions remain on the books, but some have been loosened since the terrorist attacks of 9/11. For example, the Bush administration relaxed the prohibition against assassinations, providing they are directed at terrorists and their sponsors.[42] Nonetheless, according to press reports, Congress again is contemplating additional limits on covert operations, limits that would for the first time be extended to cover clandestine military operations. More specifically, the new rules would apply the requirement of a "finding" (see below) to secret military operations.[43]

Opponents of covert action say that such operations on the whole do not work and generally go against the country's interests. They claim that the very notion of a covert operation is both a threat to civil liberties and constitutional government and contrary to international law.[44] Much of the controversy about CA, however, revolves around its oversight, particularly because CA is deemed a nonroutine intelligence activity that affects sensitive foreign policy concerns. Congress imposed an oversight process in the late 1970s, a process that has been modified and refined since then. The new process now includes both internal checks within the intelligence community and strict oversight by the relevant congressional committees. Despite some stiff public opposition to covert operations, Congress has repeatedly reaffirmed the legitimacy of CA as an American foreign policy tool.[45]

Approval of CA is difficult and time consuming.[46] Virtually all covert action proposals originate in the National Security Council or other policy departments, and various committees within the CIA exhaustively examine every covert-action proposal, on the basis of such objective criteria as feasibility, practicability, legality, and acceptability to the American public were the operation to become known. At each stage, the proposal may be nixed. Within the CIA, the Covert Action Planning Group provides the first scrub of covert-action proposals at the directorate level. The Covert Action Review Group at the agency level evaluates the proposal against given criteria and forwards it to the DCI. Even then the DCI, and now the DNI, may decide to shelve it. If he does not, he must submit it to the National Security Council, which, after careful consideration, may decide to disapprove it. If the NSC gives permission to proceed and refers it to the president, he, in turn, may kill it. The National Security Council closely reviews any covert-action proposal, as does the Intelligence Oversight Board—a committee of the National Foreign Intelligence Board—which looks at the proposal from the standpoint of legality and propriety.[47]

Only a presidentially approved proposal receives the blessing of a "finding," which is a written statement clearly stating that he, the president, finds the proposed activity to be in the national interest of the United States.[48] The finding also describes the activity and gives a rationale for it.[49] According to the Intelligence Authorization Act of 1991,[50] which repealed the Hughes-Ryan Amendment of 1974, the president is the final approving authority for all covert action programs; he gives that approval by signing a finding; and he affirms that the program supports "identifiable policy objectives." The act stipulates that no part of the program may violate American federal law, including the Constitution, and that the finding must list all government agencies that have roles to play in the program, as well as any foreign governments participating in it. Finally, it bans any covert action program that can be used to influence American political processes, policies, the media, or public opinion.[51]

Once signed by the president, the finding comes to the CIA, which is charged by law with informing the oversight committees of Congress. While Congress has no formal veto power over covert operations, the Senate Select Committee on Intelligence (SSCI) and the House Permanent Select Committee on Intelligence (HPSCI) may use their influence with the president and their leverage over funding to modify, or even kill, a covert-action proposal.[52] The CIA also routinely informs the defense subcommittees of the appropriations committees in each chamber, for the simple reason that no governmental activity—including covert action—can be undertaken without an appropriation from Congress.[53]

Current law says that the CIA must inform Congress in a timely fashion of proposed or undertaken covert operations, unless the president decides to withhold such notification. The "in timely fashion" formulation has been quite controversial in Congress and elsewhere. The legislative intent behind current law clearly favors the notion that prior notification be given, except in special circumstances. When these circumstances exist, the president may choose either to inform the top leadership of Congress or, on rare occasions, totally withhold prior notice.[54] Since the establishment of oversight procedures in the mid-1970s, the CIA has been directed by the president not to inform Congress on only a few occasions; generally Congress is apprised of even these operations subsequent to their implementation. The congressional oversight committees maintain that since 1980 the CIA has given Congress notice of all covert action proposals, with only a few exceptions.[55]

Inflection Points

Counterintelligence and covert actions contribute to intelligence failures in myriad ways. While striving to identify those who would steal American secrets and to frustrate foreign countermeasures that would skew and defeat American intelligence analyses, counterintelligence suffers from several deficiencies.[56] First, cultural precepts (see chapter 3) often work against effective counterintelligence. Americans generally oppose what counterintelligence represents; they distrust government, dislike secrets, and abhor snitches. Such opposition often is projected onto other intelligence activities, so that the public generally begins to associate intelligence with *counter*intelligence. This resistance and association dilute the potency of counterintelligence and impede the effectiveness of American intelligence.

Second, U.S. law, which is based on the 1917 Espionage Act,[57] makes difficult the prosecution of a defendant in an American court of law. The burden of proof is on the government, which must overcome a series of hurdles to prove espionage against the United States.[58] The government is also highly reluctant to reveal classified information in court, a fact often used by defendants to thwart the prosecution.

Third, the fragmentation of the counterintelligence bureaucracy in the intelligence community works against effective counterintelligence. The splintering of counterintelligence promotes isolation, parochialism, and competition, such that, as in the fragmented U.S. intelligence community generally, all issues get reduced to the most common denominator—to the specific agency and its mission. While there is something to be said for each agency pursuing its own missions, fragmentation works to defeat the central aim of counterintelligence, as it defeats the principal purpose of intelligence as a whole.

Covert action also introduces dysfunctions into the intelligence process. A keen observer of U.S. intelligence once observed that covert actions may prove operationally successful where there is opportunity, supporting policy, leadership consensus, appropriate infrastructure, agency integration, and strict review.[59] Indeed, many U.S. covert operations achieved their intended objectives because they incorporated the right mix of these principles. For example, both the 1953 overthrow of Mossadegh and the 1954 Guatemala coup were successes from an operational point of view, in that they achieved their intended purposes. Yet numerous investigations have demonstrated that while the scope and scale of such operations have been enormous, their benefits have been greatly exaggerated.[60]

The fact remains that CA is not intelligence at all but the implementation of certain aspects of American foreign policy using intelligence and other official resources. It has little to do with the principal tasks of intelligence and, as a policy instrument, is frequently the center of political and partisan disputes. These disputes often result in political complications for the U.S. intelligence community in ways that violate the policy-intelligence divide so sacrosanct to American intelligence.

In addition, the use of intelligence resources to conduct covert operations introduces policy biases into the intelligence process. The 1953 overthrow of Mossadegh, for example, solidified the American alliance with the Iranian shah. The agreement that was subsequently worked out between the U.S. government and the shah stipulated that the U.S. government would rely on his government for information about internal developments in Iran. That agreement cut the United States off from unbiased information on Iranian developments, distorted critical intelligence, and led to the failure to forecast the 1979 revolution. Manipulating events abroad for political purposes may make sense to policymakers, who have their own policy agendas, but it makes no sense from the perspective of intelligence, which policymakers insist should be timely, objective, and relevant.

10

Intelligence Priorities and Their Challenges

What keeps me awake is that we're facing a variety of sophisticated global threats of increasing complexity and lethality.
—Vice Adm. Lowell Jacoby, former head of the Defense Intelligence Agency

Priority issues are the engines of the intelligence process. Some of the issues are relatively new on the intelligence priority list, while others have been around for a long time. Some items, such as international terrorism, engage the full resources of the U.S. intelligence community, while others, like the global environment, receive only limited attention from the policy community and, therefore, the intelligence agencies. Some issues are highly technical and complicated—weapons proliferation matters, for example—while others are straightforward and less involved.

The intelligence process begins and ends with policymakers, and therefore the degree to which American intelligence agencies prioritize an issue depends in large measure on its importance to policymakers. In addition, the extent to which an issue poses particular intelligence challenges determines the ease with which it is addressed. Consequently, the more complicated the issue, the more pronounced the challenges and the greater the chances of intelligence failure.

It is now a cliché that the Cold War intelligence priorities were more manageable and easier to address than the issues that have cropped up since then. The terrorist attacks of 11 September 2001 thrust international terrorism to the forefront of the national agenda. This development in turn has catapulted a host of existing and new national security threats—such as weapons proliferation, rogue and failed states, peacekeeping operations, and various regional issues in the Middle East, North Korea, and South Asia—onto the growing intelligence priority list.

While antiterrorism provides a focal point for American intelligence, it poses the danger of forcing the intelligence agencies either to ignore or to downplay other concerns that do not receive the same kind of press play. These issues usually get short shrift in the policymakers' radar and, consequently, lie below the top priority threshold in the intelligence agenda. These include such issues as drug trafficking, money laundering, international crime, environmental issues, human rights, and international economics, just to name a few.

The New Intelligence Agenda

U.S. intelligence has undergone enormous changes in the decade and a half since the end of the Cold War. It still confronts state-specific threats from countries like Russia, the People's Republic of China, and Iran, but the threats have become overlain with sub-state political concerns like ethnic rivalries, religious extremism, and rising nationalism. Moreover, these new issues have made the traditional intelligence agenda "more complex, more subtle and harder to recognize—and [these issues] cannot be addressed by simply refocusing old capabilities on new adversaries."[1]

The following examination of the major issues on the intelligence agenda gives some sense of the types of difficulties American intelligence faces in the post-9/11 environment. These issues, in turn, spawn a series of intelligence challenges, which may serve as precursors of intelligence failure.

Rogue and Failed States

American concern over rogue and failed states links the more traditional state-centered threats with the newer sub-state issues of ethnic tensions and religious fundamentalism. During the Cold War, the superpowers managed the international system by manipulating the behaviors of their client states, some of which would have been classified as rogue states under current definitions. Once the superpowers' manipulations ended, ethnic and other internal rivalries quickly gave vent to internal political strife that often erupted into open conflict.

Outlaw or failed states are of policy concern because their internal actions or inactions affect regional stability, a dominant national security concern for the United States. For example, the internal dynamics of rogue or failed states may lead to internal strife that, in turn, may spill over into adjacent areas, thereby affecting neighboring states and destabilizing entire regions. The Somalia, Bosnian, and Kosovo crises of the 1990s are stark examples of this phenomenon. In other areas, such states as Iraq, Iran, and North Korea have been seeking advantage in the international arena by trying to enhance their own status. Iraq's Saddam Hussein not only tried to acquire additional territory by invading Kuwait in 1991, he also began a concerted weapons of mass destruction (WMD) program as a way of acquiring the necessary clout to lead the Arab world. His actions sparked intervention, first by the United Nations and then, in 2003, by the United States, bringing about further instability in an already volatile region.

In the early 1990s Afghanistan embarked on a course that brought the extreme Islamist Taliban regime to power by the mid-1990s. The Taliban regime invited in and then protected the al-Qaeda terrorist organization, sparking the Western invasion in the aftermath of the 11 September 2001 attacks to oust the regime and rout out al-Qaeda. North Korea took a different tack, seeking to develop nuclear capability in order to acquire the stature to deal with its main adversary—the United States—on an equal basis.[2]

These and other similar developments thrust the issue of rogue and failed states to top priority of the intelligence agenda. Intelligence agencies have been employing traditional methodologies in this area: identifying the intentions of the leaders of rogue states, determining their plans and capabilities, supporting American diplomacy in its dealing with these states, and devising covert ways to hinder or put a stop to

WMD developments. As such, many of the root causes of intelligence failure in the intelligence process identified in previous chapters come into play in the intelligence wars against rogue and failed states.

International Terrorism
The terrorist attacks of 11 September 2001 thrust the terrorism issue to the forefront of the American national agenda, although international terrorism has been an ongoing concern for the United States since the early 1980s. During the Cold War, international terrorism contained an ideological twinge, often associated with the machinations of the superpowers and their client states. While the roots of post–Cold War international terrorism were planted during the 1970s and 1980s—the Palestinian terrorism of the early 1970s, the ouster of the Iranian shah, and the ascendance of the Iranian clerics to power were precursors—modern international terrorism acquired its Islamist and extremist sheen after the end of the Cold War in the 1990s. Western states, particularly the United States, launched a "war on terror" as a response to such terrorism, which included the invasion of Afghanistan in 2001 to oust the Taliban and of Iraq in 2003 to oust Saddam Hussein. Additional terrorist actions after 9/11—bombings in Indonesia in 2002, in Madrid in 2004, and in London and Egypt in 2005—have made the fight against international terrorism a worldwide phenomenon.

Terrorism is an amorphous threat that has physical and psychological costs. While the physical costs include death and the destruction of property, the psychological costs include the "fear instilled in individuals, and what it leads those citizens to do,"[3] such as arming themselves or ostracizing individuals of particular ethnic backgrounds.

Because terrorism is a relatively new security threat, the role of intelligence in combating it is to identify known and likely terrorist threats, expose connections among groups and their supporters, locate the primary bases out of which terrorists operate, and forestall hostile operations against the United States and its allies. Because terrorist groups operate secretly around the globe, intelligence collection must include acquisition of information through international liaison and a new kind of espionage that requires the use of human resources to recruit terrorists to penetrate groups. But acquiring information about terrorist plots is a very difficult undertaking because, given their small and cellular nature, terrorist groups highly compartment their information.

The difficulties of recruiting individuals who might know the terrorists' plans complicate the problem. Most likely, the information necessary can only be found among the top leadership, but high-ranking sources are less likely to betray their plans. Even if intelligence agents were to penetrate a terrorist cell, they would face operational problems associated with accessing the source to provide requirements, disperse funds, and retrieve information. The source—the human agent—is also likely to have engaged in terrorism, which can embroil the American intelligence agency in the legal problems of recruiting someone with a shady past. As Paul Pillar points out, "A well-placed human source is the best possible intelligence asset for counterterrorism, but . . . such sources will be very few."[4]

To make up for these shortfalls, American intelligence relies heavily on technical collection of intelligence, such as intercepting cell phone communications, analyzing chatter from communication systems, and acquiring imagery of terrorist movements in and out of terrorist camps. However, terrorists are well aware of the monitoring capabilities of the United States and other governments and therefore either camouflage their activities or do much of their communicating through couriers and face-to-face.

There are also difficulties associated with collecting and analyzing terrorism information:

- The sheer volume of intelligence information makes the separation of the wheat from the chaff a challenge.
- Because there is so much available information, intelligence agencies are perennially short of analytic manpower to cover it all.
- Terrorist groups are so amorphous and their structures so nonhierarchical that analysts frequently are at a loss to understand terrorist organizations and their alliances.
- Because analysts rarely, if ever, get proof that their

terrorism analyses are correct, they have difficulty assessing the accuracy of intelligence information.

The inherent difficulties in collecting and analyzing terrorism-related information means that rarely do intelligence agencies issue tactical warning of most attempted terrorist attacks, or even most major attempted attacks against U.S. targets.[5]

While global in nature, international counterterrorism fuses the foreign with the domestic in ways that usually make American intelligence officials uncomfortable. U.S. law now requires the intelligence agencies to assist law enforcement, and they now do so on a routine basis. While U.S. intelligence agencies are legally barred from engaging in police functions, they have the authority to help law enforcement with expert personnel and technical knowledge and assistance.[6] To align domestic and foreign antiterror activities, the Departments of Justice and Homeland Security underwent restructuring in 2005 to better coordinate intelligence, policy, and law enforcement operations.[7] Moreover, the USA PATRIOT Act authorizes U.S. intelligence agencies, including the Federal Bureau of Investigation (FBI) and the Central Intelligence Agency (CIA), to cooperate more fully with the police at all levels. Portions of the act were renewed in 2005, and some lawmakers have introduced legislation to make the act permanent.[8]

Intelligence makes its most direct contribution to the antiterror effort through covert operations against terrorist groups and their leaders. Covert actions have the advantage of enabling the U.S. government to disassociate itself from them, if necessary. The objective of counterterrorism—disruption of terrorist actions—can also be achieved by eliciting the cooperation of willing states, and covert actions may be used to induce wavering governments to cooperate in counterterrorism efforts.

However, covert actions against terrorist targets could generate problems that can produce intelligence failure. Disrupting terrorist groups requires information about their activities, but such intelligence often is incomplete. Moreover, success depends heavily on the reliability of international liaison relationships, which are at best uncertain. In addition, there are ethical and moral considerations, especially in the area of political assassination, which continues to be against U.S. law. The USA PATRIOT Act and other legislation authorize the president to make exceptions on a case-by-case basis, and President George W. Bush has used this authority to target terrorist leaders. However, there is no evidence that assassinating terrorist leaders reduces terrorism.[9]

Weapons Proliferation
Preventing the spread of biological, chemical, nuclear, and radiological weapons has been an American policy priority since the end of the Cold War. The George W. Bush administration has set the tone for the future conduct of American counterterrorism by linking the problem of WMD proliferation to rogue and unfriendly states on one hand and to terrorist groups on the other. President Bush apparently sees the two as the flip sides of the same coin, a problem that needs to be addressed as part of the bigger international antiterror campaign. However conceived, Vice Adm. Lowell Jacoby, former head of the Defense Intelligence Agency (DIA), has dubbed WMD and missile proliferation to be "the second most immediate and significant threat to our nation and to international stability."[10]

That terrorist groups and some states have been searching for sources to acquire WMD has given the issue greater urgency in recent years. Indeed, the 9/11 Commission, which released its report on 22 July 2004, warned that "the greatest danger of another catastrophic attack in the United States will materialize if the world's most dangerous terrorists acquire the world's most dangerous weapons."[11] In addition, former CIA director Porter Goss asserted on 16 February 2005 that "it may be a matter of time before al Qaeda or another group attempts to use chemical, biological, radiological, or nuclear weapons."[12]

Intelligence has long played an important role in nonproliferation. During the Cold War, U.S. intelligence supported American diplomacy in arms control and disarmament issues. In the post–Cold War era, U.S. intelligence has taken on the role of monitoring Russia's "loose nukes" and "loose talent" that could be purchased by rogue states or subnational groups seeking to acquire such weapons. In addition, intelligence agencies are responsible for identifying weapons programs early enough to stop them before they are completed and for targeting the clandestine international commerce in some of the specialty items required to manufacture WMD. These two tasks suggest the melding of analytic and covert techniques to address the problem.

However, ambiguous information can lead analysts to wrong conclusions. Such was the case with the discovery that in fact Iraq had no WMD despite the 2003 National Intelligence Estimate claiming that Iraq possessed substantial WMD capabilities. This intelligence failure resulted in the embarrassment of the U.S. government and damage to the credibility of the intelligence agencies.[13]

This suggests that intelligence failures are an endemic part of the nonproliferation business. The CIA long possessed a unit, the Nonproliferation Center (NPC), to address the issue of WMD. Yet, in the waning months of the twentieth century, the center's failures included North Korea's unexpected test of a long-range missile; the lack of verification of a suspected weapons plant in Sudan bombed by American cruise missiles; and surprise Indian and Pakistani nuclear tests—all in 1998.[14] More recently, the George W. Bush administration, according to press reports, cooked already-faulty intelligence about Iraq's WMD programs in 2003 to justify its invasion of Iraq and the ouster of Iraq's dictator, Saddam Hussein. These intelligence failures—though offset by a much longer list of successes, many of which are classified—serve as a reminder of the uncertainties that intelligence officials and policymakers face when trying to anticipate WMD developments.

To address the shortcomings, in July 2005 the Bush administration created a National Counter Proliferation Center, aimed at helping to combat the spread of WMD to terrorist groups and rogue states. In addition, a separate executive order, released about the same time, allowed the freezing of assets of individuals, groups, or companies involved in weapons proliferation.[15] Despite these reforms, a recent assessment asserted that the United States is woefully unprepared for dangers emanating from WMD proliferation.[16]

Promoting Democracy

On 26 October 2005, the director of national intelligence (DNI) announced a national intelligence strategy listing the priority issues that were to guide future intelligence policy as well as planning, collection, analysis, budgets, and operations.[17] In this document, counterterrorism tops the list, followed by preventing and countering the spread of WMD. Following these two items is bolstering "the growth of democracy and [sustaining] peaceful democratic states," which constitutes a new intelligence priority and a departure from the kinds of more traditional, reactive issues that have previously dominated intelligence priorities.

The new emphasis probably reflects the Bush administration's focus on promoting the development of democratic principles in regions that are suffering from authoritarian rule, theocratic governments, and dictatorships. It also likely reflects the Bush administration's penchant for proactive measures abroad intended to further American foreign policy goals. While there has been speculation that this move gives covert action operatives new marching orders, intelligence officials have asserted that the new focus is not intended to affect future covert operations.[18] On the contrary, the new emphasis encourages U.S. intelligence to focus on "forging new relationships with new and incipient democracies in order to strengthen the rule of law and ward off threats to representative government."[19] This approach almost certainly will impel the U.S. government to devote more resources to human intelligence that will bolster the use of American "soft power" in unstable regions.

Support to Military Operations

Support to military operations has been one of the highest intelligence priorities since Presidential Decision Directive (PDD) 35 was issued on 2 March 1995 by the William J. Clinton White House. Under the complex terms of PDD 35, intelligence support to the military was assigned the highest priority, while providing political, economic, and military intelligence on countries hostile to the United States took second place. Third priority went to protecting American citizens from new transnational threats such as drug traffickers, terrorists, organized criminals, and WMD.

Giving high priority to supporting military operations was a direct response to failures during the 1991 Gulf War, during which military commanders issued scathing criticism of America's strategic intelligence agencies, especially the CIA, for focusing too much on national needs and failing to support military operations in the battlefield. In addition, many military commanders who received national intelligence found it to be so watered down and caveat laden that it was virtually worthless in their operations against the enemy.

To address the criticism, the CIA in the early 1990s established an Office of Military Affairs (OMA) within its Directorate of Operations (DO), and the director of central intelligence (DCI) assigned an officer of general rank to head the office and provide actionable intelligence from the CIA to commanders in the field.[20] This office also augmented coordination efforts with the military's strategic intelligence units, such as the DIA, as a way of smoothing out bureaucratic rough spots. OMA continues to be an integral part of CIA's new National Clandestine Service (NCS), which replaced the Directorate of Operations in October 2005.

Since the establishment of the Office of Military Affairs, U.S. intelligence has made great strides in collecting actionable intelligence and disseminating it to commanders in the field. This office now brings to play the lessons learned about bringing the right intelligence to the field and getting it to the right military user. One strategy is to build up the Pentagon's new espionage network to target terrorists and augment other human intelligence (HUMINT) efforts, in coordination with CIA's National Clandestine Service.[21] Another method is to use joint task forces, which bring intelligence analysts and military officers together to work on a common problem. In fact, reports indicate that joint intelligence and military operations in Afghanistan, Iraq, and elsewhere have benefited greatly from these reforms.

While an essential component of America's antiterror effort, giving the highest priority to supporting military operations may engender unrealistic expectations that may lead commanders to rely too much on intelligence as a way of dealing with the ambiguities of war. It may also allocate a greater percentage of collection assets to the task, to the detriment of other priorities elsewhere. In addition, because different levels of each of the services have different intelligence needs, identifying them and supplying the necessary intelligence to each level in the field—which often is in the midst of an unstable environment of warfare—may be nearly impossible. Intelligence may go to those who have no need for it, and too much information can flood field commanders with irrelevant intelligence, making their jobs more difficult.[22]

Cyberwar Operations
Because intelligence largely deals with the acquisition and analysis of relevant information, information warfare is a natural arena for intelligence activity. This issue has acquired added importance with the advent of information technologies, especially in the 1990s, and is now an integral part of both military and intelligence operations. Information warfare deals with the use of computer technology to wage war against state and non-state targets on one hand and to protect the United States from similar attacks on the other.

The use of information technologies to counter security threats first became an operational concept in the 1991 Persian Gulf War and is now embedded in both conceptual and operational doctrines of the U.S. military and intelligence communities. The Pentagon's counterterrorism plan, formulated in August 2005, calls for "information operations" as an inevitable dimension of warfare, augmenting the State Department's public diplomacy efforts.[23] The Defense Department's massive Information Warfare Office, established in the mid-1990s, clearly indicated that information warfare is important in military doctrine.

Intelligence agencies now routinely employ computer technologies against all intelligence targets, from terrorist groups to rogue states seeking to acquire nuclear weapons technologies.[24] Information warfare is naturally suited to intelligence activities because it involves disrupting communications and infrastructure, sending false messages, and destroying vital information. For example, cyberwar may include hacking into financial systems to interfere with financial transactions of terrorist groups and their supporters or sabotaging nuclear, biological, chemical, and radiological weapons-development programs in countries like Iran and North Korea.[25] As such, it is at the nexus of intelligence acquisition and covert action, perhaps bridging the gap between passive and active intelligence. The principal intelligence problems in this area are the fluid and complex nature of cyberspace as well as the fact that cyber warfare elevates intelligence agents from information gatherers and analysts to combatants.

Information warfare also includes countering cyber threats against the United States. The United States is heavily dependent on advanced technology in military and civilian affairs, and security officials fear that it is highly vulnerable to cyber attacks. Indeed, sub-state threats, such as terrorist groups, probably find cyberwar a highly attractive option because Western countries are woefully unprepared to counter such threats and because this kind of attack carries a low cost while having high-value results. The relevant intelligence components of FBI and the Department of Homeland Security apparently consider possible cyber attacks to be so threatening that, according to one source, they are devoting a significant portion of their funds to countering them.[26]

International Economic Competitiveness
In the post–Cold War globalized world, economic competitiveness has become an important national security priority and has thereby drawn the attention of U.S. intelligence and policy communities, which make a distinction between economic intelligence, which is acceptable, and industrial espionage, which is not. Economic intelligence is defined as economic and fiscal information about the decisions and activities of foreign governments. Industrial espionage is the acquisition of the secrets of foreign business establishments for the benefit of American companies.

Policymakers consider economic intelligence, in which U.S. intelligence has long engaged, to be important for their formulation of policies toward foreign governments. As in the past, the vast majority of economic intelligence today comes from publicly available sources, while only a tiny fraction is derived using other, especially human, assets.

The U.S. government has long rejected industrial espionage as a viable tactic for U.S. intelligence for a variety of reasons. One, American companies generally do not want the assistance of the government in this regard, rightly believing that they can perform this function better than can the government. Most American firms have marketing or public relations divisions—which gather competitive intelligence—that act well in this capacity, and the involvement of the federal government in such endeavors would complicate their work considerably. Two, the U.S. intelligence community would confront enormous legal and dissemination problems if it were to acquire information through industrial espionage. Not only would the government have difficulty ensuring that it does not provide advantage to one company over another, it in all likelihood would also face legal challenges if any favoritism of some businesses over others was perceived. Three, there is the problem of reciprocity, in that while many countries, such as France and the People's Republic of China, have active programs of industrial espionage against the United States, the American position on industrial espionage provides it the moral high ground, which can be beneficial in economic diplomacy. Were the United States to start stealing the secrets of foreign businesses to benefit its own companies, it would forgo this advantage and, in the current environment of globalization, may invite even greater espionage against American interests.

U.S. intelligence does, however, provide some assistance to American business concerns in the area of foreign economic counterintelligence, which seeks to blunt foreign efforts at economic intelligence collection. The FBI has recently identified the People's Republic of China as the "biggest [espionage] threat to the U.S. today,"[27] and has initiated programs to thwart Chinese and other economic espionage against the United States.

International Drug Traffic and International Crime
U.S. intelligence has long been in the business of monitoring the production of illicit narcotics in foreign countries, identifying drug traffickers, tracking the movement of drugs, and working cooperatively with other U.S. agencies, such as the

Drug Enforcement Administration (DEA) and the Coast Guard, to disrupt traffickers and prevent drugs from entering the country. The role of U.S. intelligence in this area falls largely in the areas of intelligence collection and analysis. Ideally, U.S. intelligence passes the analyzed information on to the other agencies, which employ it to interdict the drugs and arrest the traffickers. The official incorporation of DEA into the intelligence community in 2006 probably has facilitated such interchanges, even though cultural barriers forestall active cooperation and coordination between intelligence agencies and law enforcement bureaus.[28]

The link between the narcotics trade and international crime, and possibly terrorism, brings a new dimension to the intelligence-gathering problem. Profits from drug sales and trafficking often finance criminal activities as well as terrorist actions. This added complexity makes the work of U.S. intelligence even more difficult, as working against these targets often thrusts the agencies into crossing the line between foreign and domestic intelligence and between intelligence and law enforcement. The point at which the issue is handed from one agency to another is not always clear, raising both practical and legal questions.[29]

Global Health, the Environment, and Human Rights
Global disease and the state of the global environment are both important policy concerns for the U.S. government, and therefore constitute key parts of the intelligence requirements.[30] In the mid-1980s, working under the authority of a directive signed by President Ronald Reagan, the CIA developed a model that could predict the spread of AIDS and its demographic effects, and thus thrust global health issues onto the list of important intelligence priorities. Since then, according to intelligence expert Loch K. Johnson, U.S. intelligence has monitored and assessed global health concerns in certain regions and countries, often focusing on the impact of disease on leadership, social and political relationships, and regional stability. In addition, American intelligence has gathered and analyzed information on safe drinking water and adequate sanitation, the effects of the spread of AIDS on regime stability, and medical concerns related to peacekeeping and humanitarian operations.[31]

The global environment has also been assuming greater relevance among intelligence priorities. In this area, the basic intelligence tasks focus on determining major threats to the environment, identifying states whose policies may be harmful to the environment, and tracking major changes in the environment. Much of this intelligence comes from open sources, ranging from commercial satellites to public records, and once analyzed, it supports American diplomacy on environmental issues.

To date, the most important contribution that U.S. intelligence has made in the area of the global environment has been the MEDEA program, which is the sharing of CIA's ecological database—developed as part of the Cold War satellite and other collection efforts—with the outside scientific community for the purpose of monitoring, assessing, and addressing global environmental changes.[32]

Peace Operations

Since the end of the Cold War, the United States, as the sole superpower, has had to undertake significant peacekeeping operations around the globe that have required not only coordination at the national level but also cooperation with allies. The Pentagon's counterterrorism plan, for example, calls for embracing foreign partners as a way to institute a comprehensive global antiterror strategy.[33] Such a posture requires strong intelligence support and strong intelligence sharing.

However, some American policymakers as well as intelligence officials have been, and are, reluctant to share intelligence with former foes, with non-allies, and even with some allies. Civilian and military officials often find themselves torn between the need to keep peacekeeping partners well informed in order to carry out successful operations and the recognition that intelligence sharing may compromise sources and methods, thereby hindering U.S. intelligence from doing its job.[34]

Intelligence Challenges

These and other issues are creating significant challenges for U.S. intelligence, especially in such areas as intelligence collection and analysis. These challenges range the gamut from adapting new technologies to counter the relatively new threats all the way to protecting civil liberties in light of new security concerns. While many of these challenges have been around for a long time, the terrorist attacks of 11 September 2001 thrust them to the forefront of the intelligence failure debate.

Collection and Analytic Challenges
Terrorists, weapons proliferators, drug traffickers, and international criminals all act secretly to frustrate the ability of intelligence and security agencies to disrupt their activities. These non-state actors have become significant players in generating threat scenarios against the globe's established powers, including the United States. This suggests that U.S. intelligence agencies now must adopt new ways of collecting intelligence information against such threats, including having to move beyond the traditional way of gathering information—contacts with government officials—to penetrating political sects and terrorist cells, which often having no perceptible infrastructure. To do this, American intelligence must reorient its major collection disciplines in ways that will have major technical and organizational ramifications. The dilemma is that on one hand new and evolving technologies enable more and better intelligence collection, but on the other constantly changing technologies impose limits to success in information acquisition.

Signals intelligence (SIGINT) has emerged as the most significant collection discipline in the antiterror and anticrime efforts and, as such, requires the most adaptation among all the collection disciplines. SIGINT is particularly susceptible to criticism that it has difficulty overcoming technological advances in encryption systems and allaying allied suspicions about American communications intercept efforts.[35]

Imagery intelligence (IMINT) is also facing profound challenges, especially as new intelligence priorities demand more collection targets that, in turn, require more flexible collection platforms. The procurement of sufficient numbers of unmanned aerial vehicles (UAVs) constitutes a particular challenge because UAVs are becoming ever more important in the fight against terrorists, drug traffickers, and internal criminal organizations.[36] At the same time, the advent of high-quality commercial satellite imagery may allow the government to obtain some coverage less expensively from the private sector, which brings additional coordination and security concerns into the equation.

The HUMINT effort confronts the challenge of establishing appropriate rules for forging contacts with influential figures in rogue states, clandestine terrorist groups, or narcotics-trafficking organizations, who do their communicating in obscure languages and engage in ever-changing and ever-evolving technologies. This poses the problem of acquiring personnel trained in the appropriate languages and tradecraft, an issue that has long plagued U.S. intelligence. To overcome the deficiency, various approaches have been considered, including using civilian contract personnel or military reservists with language qualifications and offering substantial bonuses to agency personnel who maintain language proficiency.

In addition, HUMINT confronts the perennial legal and ethical problem of dealing with unsavory or undesirable persons, which has heretofore made American intelligence agents "risk averse." Although the guidelines against contacts with such individuals have been relaxed in the antiterror war, the ambiguities created by such prohibitions have not been resolved.

In the current geopolitical environment, open-source intelligence (OSINT) has become increasingly important. The use of open-source information to address new threats means greater attention to translation, dissemination, and systematic analysis, given the proliferation of intelligence priorities in the post-9/11 environment and the avalanche of open-source materials concerning them. In recognition of this reality, former CIA director Porter Goss reportedly established a large division within the CIA's Foreign Broadcast Information Service (FBIS) in mid-2005, dedicated to sorting through various forms of open data that could be vital to national security.[37] While U.S. intelligence has long employed open-source materials in its assessments, the new emphasis on open sources requires a cultural and attitudinal shift away from considering only secret information to be worthy of attention.

Collection challenges are putting the spotlight on analytic challenges as well. Former CIA official John C. Gannon asserted in June 2005 that "cognitive analytic tools are continuously under development in both the private sector and the government to facilitate management of the information glut, enhancing the IC's [intelligence community's] ability to filter, search and prioritize potentially overwhelming volumes of information."[38] Collected information must undergo analysis, but there seems to be an ever-present gap between the quantity of collected materials and how much of it ends up being analyzed, an imbalance particularly applicable to imagery intelligence. Added to that are the challenges of a largely inexperienced workforce, lack of language skills, and limited familiarity with intelligence issues, all of which are complicating the analytic task. Moreover, the antiterror emphasis has given added weight to current intelligence, a favorite of policymakers; this may further erode the ability of U.S. intelligence to conduct comprehensive strategic analysis.

Dissemination Challenges
The terrorist threat to the United States is producing some interesting effects that pose other significant challenges. One, because terrorist threats are often dealt with within law enforcement channels, more emphasis has been given to cooperation between intelligence and law enforcement. The USA PATRIOT Act[39] has generated greater cooperation between intelligence and law enforcement in accordance with guidelines established by the White House. Parts of the act have been extended beyond their December 2005 expiration date. In addition, some portions of the act have been strengthened to give the government—and the FBI, in particular—expanded powers to fight terrorism.[40] Greater cooperation between intelligence and law enforcement has raised a number of difficult issues: potential duplication of effort, the use of information obtained by intelligence agencies in court trials, the danger that the methods of secret intelligence collection might be revealed in law enforcement cases, and the undermining of legitimate foreign policy and defense initiatives.

Two, the need to provide intelligence support to military operations has encompassed numerous technical difficulties, especially in transmitting data in usable formats and in a timely manner to those in the field who need it. U.S. intelligence agencies have come a long way since the 1991 Gulf War in addressing some of the issues, but as the 2003 Iraq

War has illustrated, significant technical and organizational challenges remain.

Finally, an important new challenge is the credibility of U.S. intelligence in the eyes of policymakers and allied intelligence services. The fiasco over Iraq's WMD capability,[41] reports of abuses in Iraq and Afghanistan,[42] and mounting evidence of recent intelligence failures—including failing to anticipate the Indian nuclear tests and North Korea's launch of a three-stage missile, both in 1998, and the 9/11 terrorist attacks—all have called into question the ability of U.S. intelligence to anticipate emerging and evolving security threats. U.S. officials have acknowledged that the Iraqi WMD issue in particular has been damaging, leading a senior senator to declare in March 2005 that "our credibility has been harmed by the intelligence failure in Iraq, [and] there is less support from people and nations around the world for the United States and for the war on terrorism."[43]

The CIA's strong warning prior to the 2003 invasion of Iraq of ethnic and tribal turmoil—a warning that turned out to be accurate—has complicated the controversy. The White House apparently chose to ignore this warning in favor of concentrating on the October 2002 National Intelligence Estimate on Iraq's WMD capabilities, which appears to have been wrong.[44] As a direct result of such politicization and failures, dire intelligence assessments on Iranian and North Korean nuclear programs are encountering a good deal of skepticism from America's allies and foes alike.[45]

Inflection Points

The nature of the issue, the level of policy interest, and the resulting priority level of an issue determines the degree to which it receives money, human resources, and the attention necessary. Simply stated, the more complex an issue, the more difficult it is to address it by employing intelligence resources. Moreover, the level of difficulty tends to exacerbate the intractability of the intelligence challenges inherent in any issue. This is especially so in counterterrorism, which appears to have brought to light virtually all of the shortcomings of the intelligence process that heretofore have contributed to intelligence failures. While not all the issues are as intractable as international terrorism, globalization seems to be reinforcing both traditional and emerging issues, such that they are becoming less discrete and more a part of the mosaic of national security threats that are taxing the resources of the U.S. intelligence community. Whether or not these issues can be effectively addressed depends to a large extent on tackling the intelligence challenges that were identified in this and previous chapters.

11

Toward Smarter Intelligence

*No one can really guarantee the future. The most we can
do is size up the chances, calculate the risks involved,
estimate our ability to deal with them and then make our
plans with confidence.*
—Henry Ford

The evidence shows that the root causes of intelligence failures are embedded throughout the intelligence cycle. At the
beginning of the cycle, the manner in which consumers perceive intelligence sets the tone for what happens at the back
end—how policymakers use secret intelligence. At the front end,
the way we conceive intelligence shapes our expectations of it.
Our expectations, in turn, form the basis for judging the performance of intelligence agencies as they undertake to fulfill
their missions. In the middle stages, structure plays a major
role, defining the parameters of secret intelligence and setting
the context in which the politics of intelligence take place.
Bureaucratic imperatives combine with personality factors
everywhere in the cycle to subvert perfectly natural human
qualities, such as perception and cognition, and help distort
perfectly good intelligence. In the final stages of the intelligence cycle, issues like trust, credibility, and quality of service come into play, influencing consumers' decisions about
whether they will accept and use the products they receive.
The intelligence process envelops all of the issues mentioned

above, and in combination they create the conditions for both intelligence success and failure.

Because the roots of failures are so firmly entrenched in the intelligence process, there is little that anyone can do to address them, short of scrapping the entire apparatus and starting all over. Some proposals have embraced this pessimistic view and called for doing away with the current structure of intelligence and creating a new one. The late Senator Daniel Patrick Moynihan (D-NY) was one such advocate, holding firm to his belief that the only way to reform central intelligence was to tear it down completely and put a new and different structure in its place. But this view, shared by many thoughtful critics of U.S. intelligence, wrongly assumes that structure alone creates the conditions that lead intelligence to fail and that the only way to address them would be to uproot or change these structures.

The human element, however, has as much to do with the failures of secret intelligence as do structural factors, if not more. Some intelligence agencies, especially the CIA, have long studied the problem of human failings and have taken some remedial steps. Taking human failings into account does little good, however, for an intelligence process that intrinsically contains the seeds of failure. Nonetheless, pessimism is not synonymous with hopelessness, and there are several things reformers can do to reduce the incidence of intelligence failure or minimize their effects.

The Tragedy of Unrealistic Expectations

A critical step toward smarter intelligence is to educate the public and policymakers about what intelligence can and cannot do. Reshaping expectations toward a more pragmatic view of secret intelligence has to be part of the education of the consumer and the public. For a long time, U.S. intelligence agencies eschewed any educational outreach toward their publics, out of fear that public relations efforts might be perceived as spreading propaganda and manipulating public opinion. A small portion of the public would hold to that conviction no matter what intelligence agencies did or did not do. The majority of the public, however, would genuinely benefit from information describing the agencies' missions and activities. Some intelligence agencies took steps in this direction at the end of the Cold War, but they have a long way to go before the public really understands the purposes of intelligence agencies.

A major part of the public relations problem revolves around the terminology used to describe intelligence activities. A close examination of media reporting and policymaker attitudes reveals that in an overwhelming majority of cases, intelligence is expected to "predict" developments and events. Even intelligence officials are prone to use this term occasionally to describe what they expect of themselves. "Prediction," however, implies a degree of certainty that is rarely, if ever, present in intelligence reporting and analysis. Intelligence is based upon imperfect information and is full of complexity and ambiguity, exacerbated by secret government deliberation in foreign capitals and deception by adversaries. So long as complexities and distortions exist, secret intelligence is incapable of meeting the high standards associated with prediction. As long as people expect intelligence to predict events, the rate of intelligence failure will be high.

Agencies in the intelligence community must take the lead in providing accurate information about themselves and their activities, since the popular culture is intent on fostering a misleading picture. For a start, agencies can champion the view that a better standard with which to judge the performance of secret intelligence would be the principle enunciated in 1996 by the Working Group on Intelligence Reform of the National Strategy Information Center. In its report, the Working Group stated unequivocally that "the purpose of [intelligence] analysis is to help the policymaker shape the future, not to predict it."[1] Accordingly, a more appropriate descriptor of how intelligence can and does function is to promote the use of the word "forecast." This term incorporates all the elements of how secret intelligence serves the nation, ambiguity and complexity included. Secret intelligence works pretty much like weather forecasts, in that more, better, and timely information enables the forecaster to make better and more timely, but imperfect, judgments about the immediate future.

John Maynard Keynes, the eminent economist, once remarked that it is better to be vaguely right than precisely wrong.[2] This tongue-in-cheek comment contains a kernel of truth. American intelligence must do better than be "vaguely right," but it can never achieve the impossibly high standard of "precisely right." Forecasting, imprecise and subject to error as it is, will have to suffice. National security planners and intelligence officials would serve themselves better and promote greater understanding of secret intelligence among the public by simply adjusting their daily lexicon of intelligence-speak to include "forecasting."

Provide Strong Leadership with Unity of Command

Realistic expectations must be accompanied by some significant structural changes, the most important of which is to infuse greater cohesion into the intelligence process. The Intelligence Reform and Terrorism Prevention Act of 2004 established the position of director of national intelligence (DNI), a move favored by the Joint Inquiry, the 9/11 Commission, and other independent panels that examined the performance of U.S. intelligence prior to and after the 9/11 attacks. In the debates about the legislation, the DNI was to have full range of management, budgetary, and personnel responsibilities needed to make the entire U.S. intelligence community operate as a coherent whole.[3] The recommendation closely resembled legislation introduced in the summer of 2002 by Senator Dianne Feinstein (D-Calif.), who asserted that the new DNI position was necessary to "coordinate our intelligence and antiterrorism efforts" and to make certain that "the sort of communication problems that prevented the various elements of our intelligence community from working together effectively before 11 September never happen again."[4]

However, America's entrenched intelligence agencies opposed the proposal to create a strong "intelligence czar," even though they recognized that the plan would tackle one of the major complaints of DCIs in the past. That is, the DCIs had responsibility for the entire intelligence community and controlled the CIA but lacked budgetary power over the larger part of the community controlled by the secretary of defense.

Concerted opposition from entrenched interests, particularly the Defense Department and the CIA, served to dilute the 2004 law's intent, such that the resulting legislation established the DNI's position with little more authority than that possessed by the DCI since 1946. The law relegated the DCI to be responsible for only the CIA, freeing him to devote his energies to what the CIA does best in HUMINT, coordinated intelligence analysis, and covert operations. Some reformers also suggested that the DCI be given operational and tasking authority over the NSA, NRO, and NGA,[5] but such a proposal probably would have negated the benefits that might accrue from a strengthened DNI by further fragmenting the intelligence community.

Enhancing the DNI's authorities is now a must for comprehensive intelligence reform. A truly strong "intelligence czar" would provide U.S. intelligence with certain benefits:

- It would bring about high-quality, coordinated analysis and make resource decisions that reflect national priorities, not choices driven largely by those who oversee the technical collection programs or who are concerned with military programs alone. As such, it would focus the management and organizational structure of the intelligence community around substantive national security missions rather than the narrow and particular collection mission of each agency.
- It would allow the DNI to create new, overarching, community-wide centers to tackle new and unexpected problems.
- It would establish an undifferentiated and undisputed leader in charge.
- It would permit the imposition of uniformity in the personnel management system, thus allowing the IC to move personnel and reorganize structures on an ad hoc basis much more effectively in response to future developments. Such flexibility would augment the ability of the community to adapt flexibly and effectively to future threats.[6]

The position of a strong DNI would neither interfere with the collection competencies of the individual intelligence agencies nor be inconsistent with the principle of competitive intelligence, which must continue to undergird intelligence analysis. On the contrary, the DNI would be in a position to mediate among the parochial interests of the intelligence agencies and resolve disputes in ways that reflect national priorities, not the interests of a specific or a group of agencies. In addition, the DNI would be able to provide customers, especially the president, with intelligence advice that reflects the diversity of views within the intelligence community without having to risk upsetting the balance of power among the competing agencies.

The notion of a DNI is not new. The DNI's position is the latest iteration in a long series of similar proposals that date back to the late 1940s. The CIA was established in 1947 to be the "central" repository of all intelligence information in the U.S. government, and the first Hoover Commission in 1949 confirmed this by calling for the CIA to be the central organization of the national intelligence system. In response to charges that the DCI was not paying sufficient attention to the community, the second Hoover Commission in 1955 recommended that the DCI concentrate on his community responsibilities and that the "Executive Officer" of the CIA oversee the day-to-day operations of the agency, a recommendation that succeeding DCIs either ignored or implemented differently, with varying results. In 1971, the Schlesinger Report discussed the creation of a DNI but did not propose establishing such a position over the DCI. Instead, that report simply recommended strengthening the role of the DCI over intelligence costs and production. In 1976, the Church Committee (the Senate Select Committee to Study Government Operations with Respect to Intelligence Activities) issued a report that recommended that intelligence funding authority be delegated to the DCI, thereby giving him control over the entire intelligence community budget. The report also recommended separating the DCI from the CIA. In 1992, proposed legislation in the Senate called for a DNI with programming and reprogramming authority over the entire intelligence community and the ability to temporarily transfer personnel among the intelligence community agencies. In 1996, the House Permanent Select Committee on Intelligence produced a staff study that called for more cooperative spirit across the intelligence community and strengthened central management of the IC by providing the DCI additional administrative and resource authorities.[7]

Evidently, the intelligence community did little to implement any of these proposals except for some minor, and largely cosmetic, fixes to tweak the existing structure. Bureaucratic resistance, especially by the all-source agencies, was the culprit behind opposition to greater cohesion. Press reports indicate that despite urgency and political pressure since 11 September, intelligence agencies continued to put roadblocks in front of reforms aimed at reducing turf battles, overcoming legal stumbling blocks, streamlining the bureaucracies, and imposing greater accountability. Indeed, some insiders have asserted that, despite the passage of the 2004 act and the establishment of the DNI's office, the Bush administration has missed an excellent opportunity to untangle the nation's Cold War–era intelligence bureaucracies and retool them to fight terrorism.[8]

Refine the Fusion Center Concept

Strengthening the DNI's authorities would provide the possibility of enhancing communications and cooperation among the various agencies. The intelligence agencies undoubtedly would continue to give priority to their particular mission areas and to their own needs at the expense of the broader national security interest. Overcoming bureaucratic insularity among agencies would not be an easy task, as entrenched bureaucracies normally resist attempts to divert them from their principal mission-specific goals. Given the transnational character of contemporary national security threats, however, there is growing realization in and out of the intelligence community that fusion centers can help overcome the deleterious effects of institutional myopia, a position underscored by the George W. Bush administration when it established the National Counterterrorism Center (NCTC) in early 2005.

Surmounting institutional parochialism is a must if the chances for intelligence failure are to be reduced. The way to do that without upsetting bureaucratic sensibilities too much is to expand the use of interagency task forces and fusion centers. Task forces have been a permanent feature of the intelligence community for a long time now, used primarily for intra- rather than interagency purposes. In addition, the intelligence community currently has over ten fusion centers, operating as focal points for coordination and operations on a variety of issues. The first center was established in 1986 by then-DCI William Casey, who saw a need for a community-wide response to the terrorist problem. Since then, successive DCIs have established other centers, each focusing on a specific issue. The existing centers concentrate on terrorism, counterintelligence, international crime, the international drug trade, international environmental issues, arms control, proliferation of weapons of mass destruction, and information security matters.

Although difficult to reduce to general categories, existing fusion centers either coordinate intelligence activities or conduct operations against specific targets. The Center for Security Evaluation (CSE), the DCI Weapons Intelligence, Nonproliferation, and Arms Control Center, and the National Counterintelligence Center (NACIC) are coordinating mechanisms, in that they produce coordinated intelligence analyses. The Counterterrorism Center (CTC), the Counterintelligence Center (CIC), and the Crime and Narcotics Center (NCC) are operating centers, in that they fuse analytic and operational elements that directly support intelligence operations. The NCTC incorporated the Terrorism Threat Integration Center (TTIC), which had been established in 2002 and represented a new departure by combining domestic and foreign intelligence in one organization. Designed as an analytic effort, TTIC was supposed to provide analysis of intelligence information gathered by the CIA, the FBI, the Pentagon, and the Department of Homeland Security; it was staffed by top counterterrorism officials from each of these agencies, as is the National Counterterrorism Center. The National Counter Proliferation Center (NCPC) is likewise multiagency, with staff drawn from all relevant intelligence policy communities.[9]

The theory behind the fusion centers was to establish "community" organizations that would bring together personnel from all the relevant intelligence community agencies to work on a particular problem. In practice, however, the centers fall far short of being the focal points of all work on intelligence issues and in exhibiting community spirit. One problem is that numerous other entities within the intelligence community duplicate the work of the centers. In the case of nonproliferation, for example, three NIOs speak on various aspects of nonproliferation, as does the DNI's Community Nonproliferation Committee.[10] For another, the centers generally are located at the CIA headquarters in Virginia, are staffed predominantly by CIA employees, and are dependent on the CIA for their administrative support and operating expenses.[11] Even TTIC, which was headed by the DCI, relied heavily on CIA assets, because those were the only assets over which the DCI had control.

Even with the new focus on "national centers," existing policy on the fusion centers encompasses several problems. One, there are bureaucratic issues inherent in properly defining a center's role in the intelligence community, and turf battles often occur. Since the establishment of the first center in 1986, critics in the intelligence community have constantly complained that the centers really are not community organizations at all, since the CIA dominates them. Leo Hazelwood, former executive director of the CIA, was fond of saying that the worst thing about the centers is that they are CIA centers, and that the best thing about the centers is that they are CIA centers—the worst because CIA's dominance negates the notion of interagency cooperation, and the best because the CIA has been the one intelligence agency willing to make the resource investment in these "community" fusion centers.[12] Second, there are physical barriers to the effective work of the centers, in that the far-flung locations of the intelligence agencies can impede the detailing of employees to the centers. The integrated community-wide communications system now under development would probably ease the burden of physically locating employees from multiple agencies at CIA headquarters but would not address the bigger problem of location. Third, a host of institutional and bureaucratic rules governing employee movement, evaluations, and security hinder the realization of a center's full potential. The phrase "out of sight, out of mind" ringing in their ears, detailees from agencies other than the CIA often view a rotation to a fusion center as damaging to their careers.[13]

Strong and unified intelligence leadership in the person of the DNI would address the problems outlined above. A strong DNI would have the authority to smooth out the incongruities of the current centers and to establish new, effective inter-agency mechanisms that would respond to emerging intelligence problems. The first step in making the centers more effective would be to move them out of the CIA and put them at a neutral location accessible to all the relevant intelligence agencies. The second step would be to spell out clearly each center's mission, provide each center its own budget, and establish a personnel system in each center that would link with, but be independent of, specific agency funds and personnel systems, as was done with the National Counterterrorism Center and the National Counter Proliferation Center. The third step would be to authorize the DNI to provide incentives for people in each of the intelligence agencies to serve in the centers and make such service a positive career move.

Integrate Domestic with Foreign Intelligence

Domestic intelligence functions must be incorporated into the centers for them to be more successful. The terrorist attacks of 11 September have shown that the artificial divide between what is domestic intelligence and what is foreign intelligence is no longer tenable and must be replaced by a new conception of intelligence that seamlessly links the two. To date, the artificial division has been enshrined in the equally artificial exclusion of the FBI from foreign intelligence and of the CIA from domestic intelligence. Recognizing the new reality, some legislators recently proposed creating a domestic intelligence agency along the lines of Britain's MI-5,[14] but civil libertarians have resisted the notion on the grounds that it would be an invitation to violating the freedoms enjoyed by Americans.

For now, America's antiterrorism efforts focus more on the law enforcement aspects of the problem than on integrated counterterrorism intelligence. The FBI has acquired some new authorities under the PATRIOT Act[15] to engage in domestic intelligence, and the CIA has assigned some personnel to the

FBI and a few state and local law enforcement jurisdictions to help out in this endeavor.

Yet intelligence collection and analysis against the terrorism target requires an approach quite different from that which prevails in the law enforcement community. According to Senator Richard C. Shelby (D-Ala.), former vice chair of the Senate Select Committee on Intelligence, the FBI is "presently unequal to the challenge [of serving as a domestic intelligence agency] and provides neither first rate CT [counterterrorism] and CI [counterintelligence] competence nor the degree of civil liberty protection that would obtain were domestic intelligence collectors deprived of their badges, guns, and arrest powers and devoted wholly to CI and CT tasks."[16]

The proposal to establish a domestic intelligence agency, espoused by Senator Shelby and the independent commission investigating the 9/11 attacks, would appear to have merit. The plan would take the CT and CI portfolios out of the FBI and put them in a stand-alone organization that would be responsible for intelligence collection and analysis but would have no law enforcement powers. Alternatively, the CT and CI responsibilities could be moved to the Undersecretariat for Information Analysis and Infrastructure Protection in the Department of Homeland Security, which is well placed to bridge the span between domestic and foreign intelligence, assuming that the CIA cooperates with the shift. A third alternative would be to use the existing methodology of fusion centers and establish a mechanism that would have both operational and analytic capabilities in counterintelligence and counterterrorism.

Several task forces within the CIA are already doing precisely that, and the Defense Department too has jumped into the fray. The DIA has set up an organization, the Joint Intelligence Task Force–Counterterrorism (JITF-CT), which was established after the USS *Cole* attacks in October 2000 and was augmented by new assignments of personnel and resources after 11 September 2001. JITF-CT aspires to provide its analysts with "deep data access" sufficient to permit real all-source fusion. According to Rear Adm. Lowell E. Jacoby, DIA's aim in establishing JITF-CT was to create a "stand-alone limited access data repository accredited to host the entire range of terrorism related information, regardless of source," including not only compartmented information but also "law enforcement information related to ongoing investigations and prosecutions, and security incident reporting sometimes catalogue[d] as criminal, rather than terrorism activity."[17]

The attorney general also established his own Foreign Terrorist Tracking Task Force (FTTTF) after 11 September in order to help develop "deep access" data-mining techniques and apply these new methodologies to the formidable challenge of catching terrorists operating within the United States. FTTTF is collocated with the Pentagon's Joint Counterintelligence Assessment Group, which provides technical support.[18]

Indiscriminately proliferating task forces and fusion centers, however, poses the real danger of defeating the idea of integration. A stronger DNI can do much to stem this potentially destructive rush toward many integrative mechanisms. At a minimum, he can consolidate existing centers along functional lines and establish effective links with internal task forces for greater efficiency. Over the longer term, the DNI would have to maintain a manageable number of centers, either by expanding their missions or by imposing "sunset" regulations and letting some of them simply whither away.

Promote Total Information Awareness

Structural changes must be accompanied by new ways of doing analytic business. "Total Information Awareness" (TIA) is a promising new approach that was developed by Dr. Robert Norris of the National Defense University and Rear Admiral Jacoby. TIA is different from the Terrorist Information Awareness program that was advanced by the Department of Defense and then scrapped by Congress in September 2003.[19] Total Information Awareness aspires to create the tools that would permit analysts to "data-mine"[20] databases by using software that translates analyst queries into usable form and applies specific "business rules" to sort out relevant information. According to its developers, TIA hopes to enable an analyst to make search requests either on a name-by-name basis or apply sophisticated pattern-recognition software, such as neural net software,[21] to a "cloud" of remotely distributed databases. Each analyst user would possess a complex set of individual "credentials," which would be embedded in each query and "travel" with that query through the databases. These credentials would include information on the access permissions and the specific legal and policy authorities under which each query would be conducted. Even when the user did not have authority to see certain types of information, the system would be able to tell the analyst whether any data responsive to his query existed in any particular database, allowing him to submit a request for access to higher authority. Information responsive to user queries would then be passed back through the system to an automated data repository, where it would be stored for analysis.[22]

Such a system would provide interoperability at the data level, which, according to Rear Admiral Jacoby, "is an absolute[ly] necessary attribute of a transformed intelligence environment because it enables horizontal integration of information from all sources, not just intelligence, and at all levels of classification."[23] The Information Awareness Office of the Defense Advanced Research Projects Agency (DARPA) reportedly is on the verge of developing this promising approach to intelligence sharing. While America's counterterrorism methods will inevitably evolve in this direction, legislators must ensure that the program does not intrude on the civil liberties of Americans. Sensitivities associated with this kind of an approach were clearly demonstrated in early 2006 in the debate over President George W. Bush's authorization of the National Security Agency to collect domestic intelligence without FISA warrants.

Improve Analytic Tradecraft

Deep data mining would be only part of a larger effort to improve analytic tradecraft. Additional steps would include ensuring the quality of intelligence analysts, focusing on alternative analysis schemes, and adopting linchpin analysis throughout the intelligence community. Reforms would go a long way to addressing the kind of cognitive and analytic malfunctions that often lead to intelligence failures.

Analyst Training

If total information awareness is to be effective, analysts must have the necessary substantive know-how and tradecraft skills to "deep-mine" information. Intelligence agencies must ensure that new analysts have the necessary expertise for doing analytic work. Relying on earned degrees as the indicator of expertise can no longer suffice. Intelligence agencies must design assessment tools to determine the expertise and capabilities of the analysts and set up training programs to bring analysts up to speed. The analysts, in turn, must be up-front about their knowledge and must be capable of balancing their professional commitment to increased mastery of what can be known (substantive expertise) with their commitment to enhanced skills for dealing with what cannot be known (tradecraft expertise).[24]

In addition, managers must have the necessary resources, including funds, to bring in outside experts to train analysts in up-to-date methodologies that can be used in analytic and estimative work. Furthermore, intelligence managers need to take steps to implement the recommendations of Dr. Harold Ford, a former senior CIA officer, who suggests the following in order to make intelligence analysis more relevant:

- Share all-source intelligence, overriding the innate bureaucratic proclivity to accord turf protection the highest priority.
- Make analysis and estimates clear, brief, and unequivocal.
- Do not water down the message, and present dissenting or differing judgments sharply and unambiguously.
- Distinguish between what is fact and what is judgment, between what is evidence and what is inference.
- Venture courageously beyond evidence by discerning probable 2001 trends and contingent outcomes.
- A good estimate must reflect knowledge of the operational world.
- A good estimate must be candid, pointing out, if necessary, how others view U.S. capabilities and conduct.

- Good estimators do not merely "estimate" but offer operational officers suggestions relevant to the carrying out of policy. They do so not by treating the substance of policy but by providing "handles" that assist policymakers in their conduct of policy.
- Flag any off-chance possibility that may have momentous consequences for U.S. security interests.
- Avoid mirror-imaging, made under the assumption that others would think and behave pretty much as we do.
- Policymaking consumers with a legitimate need to know must get the estimate, and they must get it in time to act on whatever contribution it contains.[25]

Alternative Analysis

Alternative analysis is a viable technique that can enhance analysts' abilities to forecast events. In the mid-1990s, a postmortem report by retired Adm. David Jeremiah on CIA's performance on India's nuclear tests concluded that agency analysts had paid insufficient attention to alternative analysis, which would have provided for rigid testing of prevailing assumptions and taken more deliberate account of seemingly less likely but potentially high-impact developments. Jeremiah recommended two fixes: bringing in outside substantive experts in a more systematic fashion, and bringing experts into the process of analysis when the intelligence community faces a transition on a major intelligence issue. These analytic thinkers would serve, together with substantive experts, as "Red Teams" on major analytic problems, and would work with analysts to study assumptions, mirror-imaging, and complex analytic process.[26]

Intelligence experts agree that intelligence analysts must master the skills for effectively challenging their own assumptions and do some tough-minded evaluations of the authenticity and general adequacy of classified as well as open-source information—before, not after, taking on difficult substantive assignments.[27] The following are some useful techniques in alternative analysis that are available to intelligence analysts:

- Devil's advocacy—a deliberate attempt to support judgments by alternative interpretations of the meaning of available evidence and the implications of gaps in information.
- Risk-benefit analysis—as assessment of various ways the target might weigh the stakes within its own cultural and political contexts.
- High-impact/low-probability analysis—the implications for U.S. interests if the target decides to go ahead with its plans.
- Quality of information check—assessing the authenticity, comprehensiveness, and consistency of the evidence behind judgments.[28]

Linchpin Analysis
Finally, "linchpin analysis" appears to be a sound technique for dealing with some of the dysfunctional aspects of intelligence analysis. Linchpin analysis is the brainchild of Douglas MacEachin, the CIA's former deputy director for intelligence, who has argued that strategic surprise, such as Iraq's invasion of Kuwait in 1990, is often the result of assumptions so widely held by analysts that they are rarely examined critically. MacEachin criticized the prevailing analytic approach to substantive uncertainty as a "predictions sweepstake" that emphasized competition among analysts to come up with a prediction, or a "bottom-line judgment," rather than derive alternative dynamics and outcomes. To overcome this tendency, MacEachin recommends "linchpin analysis," which is the flip side of what he calls "fortune-telling"—intelligence judgments focusing on a bottom-line judgment. In linchpin analysis, analysts assess potential developments based on factors that together would logically bring about a certain future. These factors are the "drivers" or "linchpins" of the analysis. If one or more of them should change, be removed, or turn out to have been wrong to start with, the basis for the forecast would no longer hold.[29]

Identifying the role of key factors in the analytic calculus is a fundamental requirement of sound intelligence forecasts. The policymaker needs to know the potential impact of changes in these linchpins. The consumer especially needs to know whether or not the linchpins are based on assumptions of past practice or on what appear to be logical extensions of what is known; whether the evidence supporting the linchpin analysis is particularly thin or is subject to high degree of uncertainty; or if hard evidence is lacking.[30] Linchpin analysis is well on its way to becoming established doctrinal standard in the CIA, but the rest of the community has yet to sign on to using it.

The Future of Warning?

To warn effectively, analysts must understand how their key clients set their issue priorities, debate, and otherwise process decisions with their policy peers, absorb experts' views and "bad news," and deal with substantive uncertainty. Analysts must know a lot more than they now do about the policy process and about their policymaking counterparts.[31] Intelligence analysts must get into the business of customizing their products to meet the needs of the customers. According to one expert, there is no such thing as an unprofessional policymaker question for intelligence, so long as the answer reflects professional analytic tradecraft—that is, tough-minded weighing of evidence and open-minded consideration of alternatives.[32] In addition, analysts should supplement their analyses with assessments of opportunities in cost-benefit terms for incremental advancement of U.S. interests, what intelligence professionals now call "action analysis."[33]

The surprise Japanese attack on the United States at Pearl Harbor in 1941 spurred a series of measures that culminated in the creation of the U.S. intelligence community in 1947. Establishing a whole new structure out of the ashes of World War II took courage and innovative thinking. The new world order created by the 9/11 terrorist attacks requires an equal measure of creativity and determination. Secret intelligence is too valuable an asset to waste on the unrealistic expectations and fragmented structure that set up American intelligence for failure. Paying attention to proposals that would reduce the incidence of intelligence failures would bolster the argument that secret intelligence is an integral part of national security decision making.

Notes

Chapter 1: The Uncertainty Principle

1. The terrorist attacks of 11 September 2001 are frequently referred to as "9/11" in this book.
2. David E. Rosenbaum, "Years of Unheeded Alarms," *New York Times*, 12 September 2001.
3. Jack Davis, "Strategic Warning: If Surprise Is Inevitable, What Role for Analysis?" *Kent Center Occasional Papers* 2, no. 1 (January 2003): 2.
4. See Rosenbaum, "Years of Unheeded Alarms."
5. Mark M. Lowenthal, *Intelligence: From Secrets to Policy* (Washington, D.C.: Congressional Quarterly, 2000), 1–2.
6. Quoted in Jeffrey T. Richelson, *The U.S. Intelligence Community* (Boulder, Colo.: Westview, 1999), 2.
7. Remarks of DCI George J. Tenet, Oscar Iden Lecture, Georgetown University, Washington, D.C., 18 October 1999.
8. I know from personal experience that former Director of Central Intelligence William Webster was a proponent of this view. Those of us serving on his staff made sure that we included this perspective in appropriate sections of his public speeches.
9. See Jonathan D. Pollack, "Intelligence Agencies in a Swamp of Doubt," *Los Angeles Times*, 25 August 2003.
10. The budget of the U.S. intelligence community has been a closely held secret in the U.S. government, mostly because revealing it would identify classified programs and unveil the levels and types of intelligence efforts. DCI George Tenet in 1997 declassified the budget of the intelligence community for fiscal year 1998 but reclassified it in subsequent years when detractors de-

manded a breakdown of the budget figures. See John Diamond, "CIA Reveals U.S. Spy Budget," Associated Press, 15 October 1997.

11. Lowenthal, *Intelligence: From Secrets to Policy*, 1–2.

12. Robert M. Gates, *From the Shadows* (New York: Simon & Schuster, 1996), 553–75.

13. The concept of "inflection points" comes from the high-voltage world of computer science and the Internet. It refers to those major points that change the way the industry operates. (See Irwin Lazar and Arnold W. Bragg, *Perspectives on the State of the Internet*, www.computer.org/itpro/cover_stories/jan_feb/perspectives_1.htm.) Charles F. Doran considers inflection points to be those "points when a trend breaks down and forecasting is no longer possible" (Charles F. Doran, "Why Forecasts Fail: The Limits and Potential of Forecasting in International Relations and Economics," unpublished paper, n.d.). In the intelligence cycle, inflection points are those dysfunctional factors in the process that instigate intelligence failures.

14. See Loch K. Johnson, *America's Secret Power: The CIA in a Democratic Society* (New York: Oxford University Press, 1989), 76–99.

Chapter 2: Intelligence, American Style

1. Alan Axelrod, *The War between the Spies, A History of Espionage during the American Civil War* (New York: Atlantic Monthly Press, 1992), 3; and Pat M. Holt, *Secret Intelligence and Public Policy: A Dilemma of Democracy* (Washington, D.C.: Congressional Quarterly, 1995), 21.

2. Holt, *Secret Intelligence and Public Policy*, 21–22.

3. G. J. A. O'Toole, *Honorable Treachery: A History of U.S. Intelligence, Espionage, and Covert Action from the American Revolution to the CIA* (New York: Atlantic Monthly Press, 1991), 137.

4. See Axelrod, *The War between the Spies*.

5. See William A. Tidwell, James O. Hall, and David Winfred Gaddy, *Come Retribution: The Confederate Se-*

cret Service and the Assassination of Lincoln (Jackson: University Press of Mississippi, 1988).

6. Rhodri Jeffreys-Jones, *The CIA and American Democracy* (New Haven, Conn.: Yale University Press, 1989), 13.

7. Holt, *Secret Intelligence and Public Policy*, 23.

8. Henry L. Stimson and McGeorge Bundy, *On Active Service in Peace and War* (New York: Harper, 1947), 188.

9. Herbert O. Yardley, *The American Black Chamber* (New York: Blue Ribbon Books, 1931).

10. O'Toole, *Honorable Treachery*, 338; and Holt, *Secret Intelligence and Public Policy*, 23.

11. Roberta Wohlstetter, *Pearl Harbor: Warning and Decision* (Palo Alto, Calif.: Stanford University Press, 1962), passim. Also see documentation in Harold P. Ford, "The Primary Purpose of National Estimating," *Studies in Intelligence* 35 (Fall 1991): 69–79.

12. Thomas F. Troy, "CIA's British Parentage—and the Significance Thereof," paper presented at the Tenth Annual Meeting of the Society for Historians of American Foreign Relations, 3 August 1984, Washington, D.C.

13. Jeffreys-Jones, *The CIA and American Democracy*, 16.

14. For this and other traditions of America's strategic culture, see Donald Snow, *National Security* (New York: St. Martin's Press, 1995), 42–65; and Amos A. Jordan, William J. Taylor, Jr., and Michael J. Mazarr, *American National Security* (Baltimore: Johns Hopkins University Press, 1999), 48–63.

15. Quoted in Jeffreys-Jones, *The CIA and American Democracy*, 29.

16. 50 USC 401 (26 July 1947).

17. Jeffreys-Jones, *The CIA and American Democracy*, 27.

18. For an incisive discussion of these operations, see O'Toole, *Honorable Treachery*, chap. 35.

19. Jeffrey T. Richelson, *The U.S. Intelligence Community* (Boulder, Colo.: Westview, 1999), 37.

20. O'Toole, *Honorable Treachery*, 468.

21. See Loch K. Johnson, *America's Secret Power: The CIA in a Democratic Society* (New York: Oxford University Press, 89), 94.

22. Ibid.
23. See *At Cold War's End: U.S. Intelligence on the Soviet Union and Eastern Europe, 1989–1991* (Washington, D.C.: Center for the Study of Intelligence, 1999).
24. Thomas F. Troy, "The Quaintness of the U.S. Intelligence Community: Its Origin, Theory, and Problems," *International Journal of Intelligence and CounterIntelligence* 2 (Summer 1988): 258.
25. Richelson, *The U.S. Intelligence Community*, 69.
26. Ibid., 32.
27. Managing a particular collection system in U.S. intelligence means that the agency controls virtually all aspects of the system and is legally responsible for development, procurement, deployment, maintenance, use, and the consequences emanating from its use.
28. Public Law 107-56; 115 Stat. 272 (26 October 2001).
29. See *FBI Intelligence Investigations, Coordination within Justice on Counterintelligence Matters Is Limited*, GAO-01-780 (Washington, D.C.: Government Accounting Office, July 2001).
30. See David Boren, "Counterintelligence for the 1990s," *American Intelligence Journal* 10 (Summer–Fall 1989): 12–13.
31. Loch K. Johnson, *Bombs, Bugs, Drugs, and Thugs: Intelligence and America's Quest for Security* (New York: New York University Press, 2000), 109.
32. David Johnston, "CIA Director Will Lead Center to Combine Agencies' Information on Terror Danger," *New York Times*, 29 January 2003.
33. See Vernon Loeb, "9/ Failure No Obstacle to Intelligence Leaders' Success," *Washington Post*, 13 January 2003.

Chapter 3: Pitfalls of American-Style Intelligence

1. Donald Snow succinctly describes the principles of America's strategic culture in his book, *National Security* (New York: St. Martin's Press, 1995), 24–29.
2. P. Edward Haley, "Legislative-Executive Relations and the United States Intelligence Community," *Harvard Journal of Law and Public Policy* 12 (Spring 1989): 496.

3. David Ignatius, "Not a Job for Kissinger," *Washington Post*, 20 December 2002.

4. Thomas Powers, "Secrets of September 11," *New York Review of Books* 49 (10 October 2002): 50.

5. Ibid.

6. Evan Thomas, "Shadow Struggle," *Newsweek*, 14 October 2002, www.msnbc.com/news/8 647.asp?pne=msn; also see Seymour Hersh, "What Went Wrong?" *New Yorker*, 2 April 2002, www.newyorker.com/?fact/01 fa_fact.

7. Michael Warner, *Central Intelligence: Origin and Evolution* (Washington, D.C.: Center for the Study of Intelligence, 2001), 7.

8. Ibid., 7–8.

9. Statement of Eleanor Hill, Staff Director, Joint Inquiry Staff, *Joint Inquiry Staff Statement, Part 1*, 18 September 2002, 7.

10. See Robert Dreyfuss, "The Pentagon Muzzles the CIA," *American Prospect* 13 (13 December 2002): 26–29.

11. Johnson, *Bombs, Bugs, Drugs, and Thugs*, 201.

12. See Johnson's discussion of Karen Olmsted's and Steven Knott's analyses in ibid., 205–11. Also see Loch Johnson, "Covert Action and Accountability: Decision-Making for America's Secret Foreign Policy," *International Studies Quarterly* 33 (1989): 104–106. On the use of the confirmation process as an oversight tool, see Frank J. Smist, Jr., and Kyle L. Danner, "The Robert Gates Hearings: Using the Confirmation Process to Exercise Intelligence Oversight," paper prepared for delivery at the 1992 Annual Meeting of the American Political Science Association, Palmer House, Chicago, 3–6 September 1992.

13. See James Risen, "Dissent on Assigning Blame as 9/11 Panel Adopts Report," *New York Times*, 11 December 2002; and James Risen and David Stout, "Senators Urge an Overhaul of U.S. Intelligence Operations," *New York Times*, 11 December 2002, both www.nytimes.com; also see Dana Priest and Susan Schmidt, "Disciplinary Action Urged for Failures before 9/11," *Washington Post*, 11 December 2002, www.washingtonpost.com. Also see

Walter Pincus, "Shelby Urges Creating New Intelligence Service," *Washington Post*, 17 December 2002.

14. Arthur S. Hulnick and David W. Mattausch, "Ethics and Morality in United States Intelligence," *Harvard Journal of Law and Public Policy* 12 (Spring 1989): 511.

15. Lowenthal, *Intelligence: From Secrets to Policy*, 3.

16. John Macartney," Intelligence: A Consumer's Guide," paper prepared for delivery at the 1988 Annual Meeting of the American Political Science Association, Washington Hilton, Washington, D.C., 1–4 September 1988.

17. Ibid.

18. Ibid.

19. Arthur S. Hulnick, *Fixing the Spy Machine: Preparing American Intelligence for the Twenty-first Century* (Westport, Conn.: Praeger, 1999), 49–50.

20. Quoted in ibid. 49–58, and passim.

21. Lowenthal, *Intelligence: From Secrets to Policy*, 4.

22. Michael Handel, "Leaders and Intelligence," *Intelligence and National Security* 3 (July 1988): 4.

23. See Dan Eggen, "Broad U.S. Wiretap Powers Upheld," *Washington Post*, 19 November 2002, A1, and Neil A. Lewis, "Court Overturns Limits on Wiretaps to Combat Terror," *New York Times*, 19 November 2002, www.nytimes.com.

24. See Michael Moss and Ford Fessenden, "New Tools for Domestic Spying, and Qualms," *New York Times*, 10 December 2002.

25. Philip Shenon, "Sept. Panel Weighs Ideas for Domestic Intelligence," *New York Times*, 24 September 2003.

26. Don Eggen, "Mueller Defends FBI's Performance," *Washington Post*, 20 December 2002; and David Johnston, "FBI Director Rejects Agency for Intelligence in United States," *New York Times*, 20 December 2002.

27. Quoted in Jonathan D. Salant, "Terror Agency Sought So FBI Isn't Seen as 'Secret Police,'" Associated Press, 17 December 2002, www.signonsandiego.com/news/uniontrib/tue/news/news_1n fbi.html.

28. See Richard B. Schmitt, "Power of Patriot Act in Eye of the Beholder," *Los Angeles Times*, 2 September 2003.

29. Stan A. Taylor and Theodore J. Ralston explore the

myriad pathologies that result from this kind of competition in their article, "The Role of Intelligence in Crisis Management," in *Avoiding War: Problems of Crisis Management*, ed. Alexander George (Boulder, Colo.: Westview, 1991), 400–403.

30. Taylor and Ralston also examine this and other attitudinal problems that cause communications problems in ibid., 403.

31. *Additional Views of Senator Richard C. Shelby, Chair, Senate Select Committee on Intelligence, on the Joint Intelligence Inquiry,* (10 December 2002), 22.

Chapter 4: The Foreign Experience

1. Various national polls since 9/11 have illustrated this phenomenon.

2. See Shenon, "Sept. Panel Weighs Ideas for Domestic Intelligence."

3. *National Intelligence Machinery* (London: Her Majesty's Stationery Office, 2001), 6.

4. In the United Kingdom, the three services are collectively known as the "agencies."

5. "Security Service Act," at www.legislation.hmso.gov.uk.

6. "Iraq, Terrorism, and U.S. Global Leadership," speech before the Center for Strategic and International Studies, Washington, D.C., October 7, 2002.

7. S. 410, "Foreign Intelligence Collection Improvement Act of 2003," stipulates a homeland intelligence agency. See Todd Masse, "Domestic Intelligence in the United Kingdom: Applicability of the MI-5 Model to the United States," *Congressional Research Service Report,* 19 May 2003.

8. *National Intelligence Machinery,* 15–16.

9. Christopher Andrew, "Historical Research on the British Intelligence Community," in *Comparing Foreign Intelligence,* ed. Roy Godson (Washington, D.C.: Pergamon-Brassey's, 1988), 45–48.

10. *National Intelligence Machinery,* 12.

11. Ibid., 24.

12. Rodney C. Richardson, "Yom Kippur War: Grand Deception

or Intelligence Blunder," www.globalsecurity.org/military/library/report/ 91/RRC.htm.

13. See E. L. Zorn, "Israel's Quest for Satellite Intelligence," *Studies in Intelligence*, no. 10 (Winter–Spring 2001): 33–38.

14. Israel's intelligence services are described in Ephraim Kahana, "Reorganizing Israel's Intelligence Community," *International Journal of Intelligence and Counter-Intelligence* 15 (Fall 2002): 416–20.

15. "Inside Israel's Secret Organizations," *Jane's Intelligence Review* (October 1996).

16. See www.fas.org/irp/israel/mossad/index.html.

17. "Missions of Shin Bet Special Operations Unit Viewed," *Ma'ariv*, 11 April 2003.

18. See www.fas.org/irp/world/israel/shin_bet/index.html.

19. See www1.idf.il/aman/site/default.asp.

20. "Inside Israel's Secret Organizations."

21. Sandy Africa and Siyabulela Mlombile, "Transforming the Intelligence Services: Some Reflections on the South African Experience," Project on Justice in Times of Transition, Harvard University, n.d.

22. Act 94-38, 2 December 1994.

23. Act 94-39, 2 December 1994.

24. Section 4 of Act 94-39.

25. Section 7, Committee of Members of Parliament and Inspectors—General of Intelligence Act, Act 94-40, 2 December 1994.

26. Sections 2–6, Act 94-40.

27. "France: Military Intelligence Directorate's Missions Questioned," *FBIS* WEU-97-290, 17 October 1997.

28. See www.fas.org/irp/world/france/defense/dpsd/index.html.

29. See www.fas.org/irp/world/france/defense/brge/index.html.

30. See www.fas.org/irp/world/france/interieur/rg.index.html.

31. See www.fas.org/irp/world/france/interieur/dst/index.html.

32. The problems that this fusion poses for U.S. domestic intelligence are explored in Frederick P. Hitz and Brian J. Weiss, "Helping the CIA and FBI Connect the Dots in

the War on Terror," *International Journal of Intelligence and CounterIntelligence* 17 (Spring 2004): 14–22.

33. Masse, "Domestic Intelligence in the United Kingdom."
34. Article 10, Convention for the Protection of Human Rights and Fundamental Freedoms, Amended by Protocol no. 11.

Chapter 5: Requirements and Priorities

1. Senator Ted Kennedy (D-Mass.), quoted on *ABC Evenings News*, 15 July 2003.
2. Walter Pincus and Dana Priest, "Some Iraq Analysts Felt Pressure from Cheney Visits," *Washington Post*, 5 June 2003.
3. Walter Pincus, "Tenet Defends Iraq Intelligence," *Washington Post*, 31 May 2003.
4. Pincus and Priest, "Some Iraq Analysts."
5. See Eric Schmitt, "Aide Denies Shaping Data to Justify War," *New York Times*, 4 June 2003.
6. See Tom Raum, "Rice: CIA Cleared State of the Union Address," Associated Press, reported in Washingtonpost.com, 11 July 2003. Also see David E. Sanger and James Risen, "CIA Chief Takes Blame in Assertion on Iraqi Uranium," *New York Times*, 12 July 2003.
7. Statement by George Tenet, Director of Central Intelligence, 30 May 2003, www.cia.gov.
8. "In Tenet's Words: 'I Am Responsible' for Review," *New York Times*, 12 July 2003.
9. Jeffrey Goldberg, "The CIA and the Pentagon Take Another Look at al Qaeda and Iraq," *New Yorker*, 10 February 2003, from Lexis-Nexis.
10. See Carl Hulse, "White House Aide behind Uranium Claim, Senator Says," *New York Times*, 17 July 2003; and Walter Pincus, "Tenet Says He Didn't Know about Claim," *Washington Post*, 17 July 2003.
11. Much of the discussion here is based on a paper I delivered at the International Studies Association Annual Conference in San Diego, California, on 18 April 1996. The paper was subsequently published. See Michael A. Turner, "Setting Analytical Priorities in U.S. Intelligence:

A Preliminary Model," *International Journal of Intelligence and CounterIntelligence* 9 (Fall 1996): 313–27.

12. U.S. House of Representatives, Subcommittee on International Security and Scientific Affairs of the Committee on Foreign Affairs, *The Role of Intelligence in the Foreign Policy Process* (Washington, D.C.: Government Printing Office, 1980), 105.

13. Ibid., 104.

14. These issues have been dealt with by a variety of people. A cogent analysis is to be found in Robert M. Gates, "The CIA and American Foreign Policy," *Foreign Affairs* 67 (Winter 1987/88): 226–28.

15. Interview with senior National Intelligence Council official, Washington, D.C., 12 December 1995.

16. For example, see Arthur S. Hulnick, "The Intelligence Producer—Policy Consumer Linkage," *Studies in Intelligence* 29 (Winter 1985); and Reginald Hibbert, "Intelligence and Policy," *Intelligence and National Security* 5 (January 1990): 110–29.

17. Hans Heymann, "The Intelligence-Policy Relationship: From Arm's Length to Love-Hate," paper delivered at the Conference on Intelligence: Policy and Process, U.S. Air Force Academy, Colorado Springs, Colorado, 6–7 June 1984, 8.

18. See "Intelligence and Policy: Bridging the Cultural Divide," seminar report by the Center for the Study of Intelligence, Central Intelligence Agency, 19 January 1993, 4. Also see Davis, "Strategic Warning," 11–13.

19. Interview with senior NIC official, Washington, D.C., 12 December 1995.

20. Hans Morgenthau, *In Defense of the National Interest* (New York: Knopf, 1951); and Charles Beard, *The Idea of the National Interest* (New York: Macmillan, 1934).

21. Heymann, "The Intelligence-Policy Relationship," 1.

22. In U.S. House of Representatives, *The Role of Intelligence in the Foreign Policy Process*, 17.

23. For example, see Secretary of State Warren Christopher's testimony before the Senate Foreign Relations Committee on 4 November 1993, outlining the specific top foreign policy priorities of the Clinton administration. The

testimony can be found in *Vital Speeches of the Day* 60 (1 January 1994): 162–67. For an alternative view, see Walt Whitman Rostow, "The United States in a New World Order," Great Decisions Lecture at the University of St. Thomas, Houston, Texas, 1993.

24. Statement of CIA public affairs official, Washington, D.C., 12 December 1995.
25. David Gries, "New Links between Intelligence and Policy," *Studies in Intelligence* 34 (Summer 1990): 4.
26. Ronald Spiers, in U.S. House of Representatives, *The Role of Intelligence in the Foreign Policy Process*, 108.
27. See "Hill Briefing about Aristide Renews Debate on CIS Role," *Washington Post*, 24 October 1993.
28. "U.S. Fails to Use Intelligence Outlets, Critics Say," *Los Angeles Times*, 24 June 1994. Also see "From Molehill to More of a Mountain," *Washington Post National Weekly*, 9–15 January 1995, 34–35.
29. Gries, "New Links between Intelligence and Policy," 4–5.
30. Joseph S. Nye, Jr., "Peering into the Future," *Foreign Affairs* 73 (July–August 1994): 84.
31. Interview with senior NIC official, Washington, D.C., 12 December 1995. According to this official, whereas approximately 70 percent of analytical resources were devoted to the Soviet Bloc during the Cold War, Russia and Eastern Europe accounted for 8–12 percent of such resources in the 1990s. In terms of resource allocation, weapons proliferation was the dominant analytical priority.
32. Hearing before SSCI on Intelligence Issues, C-SPAN 2, 22 February 1996.
33. See former DCI James Woolsey, "The Future of Intelligence on the Global Frontier," speech before the Executive Club of Chicago, 19 November 1993.
34. See Joseph E. Persico, *Casey* (New York: Viking, 1990).
35. Interview with a senior NIC official, Washington, D.C., 12 December 1995. Also see Gates, "The CIA and American Foreign Policy," 216–18; and Nye. "Peering into the Future," 82–93.
36. Nye, "Peering Into the Future," 88.
37. U.S. House of Representatives, *The Role of Intelligence*

in the Foreign Policy Process, 157.

38. Interview with senior NIC Official, Washington, D.C., 12 December 1995.
39. The CIA's *A Consumer's Guide to Intelligence* (Washington, D.C.: CIA, 1993), 27–31, has a succinct description of the NIC.
40. See *Strategic Investment Plan for Intelligence Community Analysis*, ADCI/AP 2000–2001 (Washington, D.C.: Office of the Director of Central Intelligence).
41. Interview with senior CIA Directorate of Intelligence official, Washington, D.C., 12 December 1995.
42. For a look at the importance of these products, see Gries, "New Links between Intelligence and Policy," 1–3.
43. See U.S. House of Representatives, *The Role of Intelligence in the Foreign Policy Process*, 62.
44. Bruce Clarke, in ibid., 76.
45. Ibid., 65.
46. James N. Rosenau, "Muddling, Meddling, and Modeling: Alternative Approaches to the Study of World Politics in an Era of Rapid Change," *Millennium* 8 (Autumn 1979): 135.
47. See "Woolsey's Departure Is Symptomatic of a Troubled Agency," *Washington Post National Weekly*, 2–8 January 1995, 31.
48. Persico, *Casey*, 2–84.

Chapter 6: Perils of Intelligence Collection

1. See Jeffrey T. Richelson, "From Corona to Lacrosse: A Short History of Satellites," *Washington Post*, 25 February 1990, and Thomas E. Ricks and Alan Sipress, "Spy Planes Seek Out Philippine Guerrillas," *Washington Post*, 21 February 2002.
2. See "Written Statement from CIA Director Tenet," *Washington Post*, 10 August 2003. The white paper (a sanitized national intelligence estimate) issued in 2002 stated, "Baghdad hides large portions of Iraq's WMD efforts. Revelations since the [1991] Gulf War demonstrate the extensive efforts undertaken by Iraq to deny information." Director of Central Intelligence, *Iraq's*

Weapons of Mass Destruction Programs (Washington, D.C.: Central Intelligence Agency, October 2002), 1. The Associated Press also reported that the Hussein regime buried fighter aircraft in the desert. See John J. Lumpkin, "Iraq Fighter Jets Found Buried in the Sand," *San Diego Union Tribune*, 2 August 2003. The Associated Press also reported that the Iraqi government had destroyed its weapons of mass destruction before the 2003 war but had concealed that fact from weapons inspectors and the international community. See Slobodan Lekic, "Hussein Was Bluffing, Aide Says," *San Diego Union Tribune*, 2 August 2003; and Walter Pincus and Dana Priest, "Hussein's Weapons May Have Been Bluff," *Washington Post*, 1 October 2002.

3. Seymour Hersh, "The Intelligence Gap," *New Yorker*, 6 December 1999, 74.

4. According to the Chair of the House Permanent Select Committee on Intelligence, satellites and ground systems accounted for more than half of the National Foreign Intelligence Program (NFIP) collection budget. See U.S. House of Representatives, Staff Study, Permanent Select Committee on Intelligence, *IC21: The Intelligence Community in the 21st Century*, 104th Congress, "Collection Synergy."

5. See James Bamford, "Too Much, Not Enough: The Biggest Intelligence Agency Ought to Know Better," *Washington Post*, 2 June 2002; Ken Guggenheim, "NSA Studies Taped Sept. 10 Messages," Associated Press, 19 June 2002; and John Diamond, "Terror Group's Messengers Steer Clear of NSA Ears," *USA Today*, 18 October 2002.

6. Hersh, "The Intelligence Gap," 76.

7. Ibid.

8. Walter Pincus, "Satellite Agency Has Tradition of Secrecy," *Washington Post*, 25 August 2001.

9. See Douglas Jehl and David Stout, "Cover Story Kept Work for CIA a Secret," *New York Times*, 2 October 2003.

10. See Robert Scheer, "Bush Was All Too Willing to Use Émigrés' Lies," *Los Angeles Times*, 2 September 2003; and Douglas Jehl, "Agency Belittles Information Given

by Iraq Defectors," *New York Times*, 28 September 2003.

11. See Thomas Laird, *Into Tibet: The CIA's First Atomic Spy and His Secret Expedition to Lhasa* (New York: Grove, 2002).

12. See Stansfield Turner, *Secrecy and Democracy: The CIA in Transition* (New York: Harper and Row, 1985), 57–59.

13. Angelo Codevilla, "The CIA's Identity Crisis," *American Enterprise* (January–February 1992): 55.

14. Interview with Dr. John Gannon, former Deputy Director of Intelligence and chairman of the National Intelligence Council, Washington, D.C., April 1996.

15. Commission on the Roles and Capabilities of the United States Intelligence Community, *Preparing for the 21st Century* (Washington, D.C.: Government Printing Office, 1996), 88.

16. See www.oss.net

17. See Section 5.1 of the Director of Central Intelligence Directive 1/7, "Security Controls on the Dissemination of Intelligence Information," effective 15 June 1996.

18. See U.S. Senate, Select Committee on Intelligence and the House Permanent Select Committee on Intelligence, *Joint Inquiry into Intelligence Community Activities before and after the Terrorist Attacks of September 11, 2001* (Washington, D.C.: Government Printing Office, December 2002), xvii.

19. Quoted in Vernon Loeb, "When Hoarding Secrets Threatens National Security," *Washington Post*, 26 January 2003.

20. *A Consumer's Guide to Intelligence*, 33.

21. For an analysis of the program and the VEIL codeword, see Bob Woodward, *VEIL: The Secret Wars of the CIA, 1981–1987* (New York: Simon & Schuster, 1987).

22. John Macartney, "Intelligence: A Consumer's Guide," paper prepared for delivery at the 1988 Annual Meeting of the American Political Science Association, the Washington Hilton, Washington, D.C., 1–4 September 1988.

23. Daniel Patrick Moynihan, "Secrecy as Government Regulation," *Political Science & Politics* 30 (June 1997): 165.

24. See Dana Milbank, "Barriers to 9/11 Inquiry Decried,"

Washington Post, 19 September 2002.

25. Adam Clymer, "Government Openness at Issue as Bush Holds onto Records," *New York Times*, 3 January 2003, www.nytimes.com/ 03/01/03/politics/03SECR.html.

26. James M. Olsen, "The Ten Commandments of Counterintelligence," *Studies in Intelligence* 45 (Winter 2001), www.cia.gov/csi/studies.

27. See Vernon Loeb, "From the 'Hanssen Effect' to Sept. 11," *Washington Post*, 21 October 2002.

28. See the chapter on "Collection Synergy," House of Representatives, *IC21: The Intelligence Community in the 21st Century*.

29. Ibid.

Chapter 7: Analytic Snafus

1. Commission on the Roles and Capabilities of the United States Intelligence Community, *Preparing for the 21st Century*, 83.

2. Richard Betts, "Fixing Intelligence," *Foreign Affairs* 81 (January–February 2002): 50.

3. Richard A. Best, Jr., *Intelligence Issues for Congress* (Washington, D.C.: Congressional Research Service, 2 March 2001), CRS-7.

4. John Macartney, "Intelligence: A Consumer's Guide," paper prepared for delivery at the 1988 Annual Meeting of the American Political Science Association, Washington Hilton, Washington, D.C., 1–4 September 1988.

5. Remarks of DCI George J. Tenet, Oscar Iden Lecture, Georgetown University, Washington, D.C., 18 October 1999.

6. See Francis G. Hoffman, "Thinking Ahead Intelligently," *Naval War College Review* 56 (Winter 2003): 157.

7. David Kahn, *Hitler's Spies: German Military Intelligence in World War II* (New York: Macmillan, 1978), 39–41.

8. G. E. M. Anscombe, *Intention* (Ithaca, N.Y.: Cornell University Press, 1969), 6.

9. See Frank J. Stech, *Political and Military Intention Estimation: A Taxonometric Analysis* (Bethesda, Md.: Mathtech, November 1979), 18.

10. S. Reit, *Masquerade: The Amazing Camouflage Deceptions of World War II* (New York: Hawthorn, 1978).
11. Charles Schmidt, "Understanding Human Actions: Recognizing the Plans and Motives of Other Persons," in *Journal of Cognition and Social Behavior*, ed. S. Carroll and J. W. Payne (Hillsdale, N.J.: Erlbaum, 1976), 57.
12. Tom Robbins, *Villa Incognito* (New York: Bantam Books, 2003), 1.
13. Martin Petersen, "The Challenge for the Political Analyst," *Studies in Intelligence* 47 (Winter 2003), from www.cia.gov/studies.
14. See "Intelligence Community 'Surge' Capability," House of Representatives, *IC21: The Intelligence Community in the 21st Century*, section X.
15. See www.odci.gov/nic/about_page/index.htm.
16. The Defense Intelligence Agency also has its own defense intelligence officers (DIOs), who serve in a similar capacity but produce estimative products primarily for Defense officials. DIOs generally participate in the drafting and approving of national intelligence estimates under the auspices of the NIC.
17. See www.odci.gov/nic/about_page/index.htm
18. Ibid.
19. Richard Lehman, "The Role of Intelligence in the Foreign Policy Process," testimony to the Subcommittee on International Security and Scientific Affairs, House Committee on Foreign Affairs, 8 February 1980.
20. See Douglas Jehl, "Experts: Iraqi Trailers Produced Hydrogen," *San Diego Union Tribune*, 9 August 2003.
21. "Written Statement from CIA Director Tenet," *Washington Post*, 10 August 2003.
22. Angelo Codevilla, "The CIA's Identity Crisis," *American Enterprise* (January–February 1992): 56.
23. Commission on the Roles and Capabilities of the United States Intelligence Community, *Preparing for the 21st Century*, 90.
24. See Don Eggen and John Mintz, "Agency to Concentrate Intelligence Analysis," *Washington Post*, 30 January 2003. The "Daily Threat Matrix" has inspired a television program titled "Threat Matrix" that focuses on fic-

tional U.S. antiterror actions.

25. "CIA Director George J. Tenet Discusses the National Intelligence Estimate," *Washington Post,* 10 August 2003.

26. See "Written Statement from CIA Director Tenet," *Washington Post,* 10 August 2003.

27. Harold P. Ford, *Estimative Intelligence: The Purposes and Problems of National Intelligence Estimating* (Lanham, Md.: University Press of America, 1993), 132.

28. Ibid., 133–34.

29. Cited in Stan A. Taylor and Theodore J. Ralston, "The Role of Intelligence in Crisis Management," in *Avoiding War: Problems of Crisis Management,* ed. Alexander L. George (Boulder, Colo.: Westview, 1991), 407.

30. See Turner, *Secrecy and Democracy,* 11–118.

31. See Letter from DCI George J. Tenet, responding to House Intelligence Committee's criticism of Iraq war data (1 October 03), reprinted in the *Washington Post,* 3 October 2003.

32. T. L. Cubbage, "German Misapprehensions Regarding Overlord: Understanding Failure in the Estimative Process," *Intelligence and National Security* 2 (July 1987): 157.

33. Jack Davis," Combating Mind-Set," *Studies in Intelligence* 36 (1992): 34.

34. Richards J. Heuer, Jr., *The Psychology of Intelligence Analysis* (Washington, D.C.: Center for the Study of Intelligence, Central Intelligence Agency, 1999), xx. Heuer differentiates between inherent uncertainty and induced uncertainty, the former defined as uncertainty created by incomplete information on an issue and the latter defined as the uncertainty created by deception and denial. I am indebted to Richards Heuer's book for many of the points in this part of the chapter.

35. Cited in Heuer, Jr., *Psychology of Intelligence Analysis,* 11–12.

36. Taylor and Ralston, "The Role of Intelligence in Crisis Management," 404–405.

37. Davis, "Combating Mind-Set," 34.

38. Ibid.

39. See letter from J. Goss, Chairman, and Jane Harman, ranking Democrat on the House Permanent Select Committee on Intelligence, to George J. Tenet, Director of Central Intelligence, 25 September 2003, reprinted in the *Washington Post*, 3 October 2003. President George W. Bush in August 2004 nominated Porter Goss as his new DCI; the Senate confirmed him on 22 September 2004.

40. See "Avoiding Political and Technological Surprises in the 1980s," in *Intelligence Requirements for the 1980s: Analysis and Estimates*, ed. Roy Godson (London: Transaction Books, 1980), 85.

41. Cord Meyer, *Facing Reality: From World Federalism to the CIA* (New York: Harper and Row, 1980), 227.

Chapter 8: Getting Intelligence to the Right People

1. President Reagan was especially fond of videotaped biographies of world leaders.

2. *Additional Views of Senator Richard C. Shelby, Chair, Senate Select Committee on Intelligence, on the Joint Intelligence Inquiry*, (10 December 2002), 31.

3. Michael I. Handel, "Leaders and Intelligence," *Intelligence and National Security* 3 (July 1988): 3.

Chapter 9: Contributing Factors

1. David L. Boren, "Counterintelligence for the 1990s," *American Intelligence Journal* 10 (Summer–Fall 1989): 10.

2. See John Norton, "Reflections on Covert Action and Its Anxieties," *International Journal of Intelligence and CounterIntelligence* 4 (Spring 1990): 77–90.

3. James M. Olson, "The Ten Commandments of Counterintelligence," *Studies in Intelligence*, no. 11 (Fall–Winter 2001), www.nacic.gov.

4. Roy K. Jonkers, "Prologue," *American Intelligence Journal* 10 (Summer–Fall 1989): 7.

5. Boren, "Counterintelligence for the 90s," 12.

6. See "About NCIX," on www.nacic.gov/info/about.html.

7. "House Passes Intelligence Bill Seeking to Fix Problems

Revealed by Spy Scandals, 9- Attacks," Associated Press, 27 June 2003.

8. One commentator argues that measures like this, along with onslaughts against U.S. intelligence in the last thirty years, are sapping American counterintelligence capabilities. See W. Raymond Wannall, "Undermining Counterintelligence Capability," *International Journal of Intelligence and CounterIntelligence* 15 (Fall 2002): 321–29.

9. See U.S. Congress, House of Representatives, Committee on the Judiciary, Testimony of Larry Mefford, Executive Assistant Director, Counterterrorism and Counterintelligence, Federal Bureau of Investigation, 22 July 2003.

10. Frederick L. Wettering, "CounterIntelligence: The Broken Triad," *International Journal of Intelligence and CounterIntelligence* 13 (2000): 265.

11. Energy Secretary Bill Richardson's Address to the National Press Club, 3 March 1999.

12. The usefulness and propriety of the polygraph is a highly debated subject. U.S. courts currently do not admit into evidence any information derived from polygraph examinations. Alan P. Zelicoff, "Polygraphs: Worse than Worthless," *Washington Post*, 27 May 2003.

13. Procedures are contained in "Security Controls on the Dissemination of Intelligence Information," DCID 1/7, 15 June 1996; and "Minimum Personnel Security Standards and Procedures Governing Eligibility for Access to Sensitive Compartmented Information," DCID 1/14, 14 April 1986.

14. Michael Hurt, "Leaking National Security Secrets: Effects on Security and Measures to Mitigate," *National Security Studies Quarterly* 7 (Autumn 2001): 5.

15. U.S. Congress, Senate Committee on Energy and Natural Resources, Statement of the Honorable Kyle E. McSlarrow on the Energy Department Polygraph Program, Deputy Secretary of Energy, Department of Energy, 4 September 2003. Also see U.S. House of Representatives Permanent Select Committee on Intelligence, *Report of the Redmond Panel, Improving CounterIntelligence*

Capabilities at the Department of Energy and the Los Alamos, Sandia, and Lawrence Livermore National Laboratories (Washington, D.C.: Government Printing Office, 2000).

16. U.S. House of Representatives, Permanent Select Committee on Intelligence, *U.S. Counterintelligence and Security Concerns: A Status Report, Personnel and Information Security* (Washington, D.C.: Government Printing Office, 1988), 6.

17. Wettering, "Counterintelligence: The Broken Triad," 279.

18. Curt Andersen, "FBI Changing CounterIntelligence to Tackle Growing Economic Espionage Threat," Associated Press, 3 August 2003. Also see National Counterintelligence Executive, *Annual Report to Congress on Foreign Economic Collection and Industrial Espionage* (February 2003), NCIX 2003-100006.

19. Wettering, "Counterintelligence: The Broken Triad," 280–81.

20. Eric Lichtblau, "U.S. Uses Terror Law to Pursue Crimes from Drugs to Swindling," *New York Times*, 28 September 2003.

21. "Surveillance Program Is Killed in Committee," *New York Times*, 18 September 2003. Also see Jeffrey Rosen, "A Cautionary Tale for a New Age of Surveillance," *New York Times*, 7 October 2001.

22. James Rowley, "FBI Seeking Scores of Once-KGB Spies, Book Says," Associated Press, 3 August 1993, cited in Wettering, "Counterintelligence: The Broken Triad," 284.

23. Indeed, the foreign intelligence service of democratic Russia, the SVR, took over the handling of Aldrich Ames from its predecessor, the KGB, in 1991, and ran CIA officer Harold James Nicholson against the United States from 1994 to 1996. Olson, "The 10 Commandments of Counterintelligence."

24. Tim Weiner, "Spies Just Wouldn't Come in from the Cold," *New York Times*, 15 October 1997. Also, see John O. Koehler, *STASI: The Untold Story of the East German Secret Police* (Boulder, Colo.: Westview, 1999), 248–57.

25. Jeffrey Richelson, *A Century of Spies in the Twentieth Century* (New York: Oxford University Press, 1995), 390–91.

26. For example, see John Earl Haynes and Harvey Klehr, *VENONA: Decoding Soviet Espionage in America* (New Haven, Conn.: Yale University Press, 1999).
27. "FBI Is Monitoring War Protesters, Official Says," *Los Angeles Times*, 24 November 2003.
28. Quoted in Spenser S. Hsu, "Scholar Says U.S. Unharmed," *Washington Post*, 28 November 2003.
29. Koehler, *STASI*, 251–52.
30. Title VI, "Oversight of Intelligence Activities," Sec. 503(e) of the 91 Intelligence Authorization Act.
31. See John J. Lumpkin, "Deaths Show CIA Uses Hired Guns in Tough Battle against Terrorism," Associated Press, 27 November 2003.
32. See Frederick L. Wettering, "[C]overt Action: The Disappearing 'C,'" *International Journal of Intelligence and CounterIntelligence* 16 (Winter 2003): 561–72.
33. Roy Godson, "Intelligence: An American View," in *British and American Approaches to Intelligence*, ed. K. G. Robertson (New York: St. Martin's Press, 1987), 27.
34. 46 *Federal Register* 59941(1981). Executive Order 12333 continues to be the basic set of administrative principles governing the operations of the CIA and other U.S. intelligence agencies. Executive Order 12334-46 Federal Register 55955 (1981) addresses oversight issues. Many of EO 12334's oversight provisions were supplanted by the 1991 Intelligence Authorization Act.
35. See Stephen Kinzer, "Regime Change: The Legacy," *American Prospect* (November 2003), from Lexis-Nexis.
36. Peter Kornbluh, "The El Mercurio File: Secret Documents Shine New Light on How the CIA Used a Newspaper to Foment a Coup," *Columbia Journalism Review* (September–October 2003), from Lexis-Nexis.
37. See Robert D. Kaplan, "Special Intelligence," *Atlantic Monthly* 281 (February 1998): 61–62.
38. See Lumpkin, "Deaths Show CIA Uses Hired Guns in Tough Battle against Terrorism."
39. See Alan Sipress and Vernon Loeb, "CIA's Stealth War Centers on Eroding Taliban Loyalty and Aiding Opposition," *Washington Post*, 10 October 2001.
40. Cord Meyer, *Facing Reality: From World Federalism to the CIA* (New York: Harper and Row, 1980), 178.

41. Gregory F. Treverton, *Covert Action: The Limits of Intervention in the Postwar World* (New York: Basic Books, 1987), 201.
42. See John L. Lumpkin, "American al-Qaeda Operatives Can Be Targeted," Associated Press, 4 December 2002; James Risen and David Johnston, "Bush Has Widened Authority of CIA to Kill Terrorists," *New York Times*, 15 December 2002; Thom Shanker and Carlotta Gall, "CIA Tries to Kill Afghan Factional Leader Using Missile from Drone," *San Diego Union Tribune*, 9 May 2002. For a good discussion of U.S. assassinations in the past see the transcript of "U.S. Role in Foreign Assassinations," International Law Society panel discussion, C-SPAN, 14 April 1990.
43. Bill Gertz, "Covert-Action Curbs Fought by Pentagon," *Washington Times*, 14 August 2003.
44. Brewster C. Denny, "The Constitution and Covert Action," lecture given at the University of Washington, 8 May 1989. Also see Kenneth E. Sharpe, "Intelligence vs. Covert Action," *World Outlook*, no. 8 (Winter 1989): 173–87; Loch K. Johnson, "Covert Action and Accountability: Decision-Making for America's Secret Foreign Policy," *International Studies Quarterly* 33 (1989): 81–109; and W. Michael Reisman and James E. Baker, *Regulating Covert Action* (New Haven, Conn.: Yale University Press, 1992).
45. See Arthur S. Hulnick, "U.S. Covert Action: Does It Have a Future?" *International Journal of Intelligence and CounterIntelligence* 9 (Summer 1996): 145–57.
46. The process, over several recent administrations, is examined in detail in William J. Daugherty, "Approval and Review of Covert Action Programs since Reagan," *International Journal of Intelligence and CounterIntelligence* 17 (Spring 2004): 62–80.
47. The National Foreign Intelligence Board (NFIB) comprises sixteen individuals, appointed by the president, who review the performance of the intelligence agencies and assess the management, personnel, and organization of the intelligence community. The Intelligence Oversight Board (IOB), which was made a committee of the NFIB in 1993, prepares reports on intelligence ac-

tivities that may be unlawful or contrary to executive orders or presidential directives.

48. Prior to the Iran-Contra affair, there was ambiguity about whether findings could be oral or retroactive. Following the scandal, Congress mandated new rules stipulating only written findings prior to the commencement of a covert operation. See Johnson, "Covert Action and Accountability," 97–99.

49. Because of previous ambiguities in the regulations, various national security directives since the presidency of George H. W. Bush have required a written finding in each case of proposed covert action. The finding procedure has been in existence in some form since the Hughes-Ryan Amendment of 1974. Foreign Assistance Act of 1974. PL 93-559, Section 662, 88 Stat. 1795, 1804(1974). Hughes-Ryan was streamlined by the Intelligence Oversight Act of 1980, passed as Title V of the Intelligence Authorization Act for Fiscal Year 1981, PL 96-450, Section 501, 94 Stat. 1981(1980). The Intelligence Authorization Act of 1991 replaced Hughes-Ryan and streamlined covert-action procedures.

50. PL 102-88.

51. Twentieth Century Fund, *The Need to Know: Covert Action and American Democracy* (New York: Twentieth Century Fund, 1992), 57.

52. For an overview of congressional oversight of CA, see Gary J. Schmitt and Abram N. Shulsky, "The Theory and Practice of Separation of Powers: The Case of Covert Action," in *The Fettered Presidency*, ed. L. Gordon Crovitz and Jeremy A. Rabkin (Washington, D.C.: American Enterprise Institute, 1989), 59–81.

53. U.S. Constitution, Article I, Section 9, Clause 7.

54. The conditions and procedures governing these exceptions are enumerated in various national security directives, all based on National Security Decision Directive 286, promulgated in October 1987.

55. Interviews with several former congressional staff members (2003).

56. These three factors are developed fully in Wettering, "Counterintelligence: The Broken Triad," 289–93.

57. 18 USC 794.

58. Under the Espionage Act, the government must show that the accused person has knowingly communicated or delivered to a foreign entity material related to national security with the intent to injure the United States, for the advantage of a foreign entity, or for personal gain. Quoted in Wettering, "Counterintelligence: The Broken Triad," 289.

59. Elizabeth E. Anderson, "Covert Action and American Foreign Policy: A Case Study of the Iran-Contra Operation," paper delivered at the International Studies Association Convention, Atlanta, Georgia, 31 March–4 April 1992.

60. David Isenberg, "The Pitfalls of U.S. Covert Operations," *Policy Analysis*, no. 118 (7 April 1989), www.cato.org/pubs/pas.

Chapter 10: Intelligence Priorities and Their Challenges

1. John Seely Brown and Jeffrey R. Cooper, "Intelligence: We've Lost Our Edge," *Washington Post*, 10 May 2005.

2. For an analysis of the Iranian and North Korean perspectives on their respective nuclear programs, see Gordon Fairclough and David Crawford, "Iran, Supported by IAEA Tests, Rejects Nuke Deal," *Wall Street Journal*, 8 August 2005; William J. Cole, "Dual Policy Used to Solve Nuclear Standoff with Iran, N. Korea," Associated Press, 9 August 2005; Nazila Fathi and Thomas Fuller, "Iran Reopens Uranium Processing Plant As U.N. Agency Meets," *New York Times*, 11 August 2005; and Jay Solomon, Marc Champion, and Gordon Fairclough, "Nuclear Bargaining May Harden," *Wall Street Journal*, 11 August 2005.

3. Paul R. Pillar, *Terrorism and U.S. Foreign Policy* (Washington, D.C.: Brookings Institution Press, 2001), 25.

4. Ibid., 111.

5. Ibid., 114–15.

6. Executive Order 12333, 4 December 1981.

7. Homeland Security Secretary Michael Chertoff acknowledged in April 2005 that his department failed at times to assemble and share intelligence adequately and as-

serted that DHS must be a full partner at the table with the intelligence community. "Chertoff Says DHS Must Be Full Partner With IC," *AFIO (Association of Former Intelligence Officers) Weekly Notes*, 18 April 2005. Also see Lara Jakes Jordan, "Chertoff to Overhaul Homeland Security," *Washington Post*, 13 July 2005; Clark Kent Ervin, "Homeland Security's Intelligence Gap," *New York Times*, 17 July 2005; Douglas Jehl, "Bush to Create New Unit in F.B.I. for Intelligence," *New York Times*, 30 June 2005; and Dan Eggan and Walter Pincus, "Bush Approves Spy Agency Changes," *Washington Post*, 30 June 2005.

8. See Dan Eggan, "Permanent Patriot Act Proposed," *Washington Post*, 21 July 2005.

9. See Lisa Langdon, Alexander J. Sarapu, and Matthew Wells, "Targeting the Leadership of Terrorist and Insurgent Movements: Historical Lessons for Contemporary Policymakers," *Journal of Public and International Affairs* 15 (Spring 2004): 60–78.

10. Testimony at the Hearing of the Senate Armed Services Committee on Threats to U.S. National Security, *Federal News Service*, 17 March 2005, from Lexis-Nexis.

11. *The 9/11 Commission Report* (Washington, D.C.: Government Printing Office, 22 July 2004), 380.

12. Quoted in Corine Hegland and Greg Webb, "The Threat," *National Journal*, 5 April 2005, http://nationaljournal.com/scropts/printpage.cgi?/members/news/2005/04/0415nj.htm

13. See Walter Pincus, "CIA Finds No Evidence Hussein Sought to Arm Terrorists," *Washington Post*, 16 November 2003; and Richard W. Stevenson, "Iraq Illicit Arms Gone Before War, Departing Inspector States," *New York Times*, 24 January 2004.

14. Loch K. Johnson, *Bombs, Bugs, Drugs, and Thugs: Intelligence and America's Quest for Security* (New York: New York University Press, 2000), 23.

15. Eggen and Pincus, "Bush Approves Spy Agency Changes."

16. See John Mintz and Joby Warrick, "U.S. Unprepared Despite Progress, Experts Say," *Washington Post*, 8 November 2004.

17. News Release, National Intelligence Strategy, 26 October 2005, www.dni.gov/release_letter_102505.html.
18. Douglas Jehl, "Spy Agencies Told to 'Bolster the Growth of Democracy,'" *New York Times*, 27 October 2005.
19. News Release, National Intelligence Strategy, 26 October 2005, www.dni.gov/release_letter_102505.html.
20. See Center for the Study of Intelligence, *Intelligence and Policy: The Evolving Relationship, Roundtable Report* (Washington, D.C.: Central Intelligence Agency, June 2004).
21. Linda Robinson, "Tinker, Tailor, Soldier, Spy," *U.S. News & World Report*, 25 April 2005, 34, 37; Walter Pincus, "Pentagon to Upgrade Intelligence Structure," *Washington Post*, 24 March 2005; Barton Gellman, "Secret Unit Expands Rumsfeld's Domain," *Washington Post*, 25 January 2005; Josh White and Barton Gellman, "Defense Espionage Unit to Work with CIA," *Washington Post*, 25 January 2005; and Eric Schmitt, "Intelligence: Pentagon Sends Its Spies to Join Fight on Terror," *New York Times*, 24 January 2005.
22. Mark M. Lowenthal, *Intelligence: From Secrets to Policy* (Washington, D.C.: Congressional Quarterly Press, 2000), 180–81.
23. Linda Robinson, "Plan of Attack," *U.S. News & World Report*, 1 August 2005, 30.
24. For a comprehensive discussion of the issues in cyber- and net-war, see John Arquilla and David Ronfeldt, *In Athena's Camp: Preparing for Conflict in the Information Age* (Santa Monica, Calif.: National Defense Research Institute, RAND Corporation, 1997). For an example of the effects of information warfare on antiterrorism and individual actions, see Dionne Searcey, "Cellphone Lines Draw Scrutiny," *Wall Street Journal*, 12 August 2005.
25. Amos A. Jordan, William J. Taylor, Jr., and Michael J. Mazarr, *American National Security* (Baltimore, Md.: Johns Hopkins University Press, 1999), 168.
26. Interview with a U.S. national security official, Washington, D.C., 5 August 2005. Also see Bradley Graham, "Hackers Attack via Chinese Web Sites," *Washington Post*, 25 August 2005; and Lara Jakes Jordan, "Home-

land Security Information Network Criticized," *Washington Post*, 10 May 2005.

27. Jay Solomon, "FBI Sees Big Threat from Chinese Spies; Business Wonder," *Wall Street Journal*, 10 August 2005.

28. See Michael Isikoff and Daniel Klaidman, "Look Who's Not Talking—Still," *Newsweek*, 4 April 2005, 30–31; and Dana Priest, "Panel Warns of 'Headstrong Agencies'," *Washington Post*, 1 April 2005.

29. Lowenthal, *Intelligence: From Secrets to Policy*, 174–75.

30. See "The Role of Intelligence Services in a Globalized World," remarks by John C. Gannon, Chairman, National Intelligence Council, at the Conference Sponsored by Friedrich Ebert Stiffung, Berlin, Germany, 21 May 2001.

31. Johnson, *Bombs, Bugs, Drugs, and Thugs*, 82–83.

32. For a full description of the MEDEA Program, see ibid., 60–66.

33. Robinson, "Plan of Attack," 30.

34. Lowenthal, *Intelligence: From Secrets to Policy*, 178.

35. The press has reported that the Europeans suspect that an NSA collection effort, known as Echelon, targets communications worldwide in order to provide economic intelligence to American corporations. U.S officials have acknowledged that the United States collects information regarding the use of bribery and other illegal efforts by foreign firms in competition with American corporations. See Richard Best, *Project Echelon: U.S. Electronic Surveillance* (Washington, D.C.: Congressional Research Service Report RS20444, 2 March 2000).

36. For an example of the politics of UAV procurement, see Jonathan Karp, "Lockheed Proposes Changes to Army's Spy-Plane Program," *Wall Street Journal*, 12 August 2005. Also see Bruce V. Bigelow, "Army Chooses General Atomics' Unmanned Aircraft," *San Diego Union Tribune*, 11 August 2005.

37. "Opening Up the CIA," *Newsweek*, 8 August 2005, 5.

38. Testimony before the Homeland Security Subcommittee on Intelligence, Information Sharing, and Terrorism Risk Assessment, *Congressional Quarterly*, 21 June 2005, from Lexis-Nexis.

39. P.L. 107-56.
40. "Expanded Patriot Act to Be Proposed," *Washington Post*, 19 May 2005.
41. See "CIA Acknowledges Iraqi WMD Error," *AFIO Weekly Notes*, 8 January 2005.
42. The Abu Ghraib prison scandal in 2004, in which military intelligence and CIA officers were accused of mistreating Iraqi prisoners, is a case in point. See Josh White, "Documents Tell of Brutal Improvisation by GIs," *Washington Post*, 3 August 2005; and Kevin Sullivan, "Detainees Allege Abuse En Route to Guantanamo," *Washington Post*, 3 August 2005.
43. Senator Carl Levin (D-Mich.), Opening Comments of Hearings of the Senate Armed Services Committee on Threats to U.S. National Security, *Federal News Service*, 17 March 2005, from Lexis-Nexis.
44. David Morgan, "US Ignored Forecasts of Iraqi Turmoil-CIA," Reuters, 12 October 2005; and "White House Ignored CIA Warning on Iraq," *The National Security Archive*, 13 October 2005, http://www.gwu.edu/~nsarchiv/20051013/index.htm
45. See Kevin Whitelaw. "Getting It 'Dead Wrong,'" *U.S. News and World Report*, 11 April 2005, 32–33; and Kevin Whitelaw, "In Saddam's Ominous Shadow," *U.S. News and World Report*, 28 March 2005, 32, 34. The Iraq WMD intelligence failure has apparently inured even allies to administration claims that Iran is developing a nuclear weapons capability. See Carla Anne Robbins, "As Evidence Grows of Iran's Program, U.S. Hits Quandary," *Wall Street Journal*, 18 March 2005; and "Iran Holds Big Bargaining Chips in Dispute," *Wall Street Journal*, 18 August 2005.

Chapter 11: Toward Smarter Intelligence

1. Working Group on Intelligence Reform, *The Future of U.S. Intelligence* (Washington, D.C.: The National Strategy Information Center, 1996), cited in Jack Davis, "Improving CIA Analytic Performance: Analysts and the Policymaking Process," *Kent Center Occasional Papers*

1, no. 2 (September 2002): 6.

2. Quoted in William D. Nordhaus, "Iraq: The Economic Consequences of War," *New York Review of Books* 49 (5 December 2002): 9.

3. Recommendations of the Joint Intelligence Inquiry, 10 December 2002, 1–2.

4. Quoted in James Risen and David Johnston, "Lawmakers Want Cabinet Level Post for an Intelligence Director," *New York Times*, 8 December 2002; also see Frank Davies, "Bill to Create U.S. 'Czar' over Intelligence Agencies Offered," *San Diego Union Tribune*, 1 August 2003.

5. Richard A. Stubbing and Melvin A. Goodman, "How to Fix U.S. Intelligence," *Christian Science Monitor*, 26 June 2002.

6. This is the view of Senator Richard C. Shelby (R-Ala.), the former chair of the Senate Select Committee on Intelligence. See "September 11 and the Imperative of Reform in the U.S. Intelligence Community," *Additional Views of Senator Richard C. Shelby, Chair, Senate Select Committee on Intelligence, on the Joint Intelligence Inquiry,* (10 December 2002), 19.

7. This chronology comes from Larry C. Kindsvater, "The Need to Reorganize the Intelligence Community," *Studies in Intelligence* 47 (2003), from www.cia.gov.

8. Michael Moran, "Two Years On, U.S. Spy Landscape Little Changed," *MSNBC Special Report*, 29 August 2003, www.msnbc.com/news/948 1.asp

9. See Dan Eggen and John Mintz, "Agency to Concentrate Intelligence Analysis," *Washington Post*, 30 January 2003. The "daily threat matrix" probably refers to the *President's Daily Brief*, the principal intelligence document presented to the president and his senior officers nearly every day of the week.

10. *Additional Views of Senator Richard C. Shelby*, 19.

11. U.S. House of Representatives, *IC21: The Intelligence Community in the 21st Century*, Section XII.

12. Ibid.

13. According to a Directorate of Intelligence review in the mid-1990s, a vast majority of analytical personnel assigned to serve rotations in the centers were poor per-

formers. To alleviate this and similar problems, the DI instituted in the 1990s a policy of denying senior-level assignments without "out of directorate" experience, including rotations as the centers.

14. See Philip Shenon, "Sept. Panel Weighs Ideas for Domestic Intelligence," *New York Times*, 24 September 2003.

15. PL 107-56; 115 Stat. 272 (26 October 2001).

16. *Additional Views of Senator Richard C. Shelby*, 7.

17. Rear Adm. Lowell E. Jacoby, written statement presented to Joint Intelligence Inquiry, 1 October 2002, 2, cited in *Additional Views of Senator Richard C. Shelby*, 38.

18. Written Statement presented to the Joint Intelligence Inquiry, 1 October 2002, 15–16, in *Additional Views of Senator Richard C. Shelby*, 38.

19. See "Surveillance Program Is Killed by Committee," Reuters, 18 September 2003.

20. Data mining is a controversial procedure that many civil libertarians fear will undermine the freedoms and civil liberties of Americans. Senator Russell Fiengold (D-Wis.) introduced on 31 July 2003 the "Data Mining Reporting Act of 2003," which would require all federal agencies to report to Congress within ninety days and every year thereafter on data-mining programs used to find a pattern indicating terrorist or other criminal activity and how these programs implicate the civil liberties and privacy of all Americans. See "Statement of Senator Feingold on Introduced Bills and Joint Resolutions," *Congressional Record* 149 (31 July 2003): S10672–S10673.

21. Information from Dr. William Perry, Professor of Information Systems and Technology, Western Carolina University, Cullowhee, N.C., December 2003.

22. *Additional Comments of Senator Richard C. Shelby*, 40–42.

23. Rear Adm. Jacoby, written statement, 8, cited in Additional Comments of Senator Richard C. Shelby, 40.

24. Jack Davis, "Improving CIA Analytic Performance: Strategic Warning," *Kent Center Occasional Papers* 1, no.1 (September 2002): 8.

25. These recommendations are adapted from Harold P. Ford, "The Primary Purpose of National Estimating," *Studies in Intelligence* 35, no. 3 (Fall 1991): 76–78.

26. Adm. David Jeremiah (Ret.), *Intelligence Community's Performance on the Indian Nuclear Tests* (Washington, D.C.: Central Intelligence Agency, 1998).

27. Davis, "Improving CIA Analytic Performance: Strategic Warning," 8.

28. This list of techniques is derived from Jack Davis, "Sherman Kent's Final Thoughts on Analyst-Policymaker Relations," *Kent Center Occasional Papers* 2, no. 3 (June 2003): 10–11.

29. Davis, "Improving CIA Analytic Performance: Strategic Warning," 8.

30. Douglas J. MacEachin, "Tradecraft of Analysis," in *U.S. Intelligence at the Crossroads: Agendas for Reform*, ed. Roy C. Godson, Ernest May, and Gary Schmitt (Washington, D.C.: Brassey's, 1995).

31. Davis, "Improving CIA Analytic Performance: Strategic Warning," 8.

32. Jack Davis, "Improving CIA Analytic Performance: Analysts and the Policymaking Process," *Kent Center Occasional Papers* 1, no. 2 (September 2002): 8.

33. Jack Davis, "Strategic Warning: If Surprise Is Inevitable, What Role for Analysis?" *Kent Center Occasional Papers* 2, no. 1 (January 2003): 11.

Glossary

actionable intelligence Intelligence based on solid information and reliable sources that enables decision makers to take action with a high degree of confidence.

analysis A process preceding the production stage of the intelligence cycle in which intelligence information is systematically examined in order to identify significant facts, derive conclusions, and establish forecasts.

assessment Appraisal of the value of an intelligence activity, source, information, or product in terms of its contribution to a specific goal, or the credibility, reliability, relevance, accuracy, and usefulness of information.

briefing Presentation, usually in oral form, of intelligence information. The preparation of an individual for a specific operation by describing the situation to be encountered, the methods to be used, and the objectives to be achieved. Also the introduction of an individual into a classified, compartmented program or project by describing and explaining the program.

case officer An intelligence officer whose primary job is to identify, evaluate, assess, and recruit foreign spies to provide critical information of intelligence value. (Also see **human intelligence**.)

Central Intelligence Agency (CIA) An independent U.S. government agency and a member of the intelligence community. Established by the National Security Act of 1947 to coordinate intelligence activities, the CIA collects, analyzes, produces, and disseminates current and long-term foreign intelligence and counterintelligence; conducts counterintelligence activities abroad; conducts special activities approved by the president; and conducts research, development, and procurement of technical systems and devices.

clandestine operation A secret intelligence activity to collect information or to conduct covert political, economic, propaganda, or paramilitary action.

classification The determination that official information requires a specific degree of protection against unauthorized disclosure, accompanied by a designation that such a determination has been made; the designation results in a security classification and includes Confidential, Secret, and Top Secret. (Also see **declassification**.)

collection The exploitation of information by collection agencies, and the delivery of the information obtained to the appropriate unit in the analysis and production of intelligence. Also obtaining information in any manner, including direct observations, liaison with official foreign and domestic agencies, or solicitation from official, unofficial, or public sources, or quantitative data from the test or operation of foreign systems.

collection requirement An established intelligence need that drives intelligence collection and affects the allocation of intelligence resources. (Also see **intelligence requirement**.)

communications intelligence (COMINT) Technical and intelligence information derived from the intercept of foreign communications, but does not include the monitoring of foreign public media or the intercept of communications obtained during counterintelligence investigations within the United States. COMINT includes the fields of traffic analysis, cryptanalysis, and direction finding.

competitive intelligence Competition among agencies to collect, analyze, and produce intelligence and thereby advance their individual bureaucratic interests.

confidential Security classification applied to information that, if disclosed in an unauthorized manner, could reasonably be expected to cause damage to national security.

consumer An authorized person, such as a political leader or policymaker, who uses intelligence information directly in the decision-making process to produce other intelligence. (Also referred to as customer.)

coordination The process of seeking concurrence from one or more groups, organizations, agencies, or other national security entities regarding an intelligence activity in which they may share some responsibility. In intelligence production, the process by which producers gain the views of other producers on the adequacy of a specific assessment, estimate, or report; the intent is to increase a product's factual accuracy, clarify its judgments, and resolve or sharpen statements of disagreement on major contentious issues.

counterintelligence Information gathered and activities conducted to protect against espionage, other intelligence activities, sabotage, or assassinations conducted for or on behalf of foreign powers, organizations, persons, terrorists, or terrorist groups.

counterterrorism Intelligence analysis about and offensive measures taken to prevent, deter, and respond to a terrorist act, or the documented threat of such an act.

cover An alternative, sometimes fictitious, background and employment history provided to an intelligence officer for the purpose of facilitating his intelligence activities. A cover story may be official or unofficial, depending on the circumstance and the need.

covert action An operation designed to influence governments, events, organizations, or persons in support of foreign policy objectives in a manner that is not necessarily attributable to the sponsoring power; it may include political and economic activities, propaganda, and paramilitary action.

current intelligence Intelligence of all types and forms of immediate interest to the users of intelligence; it may be disseminated without complete evaluation, interpretation, analysis, and integration.

deception Purposeful attempt to manipulate perceptions in order to gain an advantage. Deception employs a variety of techniques, including disinformation, to affect decision-maker attitudes.

declassification Removal of official information from the protective status afforded by security classification; it requires a determination that disclosure no longer would be detrimental to national security. (Also see **classification**.)

Defense Intelligence Agency (DIA) An agency of the intelligence community responsible for providing strategic military intelligence to the secretary of defense, the Joint Chiefs of Staff, the military commands, other Defense Department components, and, as appropriate, non-Defense agencies. It provides military intelligence to national foreign intelligence and counterintelligence products and is responsible for coordinating the intelligence activities of the military services and managing the Defense Attaché System.

director of central intelligence (DCI) Until December 2004, the DCI was the primary adviser to the president and National Security Council on national foreign intelligence, appointed by the president and confirmed by the Senate; head of the intelligence community and responsible for the development and execution of the National Foreign Intelligence Program; director of the Central Intelligence Agency.

Director of Central Intelligence Directive (DCID) A directive issued by the DCI that outlines general policies and procedures to be followed by intelligence agencies and organizations that are under his direction.

director of national intelligence (DNI) A position created in December 2004 to supplant the authorities of the director of central intelligence in coordinating the intelligence community, advising the president on intelligence matters, and executing the National Foreign Intelligence program.

disinformation True or false information intended to mislead and direct recipient toward an identifiable foreign policy objective. (Also see **deception**.)

dissemination The distribution of intelligence products in any form to departmental and agency intelligence consumers. (Also see **intelligence cycle**.)

Drug Enforcement Administration Agency charged with enforcing America's laws against the production, importation, sale, and use of controlled substances.

economic intelligence Intelligence regarding foreign economic resources, activities, and policies regarding the production, distribution, and consumption of goods and services, labor, finance, taxation, and other aspects of the international economic system. Includes the economic potential of a nation to wage war.

electronic intelligence (ELINT) Technical and intelligence information derived from foreign electromagnetic transmissions other than communications. (Also see **communications intelligence**.)

energy intelligence Intelligence relating to the technical, economic, and political capabilities and programs of foreign countries to engage in the development, utilization, and commerce of basic and advanced energy technologies. It includes the location and extent of foreign energy resources and their allocation; foreign government energy policies, plans, and programs; new and improved foreign energy supply, demand, production, distribution, and utilization.

estimative intelligence A category of intelligence that attempts to project probable future foreign courses of action and developments and their implications for U.S. interests; it may or may not be coordinated and may be either departmental or national intelligence.

evaluation Appraisal of the value of an intelligence activity, information, or products to intelligence requirements and needs. An appraisal of the credibility, reliability, relevance, accuracy, or usefulness of information. Information is appraised at several stages within the intelligence cycle under different contexts. Also a process in the analysis stage of the intelligence cycle. (Also see **assessment**, **intelligence cycle**.)

exploitation The process of obtaining intelligence information from any source and taking advantage of it for intelligence purposes. In SIGINT, the production of information from messages that are encrypted in systems whose basic elements are known. Includes decryption, translation, and the solution of specific controls such as indicators and specific keys. (Also see **source**.)

finding A determination made by the president stating that a particular intelligence operation is in the national security interest of the United States in compliance with several laws, including the Intelligence Activities Act and Executive Order 12333.

finished intelligence The product resulting from the collection, integration, analysis, evaluation, and interpretation of information concerning foreign countries or issues. The final result of the production step of the intelligence cycle; the intelligence product.

flexible accountability Practice of varying the amount and degree of intelligence accountability in order to provide intelligence agencies with the flexibility to accomplish their objectives.

geospatial intelligence (GEOINT) The complete digital visualization of geographical areas of the earth, enabling intelligence analysts and military commanders to "see" target areas remotely in complete detail. This new "int" is now under the jurisdiction of the National Geospatial Intelligence Agency (NGA), the successor to the National Imagery and Mapping Agency (NIMA).

human intelligence (HUMINT) Intelligence information acquired by human sources through clandestine collection techniques and open-source data from foreign media; espionage.

imagery intelligence (IMINT) The products of imagery and imagery interpretation processed for intelligence use.

intelligence assessment A category of intelligence production that encompasses most analytic studies dealing with subject of policy significance; it is thorough in its treatment of subject matter but, unlike estimative intelligence, does not attempt to project the future.

intelligence cycle The process by which information is acquired and converted into intelligence and made available to consumers. There are four steps in the cycle, although the CIA asserts that it has five stages.

intelligence estimate The product of estimative intelligence. In military usage, an appraisal of available intelligence relating to a specific situation or condition with a view to determining the course of action open to the enemy or potential enemy and the probable order of their adoption. (Also see **estimative intelligence**.)

intelligence information Information of potential intelligence value concerning the capabilities, intentions, and activities of any foreign power, organization, or associated personnel.

intelligence officer A professional employee of an intelligence organization engaged in intelligence activities.

Intelligence Oversight Board (IOB) A committee of the National Foreign Intelligence Board, the Intelligence Oversight Board oversees the legality and propriety of U.S. intelligence activities.

intelligence producer An organization or agency that participates in the production stage of the intelligence cycle.

intelligence requirement Any subject—general or specific—on which there is a need for the collection of intelligence or the production of intelligence.

measurement and signature intelligence (MASINT) Scientific and technical information obtained by quantitative and qualitative analysis of data derived from specific technical sensors for the purpose of identifying any distinctive features associated with the source, emitter, or sender and to facilitate subsequent identification or measurement of the source.

National Foreign Intelligence Board (NFIB) The senior intelligence community advisory body to the DNI on the substantive and legal aspects of national intelligence. The board advises the DNI on production, review, and coordination of national intelligence; interagency exchanges of foreign intelligence information; arrangements with foreign governments on intelligence matters; the protection of sources and methods; activities of common concern; and such matters as are referred to it by the DNI. The Oversight Intelligence Board (OIB) is a committee of the NFIB. (Also see **Intelligence Oversight Board**.) The NFIB is composed of the principals of the civilian intelligence community agencies; senior officers of the military intelligences participate as observers, as does the representative of the adviser to the president on national security affairs.

National Intelligence Council (NIC) The National Intelligence Council is composed of the NIOs, their staffs, and an analytic group. The NIOs support the DNI by producing national intelligence estimates, other interagency assessments, and by advising him on intelligence needs of policy consumers. (See **NIO.**)

national intelligence estimate (NIE) A thorough assessment of a situation in the foreign environment that is relevant to the formulation of foreign, economic, and national security policy and that projects probable future courses of actions and developments; it illuminates differences of view within the intelligence community; it is issued by the DNI with the advice of the NFIB. The NIE is a strategic estimate of capabilities, vulnerabilities, and probable courses of action of foreign nations that is produced at the national level as a composite of the views of the intelligence community agencies. Special NIEs (SNIEs) focus on immediate concerns and have shorter time frames.

National Intelligence Officer (NIO) The senior staff officer of the DNI for an assigned area of functional or geographic responsibility. The NIO manages the estimative process and interagency intelligence production on behalf of the DNI; is the principal point of contact between the DNI and intelligence consumers below the cabinet level; and is a primary source of national-level substantive guidance to intelligence community planners, collectors, and resource managers.

national security The territorial integrity, sovereignty, and international freedom of action of the United States. Intelligence activities relating to national security encompass all the military, economic, political, scientific, technological, and other aspects of foreign developments that pose actual or potential threats to U.S. national interests.

National Security Agency (NSA) An agency of the intelligence community responsible for highly specialized technical collection of intercepted communications, decryption of foreign communication systems, and provision of communications security to U.S. government agencies.

need A general or specific request for intelligence information made by a member of the intelligence community.

Open Source Center Established in November 2005 within the CIA to coordinate the exploitation of open-source materials and devise new and creative mechanisms for the use of open-source materials in intelligence products.

production The preparation of reports based on analysis of information to meet the needs of intelligence users—consumers—within and outside the intelligence community.

raw intelligence A colloquial term meaning collected intelligence information that has not yet been converted into finished intelligence.

requirements category A category of substantive foreign intelligence information that is of interest to the U.S. government. The DNI approves priorities for requirements categories that are reference points for actions in the intelligence cycle.

secret Security classification applied to information which, if disclosed in an unauthorized manner, could reasonably be expected to cause serious damage to national security.

signals intelligence (SIGINT) Intelligence information derived from signals intercepts comprising all communications intelligence, electronic intelligence, and foreign instrumentation signals intelligence, however transmitted.

telemetry intelligence (TELINT) Intelligence derived from the interception, processing, and analysis of electronic signals emanating from foreign test equipment, such as space launch rockets and weapons systems.

top secret Security classification applied to information that, if disclosed in an unauthorized manner, could reasonably be expected to cause exceptionally grave damage to national security.

Portions adapted from *A Consumer's Guide to Intelligence* (Washington, D.C.: Central Intelligence Agency, 1994), 37–43.

Bibliography

General Works

Ameringer, Charles. *U.S. Foreign Intelligence, The Secret Side of American History* (Lexington, Mass.: Lexington Books, 1990).

Andrew, Christopher. *For the President's Eyes Only: Secret Intelligence and the American Presidency from Washington to Bush* (New York: HarperCollins, 1995).

Axelrod, Alan. *The War between the Spies: A History of Espionage during the American Civil War* (New York: Atlantic Monthly Press, 1992).

Babbington-Smith, Constance. *Air Spy: The Story of Photo Intelligence in World War II* (New York: Harper and Brothers, 1957).

Barnett, Thomas P. M. *The Pentagon's New Map* (New York: Berkley Books, 2004).

Berkowitz, Bruce, and Allan E. Goodman. *Strategic Intelligence for American National Security* (Princeton, N.J.: Princeton University Press, 1989).

Best, Jr., Richard A. *Intelligence Issues for Congress* (Washington, D.C.: Congressional Research Service, March 2, 2001).

Betts, Richard. "Fixing Intelligence." *Foreign Affairs* 81 (January–February 2002).

Born, Hans, Loch K. Johnson, and Ian Leigh. *Who's Watching the Spies? Establishing Intelligence Service Accountability* (Washington, D.C.: Potomac Books, 2005).

Breckenridge, Scott D. *The CIA and the U.S. Intelligence Community* (Boulder, Colo.: Westview, 1986).

Cimbala, Stephen J., ed. *Intelligence and Intelligence Policy in a Democratic Society* (Dobbs Ferry, N.Y.: Trans-National, 1987).

Clarke, Richard. *Against All Enemies: Inside America's War on Terror* (New York: Free Press, 2004).

Cline, Ray. *The CIA: Reality vs. Myth: The Evolution of the Agency from Roosevelt to Reagan* (Washington, D.C.: Acropolis Books, 1982).

Cobban, Alfred. *Ambassador and Secret Agents: The Diplomacy of the First Earl of Malmesbury at the Hague* (London: Jonathan Cape, 1954).

Codevilla, Angelo. "The CIA's Identity Crisis." *American Enterprise* (January–February 1992).

———. *Informing Statecraft, Intelligence for a New Century* (New York: Free Press, 1992).

Coll, Steve. *Ghost Wars: The Secret History of the CIA, Afghanistan, and Bin Laden, from the Soviet Invasion to September 10, 2001* (New York: Penguin Books, 2004).

A Consumer's Guide to Intelligence (Washington, D.C.: Central Intelligence Agency, 1993).

Corson, William R. *The Armies of Ignorance: The Rise of the American Intelligence Empire* (New York: Dial, 1977).

Darling, Arthur. *The Central Intelligence Agency: An Instrument of Government to 1950* (State College: Pennsylvania State University Press, 1990).

Dorwart, Jeffery. *The Office of Naval Intelligence: The Birth of America's First Intelligence Agency, 1865–1918* (Annapolis, Md.: Naval Institute Press, 1979).

Dulles, Allen. *The Craft of Intelligence* (New York: Harper and Row, 1963).

———, ed. *Great True Spy Stories* (New York: Harper and Row, 1968).

Dvornik, Francis. *Origins of Intelligence Services: The Ancient Near East, Persia, Greece, Rome, Byzantium, the Arab Muslim Emirates, the Mongol Empire, China, Muscovy* (New Brunswick, N.J.: Rutgers University Press, 1974).

Fergusson, Thomas G. *British Military Intelligence, 1870–1914: The Development of a Modern Intelligence Organization* (Frederick, Md.: University Publications of America, 1984).

Fishel, Edwin. *The Secret War for the Union* (New York: Houghton Mifflin, 1996).

———. "The CIA and American Foreign Policy." *Foreign Affairs* 67 (Winter 1987/1988).

Gates, Robert M. *From the Shadows: The Ultimate Insider's Story of Five Presidents and How They Won the Cold War* (New York: Simon & Schuster, 1996).

Godson, Roy, ed. *Comparing Foreign Intelligence: The U.S., the U.S.S.R., the U.K., and the Third World* (McLean, Va.: Pergamon-Brassey's, 1988).

————, ed. *Intelligence Requirements for the 1980s, no. 1 Books: Elements of Intelligence* (New Brunswick, N.J.: Transaction, 1979).

————, ed. *Intelligence Requirements for the 1980s: Intelligence and Policy* (Lexington, Mass.: Lexington Books, 1985).

Graham, Bob. *Intelligence Matters: The CIA, the FBI, Saudi Arabia, and the Failure of America's War on Terror* (New York: Random House, 2004).

Haley, P. Edward. "Legislative-Executive Relations and the United States Intelligence Community." *Harvard Journal of Law and Public Policy* 12 (Spring 1989).

Helms, Richard. *A Look over My Shoulder: A Life in the Central Intelligence Agency* (New York: Ballentine Books, 2003).

Hersh, Burton. *The Old Boys, The American Elite and the Origins of the CIA* (New York: Charles Scribner's Sons, 1992).

Holt, Pat M. *Secret Intelligence and Public Policy: A Dilemma of Democracy* (Washington, D.C.: Congressional Quarterly, 1995).

Hulnick, Arthur S. *Fixing the Spy Machine: Preparing American Intelligence for the Twenty-first Century* (Westport, Conn.: Praeger, 1999).

"Inside Israel's Secret Organizations." *Jane's Intelligence Review* (October 1996).

Jeffreys-Jones, Rhodri. *American Espionage: From Secret Service to CIA* (New York: Free Press, 1977).

————. *The CIA and American Democracy* (New Haven, Conn.: Yale University Press, 1989).

————. *America's Secret Power, The CIA in a Democratic Society* (New York: Oxford University Press, 1989).

Johnson, Loch K. *A Season of Inquiry: Congress and Intelligence* (Chicago: Dorsey, 1988).

Johnson, Loch K., and James J. Wirtz, eds. *Strategic Intelligence, Windows into a Secret World* (Los Angeles: Roxbury Publishing Company, 2004).

Jordan, Amos A., William J. Taylor, Jr., and Michael J. Mazarr. *American National Security* (Baltimore: Johns Hopkins University Press, 1999).

Kahana, Ephraim. "Reorganizing Israel's Intelligence Community." *International Journal of Intelligence and CounterIntelligence* 15 (Fall 2002).

Kahn, David. *Hitler's Spies: German Military Intelligence in World War II* (New York: Macmillan, 1978).

Katz, Barry M. *Research and Analysis in the Office of Strategic Services, 1942–1945* (Cambridge, Mass.: Harvard University Press, 1989).

Kent, Sherman. *Strategic Intelligence for American World Policy* (Princeton, N.J.: Princeton University Press, 1949).

————. *The FBI* (New York: Pocket Books, 1993).

Kessler, Ronald. *Inside the CIA* (New York: Pocket Books, 1992).

Kindsvater, Larry C. "The Need to Reorganize the Intelligence Community." *Studies in Intelligence* 47 (2003).

Knightley, Philip. *The Second Oldest Profession* (New York: W. W. Norton, 1986).

Knott, Stephen F. *Secret and Sanctioned: Covert Operations and the American Presidency* (New York: Oxford University Press, 1996).

Koehler, John O. *STASI: The Untold Story of the East German Secret Police* (Boulder, Colo.: Westview, 1999).

Lacqueur, Walter. *A World of Secrets: The Use and Limits of Intelligence* (New York: Basic Books, 1985).

Leary, William M. *The Central Intelligence Agency: History and Documents* (Tuscaloosa: University of Alabama Press, 1984).

Lefever, Ernest W., and Roy C. Godson. *The CIA and the American Ethic: An Unfinished Debate* (Washington, D.C.: Georgetown University, Ethics and Public Policy Center, 1979).

Lowenthal, Mark M. *Intelligence: From Secrets to Policy* (Washington, D.C.: Congressional Quarterly, 2000).

————. *U.S. Intelligence: Evolution and Anatomy* (Westport, Conn.: Praeger, 1992).

Masse, Todd. "Domestic Intelligence in the United Kingdom: Applicability of the MI-5 Model to the United States." *Congressional Research Service Report* (19 May 2003).

Mauer, Alfred C., Marion D. Turnstall, and James M. Keagle,

eds. *Intelligence: Policy and Process* (Boulder, Colo.: Westview, 1985).

Meyer, Cord. *Facing Reality: From World Federalism to the CIA* (New York: Harper and Row, 1980).

Miller, Nathan. *Spying for America: The Hidden History of U.S. Intelligence* (New York: Paragon House, 1989).

Moynihan, Daniel Patrick. "Secrecy as Government Regulation." *Political Science and Politics* 30 (June 1997).

Oseth, John M. *Regulating U.S. Intelligence Operations: A Study in Definition of the National Interest* (Lexington: University Press of Kentucky, 1985).

O'Toole, G. J. A. *Honorable Treachery: A History of U.S. Intelligence, Espionage and Covert Action from the American Revolution to the CIA* (New York: Atlantic Monthly Press, 1991).

Perry, Mark. *Eclipse: The Last Days of the CIA* (New York: William Morrow, 1992).

Persico, Joseph E. *Casey: From OSS to the CIA* (New York: Viking Penguin, 1990).

Pincher, Chapman. *Their Trade Is Treachery* (London: Sidgwick and Jackson, 1981).

Powers, Thomas. "Secrets of September 11." *New York Review of Books* 49 (October 10, 2002).

Ranelagh, John. *The Agency: The Rise and Decline of the CIA* (New York: Simon & Schuster, 1986).

Richelson, Jeffrey T. *A Century of Spies: Intelligence in the Twentieth Century* (New York: Oxford University Press, 1995).

———. *The U.S. Intelligence Community* (Boulder, Colo.: Westview, 1999).

Robertson, K. G., ed. *British and American Approaches to Intelligence* (New York: St. Martin's Press, 1987).

Rothkopf, David. *Running the World: The Inside Story of the National Security Council and the Architects of American Power* (New York: Public Affairs, 2005).

Shulsky, Abram N., and Gary J. Schmitt. *Silent Warfare: Understanding the World of Intelligence* (Washington, D.C.: Brassey's, 2003).

Smith, R. Harris. *OSS: The Secret History of America's First Central Intelligence Agency* (Berkeley: University of California Press, 1972).

Snow, Donald. *National Security* (New York: St. Martin's Press, 1995).

Stimson, Henry L., and McGeorge Bundy. *On Active Service in Peace and War* (New York: Harper, 1947).

Tidwell, William A., James A. Hall, and David Winfrey Gaddy. *Come Retribution: The Confederate Secret Service and the Assassination of Lincoln* (Jackson: University Press of Mississippi, 1988).

Tovar, B. Hugh. "The Not-So-Secret War, or How State-CIA Squabbling Hurts U.S. Intelligence." *Studies in Intelligence* 25, no. 1 (Spring 1981).

Troy, Thomas F. *Donovan and the CIA: A History of the Central Intelligence Agency* (Frederick, Md.: Aletheia Books, 1981).

―――. "The Quaintness of the U.S. Intelligence Community: Its Origin, Theory, and Problems." *International Journal of Intelligence and CounterIntelligence* 2 (Summer 1988).

Turner, Michael A. "A Distinctive U.S. Intelligence Identity." *International Journal of Intelligence and CounterIntelligence* 17 (Spring 2004).

―――. *Historical Dictionary of United States Intelligence* (Lanham, Md.: Scarecrow Press, 2006).

―――. "Understanding CIA's Role in Intelligence." *International Journal of Intelligence and CounterIntelligence* 4 (1990).

Turner, Stansfield. *Secrecy and Democracy: The CIA in Transition* (New York: Houghton Mifflin, 1985).

Sun Tzu. *The Art of War* (New York: Oxford University Press, 1963).

Warner, Michael. *Central Intelligence: Origin and Evolution* (Washington, D.C.: Center for the Study of Intelligence, 2001).

West, Nigel. *Games of Intelligence, The Classified Conflict of International Espionage* (London: Weidenfeld and Nicolson, 1989).

Westerfield, H. Bradford, ed. *Inside the CIA's Private World, Declassified Articles from the Agency's Internal Journal, 1955–1992* (New Haven, Conn.: Yale University Press, 1995).

Winks, Robin. *Cloak and Gown: Scholars in the Secret War, 1939–1961* (New York: Morrow, 1987).

Zorn, E. L. "Israel's Quest for Satellite Intelligence." *Studies in Intelligence*, no. 10 (Winter–Spring 2001).

The Intelligence Cycle

Gordon, Don E. "Winners and Losers." *International Journal of Intelligence and CounterIntelligence* 1, no. 3 (1986).

Gries, David. "New Links between Intelligence and Policy." *Studies in Intelligence* 34 (Summer 1990).

Hastedt, Glenn. "Controlling Intelligence: The Role of the DCI." *International Journal of Intelligence and CounterIntelligence* 1, no. 4 30 (1986).

Johnson, Loch K. "Making the Intelligence Cycle Work." *International Journal of Intelligence and CounterIntelligence* 1, no. 4 (1986).

Priorities, Requirements, and Use of Intelligence

Beard, Charles. *The Idea of the National Interest* (New York: Macmillan, 1934).

Bozeman, Adda B. *Strategic Intelligence and Statecraft* (Washington, D.C.: Brassey's, 1992).

Dreyfuss, Robert. "The Pentagon Muzzles the CIA." *American Prospect* (16 December 2002).

Gardiner, L. Keith. "Dealing with Intelligence-Policy Disconnects." *Studies in Intelligence* 33, no. 2 (Summer 1989).

Godson, Roy. *Intelligence Requirements for the 1990s* (Lexington, Mass.: Lexington Books, 1989).

Gries, David D. "New Links between Intelligence and Policy." *Studies in Intelligence* 34, no. 2 (Summer 1990).

Handel, Michael I. "Leaders and Intelligence." *Intelligence and National Security* 3 (July 1988).

———, ed. *Leaders and Intelligence* (London: Frank Cass, 1989).

———, ed. *War, Strategy and Intelligence* (London: Frank Cass, 1989).

Hibbert, Reginald. "Intelligence and Policy." *Intelligence and National Security* 5 (January 1990).

Hulnick, Arthur S. "The Intelligence Producer-Policy Consumer Linkage." *Studies in Intelligence* 29 (Winter 1985).

Johnson, Loch. *Bombs, Bugs, Drugs, and Thugs: Intelligence and America's Quest for Security* (New York: New York University Press, 2000).

Morgenthau, Hans. *In Defense of the National Interest* (New York: Knopf, 1951).

Pillar, Paul R. *Terrorism and U.S. Foreign Policy* (Washington, D.C.: Brookings Institution, 2001).

Intelligence Collection

Andrew, Christopher, and Oleg Gordievsky. *KGB: The Inside Story* (New York: HarperPerennial, 1990).

Axelrod, Alan. *The War between the Spies: A History of Espionage during the American Civil War* (New York: Atlantic Monthly Press, 1992).

Babcock, Fenton. "Assessing DDO Human Source Reporting." *Studies in Intelligence* 22, no. 3 (Fall 1978).

Bamford, James. *Body of Secrets: Anatomy of the Ultra-Secret National Security Agency* (New York: Doubleday, 2001).

———. *The Puzzle Palace: A Report on America's Most Secret Agency* (Boston: Houghton Mifflin, 1982).

Beschloss, Michael R. *Mayday: Eisenhower, Khrushchev, and the U-2 08 Affair* (New York: Harper and Row, 1986).

Burrows, William E. *Deep Black: Space Espionage and National Security* (New York: Random House, 1986).

Constantinides, George C. "Tradecraft: Follies and Foibles." *International Journal of Intelligence and Counterintelligence* 1, no. 4 (1986).

Godson, Roy., ed. *Intelligence Requirements for the 1980s: Clandestine Collection* (New Brunswick, N.J.: Transaction, 1980).

Haynes, John Earl, and Harvey Klehr. *VENONA: Decoding Soviet Espionage in America* (New Haven, Conn.: Yale University Press, 1999).

Kessler, Ronald. *The Bureau: The Secret History of the FBI* (New York: St. Martin's, 2002).

Laird, Thomas. *Into Tibet: The CIA's First Atomic Spy and His Secret Expedition to Lhasa* (New York: Grove, 2002).

McKee, W. J. "The Reports Officer: Issues of Quality." *Studies in Intelligence* 27, no. 1 (Spring 1983).

Peebles, Curtis. *Guardians: Strategic Reconnaissance Satellites* (Novato, Calif.: Presidio, 1987).

Richelson, Jeffrey. *America's Secret Eyes in Space* (New York: Ballinger Books, 1989).

———. "The Keyhole Satellite Program." *Journal of Strategic Studies* 7 (June 1984).

Singer, Kurt D., ed. *Three Thousand Years of Espionage: An Anthology of the World's Greatest Spy Stories* (Freeport, N.Y.: Books for Libraries, 1970).

Wise, David, and Thomas B. Ross. *The U-2 Affair* (New York: Random House, 1962).

Yardley, Herbert O. *The American Black Chamber* (New York: Blue Ribbon Books, 1931).

Analysis and Estimates

Anscombe, G. E. M. *Intention* (Ithaca, N.Y.: Cornell University Press, 1969).

Armstrong, Willis C., William Leonhart, William F. McCaffrey, and Herbert C. Rothenberg. "The Hazards of Single-Outcome Forecasting." *Studies in Intelligence* 28, no. 3 (Fall 1984).

Betts, Richard. *Surprise Attack: Lessons for Defense Planning* (Washington, D.C.: Brookings Institution, 1982).

Clark, Robert M. "Scientific and Technical Intelligence Analysis." *Studies in Intelligence* 19, no. 1 (Spring 1975).

Cremeans, Charles D. "Basic Psychology for Intelligence Analysts." *Studies in Intelligence* 15, no. 1 (Winter 1971).

Cubbage, T. L. "German Misapprehensions Regarding Overlord: Understanding Failure in the Estimative Process." *Intelligence and National Security* 2 (July 1987).

Daniels, Donald C., and Katherine L. Herbig, eds. *Strategic Military Deception* (New York: Pergamon, 1982).

Davis, Jack. "Combating Mind-Set." *Studies in Intelligence* 36 (1992).

———. "Improving CIA Analytic Performance: Analysts and the Policymaking Process." *Kent Center Occasional Papers* 1, no. 2 (September 2002).

———. "Improving CIA Analytic Performance: Strategic Warning." *Kent Center Occasional Papers* 1, no. 1 (September 2002).

———. "Sherman Kent's Final Thoughts on Analyst-Policymaker Relations." *Kent Center Occasional Papers* 2, no. 3 (June 2003).

———. "Strategic Warning: If Surprise Is Inevitable What Role for Analysis?" *Kent Center Occasional Papers* 2, no. 1 (January 2003).

Ford, Harold. *Estimative Intelligence: The Purposes and Problems of National Intelligence Estimating* (Lanham, Md.: University Press of America, 1993).

———. "The Primary Purpose of National Estimating." *Studies in Intelligence* 35 (Fall 1991).

Godson, Roy, ed. *Intelligence Requirements for the 1980s, no. 2: Analysis and Estimates* (New Brunswick, N.J.: Transaction Books, 1980).

———. *Intelligence Requirements for the 1980s, no. 3: Counterintelligence* (New Brunswick, N.J.: Transaction Books, 1980).

Helgerson, John L. *Getting to Know the President: CIA Briefings of Presidential Candidates* (Washington, D.C.: Center for the Study of Intelligence, 1997).

Herman, Michael. *Intelligence Power in Peace and War* (Cambridge: Cambridge University Press, 1996).

Heuer, Richards J., Jr. "Do You Really Need More Information?" *Studies in Intelligence* 23, no. 1 (Spring 1979).

———. *Psychology of Intelligence Analysis* (Washington, D.C.: Center for the Study of Intelligence, 1999).

Hoffman, Francis G. "Thinking Ahead Intelligently," book review, *Naval War College Review* 56 (Winter 2003).

Jordan, Amos, William Taylor, and Michael Mazarr. *American National Security* (Baltimore: Johns Hopkins University Press, 1999).

Kent, Sherman. *Strategic Intelligence for American World Policy* (Princeton, N.J.: Princeton University Press, 1966).

Levite, Ariel. *Intelligence and Strategic Surprise* (New York: Columbia University Press, 1987).

MacEachin, Douglas J. *CIA Assessments of the Soviet Union: The Record vs. the Charges* (Washington, D.C.: Center for the Study of Intelligence, 1996).

————. "Tradecraft of Analysis." In *U.S. Intelligence at the Crossroads: Agendas for Reform*, ed. Roy C. Godson, Ernest May, and Gary Schmitt (Washington, D.C.: Brassey's, 1995).

Martin, Joseph W. "What Basic Intelligence Seeks to Do." *Studies in Intelligence* 14, no. 2 (Fall 1970).

May, Ernest R. ed. *Knowing One's Enemies: Intelligence Assessment before the Two World Wars* (Princeton, N.J.: Princeton University Press, 1985).

Nye, Joseph S., Jr. "Peering into the Future." *Foreign Affairs* 73 (July–August 1994).

Petersen, Martin. "The Challenge for the Political Analyst." *Studies in Intelligence* 47 (Winter 2003).

Pipes, Richard. "Team B: The Reality behind the Myth." *Commentary*, no. 10 (October 1986).

Prados, John. *The Soviet Estimate: U.S. Intelligence Analysis and Russian Military Strength* (New York: Dial, 1982).

Rosenau, James N. "Muddling, Meddling, and Modeling: Alternative Approaches to the Study of World Politics in an Era of Rapid Change." *Millennium* 8 (Autumn 1979).

Schmidt, Charles. "Understanding Human Actions: Recognizing the Plans and Motives of Other Persons." In *Cognition and Social Behavior*, ed. J. S. Carroll and J. W. Payne (Hillsdale, N.J.: Erlbaum, 1976).

Stech, Frank J. *Political and Military Intention Estimation: A Taxonometric Analysis* (Bethesda, Md.: Mathtech, November 1979).

Taylor, Stan A., and Theodore J. Ralston. "The Role of Intelligence in Crisis Management." In *Avoiding War: Problems of Crisis Management*, ed. Alexander George (Boulder, Colo.: Westview, 1991).

Turner, Michael A. "Setting Analytical Priorities in U.S. Intelligence: A Preliminary Model." *International Journal of Intelligence and CounterIntelligence* 9 (Fall 1996).

Wohlstetter, Roberta. *Pearl Harbor: Warning and Decision* (Palo Alto, Calif.: Stanford University Press, 1962).

Ziegler, David W. "Yellow Rain: An Analysis That Went Awry." *International Journal of Intelligence and CounterIntelligence* 2, no. 1 (1988).

Counterintelligence

Boren, David L. "Counterintelligence for the 1990s." *American Intelligence Journal* 10 (Summer–Fall 1989).

Hurt, Michael. "Leaking National Security Secrets: Effects on Security
and Measures to Mitigate." *National Security Studies Quarterly* 7
(Autumn 2001).

Jonkers, Roy K. "Prologue." *American Intelligence Journal* 10 (Summer– Fall 1989).

Olsen, James M. "The Ten Commandments of Counterintelligence." *Studies in Intelligence* 45 (Winter 2001).

Wannall, W. Raymond. "Undermining Counterintelligence Capability." *International Journal of Intelligence and CounterIntelligence* 15 (Fall 2002).

Wettering, Frederick L. "Counterintelligence: The Broken Triad." *International Journal of Intelligence and CounterIntelligence* 13 (2000).

Covert Action

Hulnick, Arthur S. "U.S. Covert Action: Does It Have a Future?" *International Journal of Intelligence and CounterIntelligence* 9 (Summer 1996).

Hulnick, Arthur S., and David W. Mattausch. "Ethics and Morality in United States Intelligence." *Harvard Journal of Law and Public Policy* 12 (Spring 1989).

Isenberg, David. "The Pitfalls of U.S. Covert Operations." *Policy Analysis*, no. 118 (April 7, 1989).

Johnson, Loch K. "Covert Action and Accountability: Decision-Making for America's Secret Foreign Policy." *International Studies Quarterly* 33 (1989).

Kaplan, Robert. "Special Intelligence." *Atlantic Monthly* 281 (February 1998).

Kinzer, Stephen. "Regime Change: The Legacy." *American Prospect* (November 2003).

Kornbluh, Peter. "The El Mercurio File: Secret Documents Shine New Light on How the CIA Used a Newspaper to Foment a Coup." *Columbia Journalism Review* (September–October 2003).

Norton, John. "Reflections on Covert Action and Its Anxieties." *International Journal of Intelligence and CounterIntelligence* 4 (Spring 1990).

Reisman, W. Michael, and James E. Baker. *Regulating Covert Action* (New Haven, Conn.: Yale University Press, 1992).

Reit, S. *Masquerade: The Amazing Camouflage Deceptions of World War II* (New York: Hawthorn, 1978).

Schmitt, Gary J., and Abram N. Shulsky. "The Theory and Practice of Separation of Powers: The Case of Covert Action." In *The Fettered Presidency*, ed. L. Gordon Crovitz and Jeremy A. Rabkin (Washington, D.C.: American Enterprise Institute, 1989).

Sharpe, Kenneth E. "Intelligence vs. Covert Action." *World Outlook*, no. 8 (Winter 1989).

Treverton, Gregory F. *Covert Action: The Limits of Intervention in the Postwar World* (New York: Basic Books, 1987).

Twentieth Century Fund. *The Need to Know, Covert Action and American Democracy* (New York: Twentieth Century Fund, 1992).

Wettering, Frederick L. "[C]overt Action: The Disappearing 'C.'" *International Journal of Intelligence and CounterIntelligence* 16 (Winter 2003).

Woodward, Bob. *VEIL: The Secret Wars of the CIA, 1981–1987* (New York: Simon & Schuster, 1987).

Official Assessments and Reform Proposals

Additional Views of Senator Richard C., Shelby, Chair, Senate Select Committee on Intelligence, on the Joint Intelligence Inquiry (10 December 2002).

At Cold War's End: U.S. Intelligence on the Soviet Union and Eastern Europe, 1989–1991 (Washington, D.C.: Center for the Study of Intelligence, 1999).

Commission on the Roles and Capabilities of the United States Intelligence Community. *Preparing for the 21st Century* (Washington, D.C.: Government Printing Office, 1996).

Director of Central Intelligence, *Iraq's Weapons of Mass Destruction* (Washington, D.C.: Central Intelligence Agency, 2002).

FBI Intelligence Investigations, Coordination within Justice on

Counterintelligence Matters Is Limited, GAO-01-780 (Washington, D.C.: Government Accounting Office, July 2001).

Jeremiah, David. *Intelligence Community's Performance on the Indian Nuclear Tests* (Washington, D.C.: Central Intelligence Agency, 1998).

National Counterintelligence Executive. *Annual Report to Congress on Foreign Economic Collection and Industrial Espionage* (NCIX 2003-26 100006, February 2003).

National Intelligence Machinery (London: Her Majesty's Stationery Office, 2001).

U.S. House of Representatives. Hearings before the Select Committee on Intelligence. *U.S. Intelligence Agencies and Activities: Risks and Control of Foreign Intelligence* 94th Congress, 1st session, November 4–December 17, 1975.

U.S. House of Representatives. Permanent Select Committee on Intelligence. *Report of the Redmond Panel, Improving Counterintelligence Capabilities at the Department of Energy and the Los Alamos, Sandia, and Lawrence Livermore National Laboratories* (Washington, D.C.: Government Printing Office, 2000).

U.S. House of Representatives. Permanent Select Committee on Intelligence. *U.S. Counterintelligence and Security Concerns: A Status Report, Personnel and Information Security* (Washington, D.C.: Government Printing Office, 1988).

U.S. House of Representatives. Permanent Select Committee on Intelligence, Subcommittee on Evaluation. *Iran: Evaluation of U.S. Intelligence Performance prior to November 1978* Staff Report 38-745, 96th Congress, 1st session, 1979.

U.S. House of Representatives. Staff Study, Permanent Select Committee on Intelligence. *IC21: The Intelligence Community in the 21st Century,* 104th Congress.

U.S. House of Representatives. Subcommittee on International Security and Scientific Affairs of the Committee on Foreign Relations. *The Role of Intelligence in the Foreign Policy Process* (Washington, D.C.: Government Printing Office, 1980).

U.S. Senate. Committee on Foreign Relations, Subcommittee on International Security and Scientific Affairs. *The Role of Intelligence in the Foreign Policy Process* Hearings, 1980.

U.S. Senate. Select Committee on Intelligence and the House Permanent Select Committee on Intelligence. *Joint Inquiry into Intelligence Community Activities before and after the Terrorist Attacks of September 11, 2001* (Washington, D.C.: Government Printing Office, December 2002).

U.S. Senate. Select Committee to Study Governmental Operations with Respect to Intelligence Activities. *Final Report* Senate Report 94-755, 94th Congress, 2nd session, 1976.

Index

Page numbers in italics refer to entries in figures.

A

actionable intelligence, 51, 75, 161, 188, 220

Adams, John, 18

Afghanistan, 26, 29, 96, 145, 147, 154, 155, 161, 170; and Taliban, 154

African National Congress (ANC), 66

AIDS, 86, 165

Air Force, 24, 29, 30, 31, 32, 142

Allende, Salvador, 147

all-source intelligence, 30, 31, 37, 88, 108, 182, 185

Aman (Israel), 65

Ames, (Aldrich) Rick, 39, 105, 141, 142, 143

analysis, definition of, 220

analysis types: alternative, 16, 18, 184, 186–187; devil's advocacy, 187; high impact–low probability, 187; linch-pin, 184, 187–188; opportunity, 76; quality of information check, 187; risk-benefit, 187

Analysis and Forecasting Center (France), 68

Angleton, James J., 142

Arab-Israeli: War of 1967, 25, 29; (Yom Kippur) War of 1973, 26, 64, 65

Arbenz, Alfonso, 23, 29, 146

Aristide, Jean Bertrant, 78

Army, 19, 20, 29, 30, 31, 32, 142

assassinations, 26, 37, 145, 158,

assessment, definition of, 220

asset, 94

B

background investigations, 39, 136, 141

Baer, Robert, 46

Barnett, David, 142

Bay of Pigs, 25, 29

Beard, Charles, 76

Bell, William, 142

Betts, Richard, 77

Black Chamber, 20

Bloch, Felix, 142

Boone, David, 142

Boren, David, 134

Bosnia, 29, 80, 91, 96, 154

briefing, definition of, 220

Bureau of Intelligence and Research (INR), 30, 31, 37, 38, 65, 83, 88

Bureau of Narcotics and Dangerous Drugs (BNDD), 35

bureaucratic: competition, 15, 105; dys-functions, 14; imperatives, 30, 72, 77, 172; interests, 44; pathologies; 44, 52–55, 57, 122; politics, 41, 53; procedures, 81, 84, 86, 87; rivalries, 55; snafus, 14; tensions, 23; turf battles, 15, 104, 105, 135

Bush, George W., 42, 73, 78, 103, 117, 146, 147, 158, 160, 178, 184

C

Canada, 62

"can do" attitude, 45–46

capabilities, 6, 7, 8, 92, 94, 99, 105, 107, 110, 111, 112, 154, 156

Carney, Jeff Martin, 142

Carter, Jimmy, 26, 125

case officers, 82, 94, 95, 97, 220

Casey, William, 42, 81, 86, 117, 118, 179

Castro, Fidel, 25–26

Center for Security Evaluation (CSE), 179

Central Directorate of General Informa-tion (RG, France), 68

Central Directorate Judicial Police (DCPJ, France), 68

Central Imagery Office (CIO), 33

Central Intelligence Agency (CIA); 8, 9, 13, 17, 22–24, 26–27, 30, 31, 32–33, 35, 37–39, 40, 41, 44, 46, 48, 54, 55, 56, 73, 74, 78, 82, 86, 88,

91, 94, 95, 97, 98, 100, 104, 105, 107, 108, 113, 118, 121, 125, 126, 130, 134, 136, 138, 141, *142*, 143, 145–149, 150, 157, 159, 161, 166, 168, 170, 173, 176, 177, 179, 180, 181, 182, 185, 188, 220; CIASOURCE, 128; chief of station, 95; and its golden age, 23, 25; station, 95

Central Service for Information Systems Security (SCSSI, France), 68

Cheney, Vice President Dick, 73

Chile, 146

Chin, Larry Wu-Tai, *142*

China, People's Republic of, 57, 142, 153, 164; and its atomic bomb; 25, *29*; entry into Korean War, 23, *29*; invasion of Vietnam in 1978, 26, *29*; occupation of Tibet, 96

civil liberties, 16, 22, 28, 35, 46, 51, 52, 60, 61, 69, 148, 167

Civil War, 19

clandestine operation, definition of, 221

clandestine SIGINT, 91

Clark, James, *142*

Clarke, Bruce, 75

classification, 41, 221; regulations, 99, 105; system, 101–103

classification categories: confidential, 101, 221; secret, 102, 228; top secret, 102, 228

Clinton, Bill, 27, 46, 78, 79, 125, 134, 160

Coast Guard, 29, *31*, 34, 165

code: breaking (decoding); 20, 24, 32, 92, 143; making; 20, 24, 32

COINTELPRO, 144

Cold War, 23, 27, 33, 53, 57, 77, 84, 96, 109, 140, 142, 143, 147, 152–154, 155, 163, 166, 174

collection, definition of, 221

collection disciplines; 37, 55, 89–99, 105, 106

collection requirement, definition of, 221

Commerce, Department of, 8

Committee of Members of Parliament (South Africa), 67

communication: gaps, 56; problems, 57, 134

communications intelligence (COMINT), 91, 92, 221

communications security (COMSEC), 24, 32

Community Nonproliferation Committee, 180

Companies for Republican Security (CRS, France), 68

compartmentation, 15, 41, 54, 56, 102, 106, 139, 156, 183

competitive intelligence, 48, 106, 164, 221

Confederate States of America (CSA), 19

Congress, 53; and oversight, 4, 26, 27, 49, 62, 64, 126, 148, 149, 150

Conrad, Clyde Lee, *142*

consumer-producer relations. *See* policy-intelligence relationship

consumers of intelligence, 51, 75, 81, 87, 126, 128–130, 221. *See also* intelligence consumers

Contra war, 27, *29*

Convention for a Democratic South Africa, 66

coordination, definition of, 221–222

Coordinator of Information (COI), 21

CORONA, 24

counterintelligence (CI), 13, 15, 16, 18, 30, 34–41, 65, 67, 68, 103–105, 132–144, 150, 164, 179, 182, 222

Counterintelligence Center (CTC), 40, 179

countermeasures, 13, 138, 141

counterterrorism, 35, 41, 42, 48, 49, 64, 68, 135, 136, 157–158, 160, 162, 166, 170, 175, 181, 182, 184, 222

Counterterrorism Center (CTC), 42, 179

cover; 21, 95, 222; "backstopping" of, 95; pocket litter for, 95

cover types: official, 95, 139, 222; nonofficial, 95, 222

covert action (CA); 3, 5, 13, 16, 19, 26, 37, 39, 64, 67, 97, 128, 132, 133, 144–150, 151, 160, 163, 222; and "blowback," 146; and counterinsurgency, 147; and "dirty tricks," 26, 37; and "overt-covert operations," 145, 157, 176; the "quiet option," 23; as the third option, 145

Covert Action Planning Group, 148

Covert Action Review Group, 148

covert action types: economic action, 146, 221; paramilitary activity, 146, 221; political action, 146, 221; propa-

ganda, 23, 65, 146, 173, 221
Cox, Frank, 21
crime, 82, 94, 95, 134, 153, 161, 164–165, 179
Crime and Narcotics Center (NCC), 55, 179,
cryptology, 20, 24, 93
"cry wolf syndrome," 113, 114
Cuba, 25, 89, 96, 112, 140, *142*
Cuban Missile Crisis, 118
current intelligence, 35, 465, 82, 84, 108, 109, 169, 220, 222
cyberwar operations, 162–163

D
Daily Threat Matrix, 116
Davis, Jack, 120
decentralization, 18
deception, 2, 45, 91, 93, 97, 102, 174, 222
decision makers, 9, 10, 12, 37, 88. *See also* policymakers
declassification, definition of, 222
deep data access (deep data mining), 16, 182, 183
defectors, 96, 143
Defense Advanced Research Projects Agency (DARPA), 24, 184; and Information Awareness Office, 184
defense attaché program, 31, 223
Defense, Department of (Pentagon), 22, 24, 25, 30, 32, 34, 37, 39, 48, 125, 138, 166, 176, 179, 182, 183
Defense HUMINT Service, 32, 94
Defense Intelligence Agency (DIA), 25, 27, 29, 30, 31, 32, 38, 88, 100, 108, 115, 158, 161, 183, 223
Defense Mapping Agency, 33
Defense Reorganization Act of 1958, 25
democracy, promotion of, 160
Deutch, John, 80
diplomacy, 6, 109, 132, 145, 158, 164; diplomatic reports, 37, 166
director of central intelligence (DCI), 1, 5, 11, 23, 33, 39, 40–41, 45, 47, 74, 80, 90, 91, 96, 99, 103, 109–110, 115–119, 148, 161, 175–178, 180, 223
director of the Central Intelligence Directive (DCID), 89, 223
director of national intelligence (DNI), 28, 33, 38, 39–41, 79, 80, 98, 99, 102,

104, 114, 116, 125, 134, 139, 148, 160, 176, 177, 181, 183, 223
Directorate of Defense Protection and Security (DPSD, France), 68
Directorate of Intelligence (DI), 75, 82, 100, 107
Directorate of Military Intelligence (DRM, France), 67
Directorate of Operations (DO), 94, 161
Directorate of Science and Technology (DS&T), 98
Directorate of Territorial Security (DST, France), 68
disinformation, definition of, 223
dissemination list (DISSEM LIST), 83, 130
domestic intelligence, 16, 52, 60, 65–66, 68–69, 181, 182
Donovan, William, 21
double agent, 18, 97, 104, 139, 143
Drug Enforcement Administration (DEA), 30, 31, 35–36, 52, 165, 223
drug trafficking, 82, 153, 161, 164–165, 167, 168, 179

E
East Germany, 142; Security Service (STASI), 143, 144
economic espionage, 68, 135, 139, 163, 164
economic intelligence, 98, 135, 163, 223–224
Edwards, John, 62, 70
Egypt, 64
El Paso Intelligence Center, 36
electronic intelligence (ELINT), 67, 83, 92, 224
émigrés, 96
encryption, 20, 92, 138, 167
Energy, Department of, 30, 31, 36, 138
energy intelligence, definition of, 224
Enigma, 61
environmental issues, 153, 165–166, 179
espionage, 6, 17, 19, 32, 37–39, 45, 91, 94, 97, 103–104, 133, 139–142, 156. *See also* spying
Espionage Act of 1917, 150
estimative intelligence, 114–118, 185, 186, 224
estimative process, 113, 114–118
European Union, 70
evaluation, definition of, 224

exclusive distribution (EXDIS), 127
Executive Order 12333, 26, 145, 224
Executive Order 12958, 99
exploitation, definition of, 224

F

failed and rogue states, 53, 82, 153–155, 168
Federal Bureau of Investigation (FBI), 22, 30, *31*, 32, 34–35, 38–40, 46, 52, 56, 69, 79, 104–105, 134–135, 138–141, *142*, 143–144, 157, 163, 164, 169, 179, 181, 182; its Office of Counterterrorism and Counterintelligence, 135
Feinstein, Diane, 175
Feith, Douglas, 74
finished intelligence, 13, 27, 38, 55, 86, 220, 225
flexible accountability, 49, 225
for official use only (FOUO), 102
Ford, Gerald, 26
Ford, Harold, 185
forecast, 6, 8, 98, 110, 111, 112, 174, 175, 187
Foreign and Commonwealth Office (FCO, UK), 61
Foreign Broadcast Information Service (FBIS), 98, 168
foreign intelligence, 16, 22, 34, 35, 38, 132, 133, 136, 139, 140, 141, 143, 181
Foreign Intelligence Surveillance Act, 184
Foreign Intelligence Surveillance Court, 52, 63, 69
foreign secretary, 61
Foreign Terrorist Tracking Task Force (FTTTF), 183
fragmentation, 18, 30, 48, 57, 59, 134, 139, 150
France, 60, 67–69, 70, 164
Franklin, Benjamin, 18
fusion center, 55, 178, 180–182

G

Gannon, John, 168
Gates, Robert, 11, 76, 77, 118
General Directorate for External Security (DGSE, France), 67
geospatial intelligence (GEOINT), 33, 225
Gestapo, 51
Ghana, *142*

Gilmore, James, 52
global health, 165–166
Global Positioning System, 90
globalization, 164, 171
Goss, Porter, 158, 168
Government Code and Cipher School (UK), 61
Government Communications Headquarters (GCHQ), 60, 61
Great Britain. *See* United Kingdom
Gries, David, 78
Groat, Douglas, *142*
Guatemala, 23, 146, 151
guerrilla warfare, 19

H

Haiti, 79
Hale, Nathan, 18
Hall, James, *142*
Hannsen, Robert, 39, 141, *142*; "Hannsen effect," 39, 105
Harper, James, *142*
Hazelwood, Leo, 180
Heuer, Jr., Richards, 120
Hill, Eleanor, 47
Homeland Security, Department of, 28, 29–30, *31*, 34, 157, 163, 179, 182
Hoover, J. Edgar, 35
Hoover commissions: of 1949, 177; of 1955, 177
House Permanent Select Committee on Intelligence (HPSCI), 26, 105, 149, 177
Howard, Edward, *142*, 143
Hughes-Ryan Amendment of 1974, 149
Hulnick, Arthur, 50, 76
human intelligence (HUMINT), 37, 55, 64, 83, 93–97, 160, 161, 168, 225
human rights, 153, 165–166, 176
Hussein, Saddam, 73, 74, 155, 159

I

Ignatius, David, 46
imagery intelligence (IMINT), 33, 34, 67, 89, 90–93, 156, 167–169, 225
India-Pakistan War of 1971, 26, *29*
Indian nuclear tests (1998), 27, *29*, 170, 186
indicators, 112
industrial espionage. *See* economic espionage
information: deep mining of, 16, 183,

185; hoarding, 15; security (INFOSEC), 32, 179; warfare, 162; warfare office, 162
Institute for Intelligence and Special Tasks (Mossad), 64, 65
INTELINK, 55, 128
intelligence: agenda, 76; agents, 11, 80, 82, 84, 85, 87, 153; analysis, 3, 4, 8, 9, 11, 12, 36, 37, 47, 50, 55, 73–75, 78–79, 82, 84, 85, 90, 101, 106, 108–123, 124, 126, 129–130, 138, 139, 157, 160, 166, 169, 174, 176, 179, 182, 186, 187; analysts, 11, 12, 14, 15, 38, 51, 56, 57, 76, 77, 82–84, 92, 98, 106, 107–123, 125–128, 144, 146, 165, 183–184, 185; assessments, 78, 85, 94, 100, 109, 125, 225; budgets, 8, 90, 92; challenges, 166–170, 171; charter, 26; collection, 3, 4, 9, 11, 15, 37, 47, 74, 75, 83, 88–106, 107, 124, 129, 157, 160, 165, 166, 182; community (IC), 2, 14, 17, 24, 26, 28, 32, 34, 35–37, 39, 42, 44, 47, 55–57, 67, 71, 77, 80, 81, 84, 86, 89, 90, 92, 94, 98, 100, 105–108, 113–115, 123–124, 128, 139, 148, 151–152, 162, 164, 169, 171, 175–180, 184, 186, 188; competition, 18; consumer, 12, 15, 56, 57; cooperation; 14, 39, 42, 104, 134; coordination, 20, 23, 28, 36, 39, 71, 113, 115, 134; criticism of, 13; culture, 18; cycle, 4, 8–13, 14–15, 37, 122, 130, 131, 132, 172, 225; czar of, 16, 175–176; definition of, 3–5; dissemination, 3, 9, 4, 15, 47, 83, 126–128, 223; ethos, 14, 43, 57; exceptionalism, 45; gaps, 7, 104; guidance, 14; history, 18–28; memorandum, 125; mission, 4, 9, 30, 41, 43–44, 77, 80, 104, 109; need for, 227; officer, 10, 226; operations, 19; oversight, 4, 26, 27, 49, 62, 64, 126, 148–150; pathologies, 14; planning, 9; politicization of, 10, 51, 117, 118–119; priorities, 15, 33, 42, 53, 54, 67, 71, 72, 75, 79, 80, 84, 87, 152–166; process, 2, 9, 13, 14, 16, 40, 44, 53, 75, 87, 92, 101, 122, 151, 152, 170, 172, 173; processing, 3, 4, 9; producer, 15, 57, 226; prod-

uct, 12, 15, 37, 38, 54, 75, 76, 78, 83, 125; production, 9, 75, 124, 129, 228; professionals, 3, 10, 12, 13; requirements, 4, 11, 13, 15, 33, 40, 53, 67, 76, 78, 80, 85, 90, 95, 108, 226; resources, 105, 133; risks, 45; sharing, 7, 36, 101, 106, 128, 139, 166, 184; structure, 28; theory, 6, 13
Intelligence and Electronic Warfare Brigade (BRGE, France), 68
Intelligence Authorization Act of 1991, 149
Intelligence Community-Wide System for Information Sharing (ICSIS), 128
Intelligence Oversight Act of 1980, 26
Intelligence Oversight Board (IOB), 148, 226
Intelligence Reform AND Terrorism Prevention Act of 2004, 28, 39–40, 175
Intelligence Services Act of 1994 (UK), 62
Intelligence Services Act of 1994 (South Africa), 61, 66
Intelligence Services Commissioner, 63
intentions, 6–8, 91, 92, 94, 96, 105, 107, 110–112
interagency communication, 18, 55, 106
interagency cooperation, 18, 116
interagency process, 80, 86
interagency task forces, 179
interception commissioner, 63
intercepts, 21, 24, 32, 63, 65, 82, 86, 140, 156
international system, 6
intifadah. See Palestinian insurgency
Investigatory Powers Tribunal (UK), 63
Iran, 223, 29, 55, 119, 146, 153, 154, 163: hostage crisis of 1979, 91, 96, 121; revolution in 1979, 55, 151; shah of, 26, 29, 85, 119, 151, 155
Iran-Contra Affair, 27
Iraq, 74, 75, 78, 96, 147, 154, 161; war, 117, 169–170
Iraq's invasion of Kuwait in 1990, 27, 187
Islamic insurgency, 78
Israel, 60, 63–65, 69, 70, 142; Center for Pollitical Research, 65; invasion of Lebanon in 1983, 65; Security Service (Shin Bet or Shabak), 64, 65
Italy, 23; 1948 election, 23, 29, 146

J

Jacoby, Lowell E., 158, 182, 184
Jefferson, Thomas, 18
Jeffrey-Jones, Rhodri, 22
Jeremiah, Admiral David, 186
Jervis, Jr., Robert, 120
Johnson, Loch K., 14, 49, 165
Johnson, Lyndon B., 117, 130
Joint Chiefs of Staff (JCS), 4, 22, 25, 31
Joint Counterintelligence Assessment Group, 183
Joint Deployable Intelligence Support System (JDISS), 128
Joint Intelligence Committee (JIC), 62, *63*
Joint Intelligence Inquiry, 47, 48, 101, 103, 175
Joint Intelligence Task Force–Counterterrorism (JITF-CT), 182, 183
joint intelligence task forces, 33, 161
Joint Military Intelligence College, 31
Joint Military Intelligence Program (JMIP), 40

K

Kennedy, John F., 86,117
Kennedy, Robert, 118
Kerry, John, 80
key intelligence questions (KIQs), 81
Keynes, John Maynard, 175
KGB, 51, 143
Khomeini, Ayatollah, 55
Khrushchev, Nikita, 23; secret speech of, 23, *29*
Kim, Robert, *142*
Kissinger, Henry, 146
Korean War, 23, 29, 121
Kosovo, *29*, 91, 154

L

law enforcement, 28, 34, 35, 51, 52, 56, 61, 68, 70, 104, 127, 157, 165, 179, 181–183
Lexis Nexis, 99
liaison, 35, 138, 155, 157
Libya, 102
limited distribution (LIMDIS), 127
linchpin analysis. *See* analysis
Lipka, Ronald, *142*
long-term intelligence, 37, 82, 84, 108, 109
Lowenthal, Mark, 4, 9

M

MacEachin, Douglas, 187
Madison, President James, 19
MAGIC, 20
Mahnken, Thomas, 110
Marine Corps Intelligence, 29, 30, *31*, 32
materiel exploitation, 33
McCone, John, 117
McNamara, Robert, 25
measurement and signature Intelligence (MASINT), 93, 226
MEDEA program, 166
Mexican War of 1848, 19
Mexico, 117
Meyer, Cord, 121, 147
MI-5. *See* Security Service
MI-6. *See* Secret Intelligence Service
Middle East, 64, 96, 153
Military Intelligence Division (MID), 19, 22
Miller, Richard William, *142*
Ministerial Committee on the Intelligence Services (UK), 62
Ministry of Defense (France), 67
Ministry of Home Affairs (UK), 61
mission specific tasks, 49
Montes, Ana Belen, *142*
Morgenthau, Hans, 76
Morning Summary, 37, 108
Mossadegh, Mohammad, 23, *29*, 146, 151
Moynihan, Daniel Patrick, 173
Mueller, Robert, 52

N

National Clandestine Service, 94, 95, 100, 107, 161. *See also* Directorate of Operations
National Commission for the Control of Security Interceptions (France), 68
National Commission on Terrorist Threats Upon the United States (9/11 Commission), 52, 158, 175, 182
National Counter Proliferation Center, 159, 179, 181
National Counterintelligence Center (NCIC), 134, 179
National Counterintelligence Executive (NCIX), 40, 134–135
National Counterterrorism Center (NCTC), 28, 42, 116, 178, 181
National Defense Force (South Africa), 67

National Defense University, 183
National Endowment for Democracy, 145
National Foreign Assessment Center (NFAC), 75
National Foreign Intelligence Board (NFIB), 62, 116, 148, 226
National Foreign Intelligence Program (NFIP), 40, 223
National Geospatial Intelligence Agency (NGA), 29, 30, *31*, 33, 88, 176, 225
National Imagery and Mapping Agency (NIMA), 33, 225
National Intelligence Agency (South Africa), 66,
National Intelligence Coordinating Committee (South Africa), 67
National Intelligence Council (NIC), 62, 68, 81–82, 226–227
national intelligence estimate (NIE), 15, 38, 65, 81–82, 109, 114–118, 128, 159, 225, 227; on Iraqi WMD, 170; on Mexico, 117, 118; on Soviet Strategic Forces, 118
national intelligence officer (NIO), 81–82, 84, 87, 114–118, 180, 227; for warning, 114
National Intelligence Strategy, 160
national intelligence topics (NITs), 81
National Narcotics Intelligence System (NADDIS), 36
National Photographic Interpretation Center (NPIC), 24, 33
National Reconnaissance Office (NRO), 24, 25, 29, 30, *31*, 33–34, 88, 90, 92, 176
national security, definition of, 227
National Security Act of 1947, 22, 23, 30, 47, 133, 145
national security adviser, 146
National Security Agency (NSA), 24, 29, 30, *31*, 32–33, 61, 88, 91, 93, *142*, 176, 184, 227
National Security Archive, 4
National Security Council (NSC), 23, 30, 39, 62, 126, 145, 148
National Security Directive 286, 145
National Security Presidential Directive (NSPD), 81
National Strategic Intelligence Act of 1994 (South Africa), 66
national technical means, 55, 89, 96
Navy, 19, 20, 29, 30, *31*, 32, *142*

"need to know", 12, 32, 37, 102, 108, 126, 135–136, 138
Nicaragua, 27
Nicholson, Harold James, *142*
9/11 attacks. *See* terrorist attacks of 11 September 2001
no distribution (NODIS), 127
Nonproliferation Center (NPC), 159
Norris, Robert, 183
North Korea, 7, 78, 96, 153, 154, 159, 163, 170; invasion of South Korea, 23, *29*
not releasable to contractors (NOCONTRACT), 102
not releasable to foreign services (NOFORN), 102

O

Office of Military Affairs (OMA), 161
Office of Missile and Satellite Systems, 24
Office of Naval Intelligence (ONI), 19, 22
Office of Strategic Services (OSS), 21
Official Secrets Act (UK), 62
Organizational of Petroleum Exporting States (OPEC), 120
"open diplomacy," 20
Open Source Center, 98, 227–228
open source intelligence (OSINT), 97–99, 166, 168, 186
Open Source Solutions, 99
openness, 27
originator controlled (ORCON), 99–101
O'Toole, G. J. A., 25

P

Palestinian insurgency, 63, 64, 155
peace dividend, 27
peacekeeping operations, 153, 166
Pearl Harbor: Japanese attack on, 2, 20–21, 188
Pelton, Ronald, *142*, 143
Persian Gulf War of 1991, 68, 74, 91, 116, 161, 162, 169
Philippines, 21
PHOENIX program, 26
photographic intelligence (PHOTINT), 89, 90
physical intelligence, 110–111
Pillar, Paul, 156
Pitts, Earl, *142*
Poland, *142*

policy-intelligence relationship, 11, 75, 77, 79, 151
policymakers, 10–12, 15, 20, 38, 40, 48, 54, 56, 68, 74–75, 77–79, 85–86, 88, 113, 118, 120, 128, 152, 169, 170, 172–174. *See also* decision makers
Pollard, Jonathan, *142*, 144
polygraph, 39, 136–138, 141
Posse Comitatus Act, 51
Powers, Francis Gary, 24, 46
president, 23, 38
Presidential Decision Directive (PDD): 78, 134, 160
President's Daily Brief (PDB), 38, 82, 108, 125, 127
profiles, 112
public diplomacy, 162

Q
al-Qaeda, 122, 154, 158

R
Rabin, Yitzak, 65
raw intelligence, 11, 12, 15, 31, 37, 55, 86, 107, 118, 127, 228
Reagan, Ronald, 26, 81, 86, 102, 125, 165
reinvestigation, 137
reports officer, 107
Richardson, Bill, 135
Richelsen, Jeffrey, 4, 32
risk aversion, 46
risk taking, 463
Robbins, Tom, 112
Roosevelt, Franklin, 21
Russia, 57, 105, 136, 141, *142*, 153
Rwanda, *29*

S
sabotage, 19, 21, 38, 133–134, 147
satellites, 24, 33–34, 64, 89, 90, 92, 166, 168
Schlesinger Report of 1971, 177
Schwartzkopf, Norman, 116
Scranage, Sharon, *142*
secrecy, 2, 3, 6, 11, 13, 15, 17, 18, 40, 45, 57, 60, 69, 70, 100, 102–104
secret intelligence, 2, 3, 5, 6, 14, 133, 169, 172–174, 188
Secret Intelligence Service (SIS or MI-6), 60
secret military operations, 148

secret police, 18, 61
Secure Compartmented Intelligence Facility (SCIF), 137
security facility, 133
security personnel, 133, 135, 136, 138
Security Service (MI-5), 60, 65, 181
Security Services Act of 1989 (UK), 61
security violation, 137
Senate Select Committee on Intelligence (SSCI), 26, 57, 80, 117, 134, 149, 182
Senate Select Committee to Study Government Operations With Respect to Intelligence Activities, 177
Senior Executive Intelligence Review (SEIR), 82, 108
Shelby, Richard, 57, 101, 182
signals intelligence (SIGINT), 32, 67, 68, 83, 91–93, 98, 167, 228
signatures, 112
Sino-Soviet split, 25, *29*, 96
Situation Room, 86
Somalia, 27, *29*, 91, 154
sources and methods, 39, 40, 41, 100, 103
South Africa, 60, 66–67, 69, 70, *142*
South African Secret Service, 66
South Asia, 153
South Korea, 23, *29*, *142*
Southeast Asia, 19, 145
Souther, Glen, *142*
Soviet Union, 21, 23, 24, 25, *27*, *29*, 84, 85, 91, 96, 105, 112, 116, 119, 140, *142*, 143; invasion of Afghanistan (1979), 26, *29*, 96; invasion of Czechoslovakia, 25; strategic weapons, 25, *29*, 89
space SIGINT, 33
special activities, 23, 39, 145. *See also* covert action
Special National Intelligence Estimates (SNIEs), 109, 114, 116, 227
Sputnik, 23, 24, *29*
spying, 17, 97, 132, 133, 135, *142*. *See also* espionage
Squillacote, Teresa, *142*
SR-71 Blackbird, 89
staff notes, 82, 126
Stalin, Josef, 23
Stand, Kurt, *142*
State, Department of, 20, 32, 39, 48, 65, 82, 125, 138, *142*, 162

Stimpson, Henry, 20
stovepipe, 15, 55, 105
strategic analysis, 169
strategic intelligence, 35–36
strategic military intelligence, 22, 25, 31, 67
strategic surprise, 8, 187
stress, 119
Sudan, 159
Suez Crisis of 1956, 24, *29*
support to military operations, 160–162, 169
surge capability, 113

T
tactical intelligence, 25, 32
Tactical Intelligence and Related Activities (TIARA), 40
tactical military intelligence, 19, 67
technical means. *See* national technical means
telemetry intelligence (TELINT), 92, 228
telephone taps, 140
Tenet, George, 1, 2, 5, 45, 74, 91, 100, 103, 109, 116, 119
terrorism, 2, 52, 53, 54, 62, 68, 82, 85, 94, 95, 127, 134, 135, 140, 152, 155–158, 161, 165, 167–168, 171, 182, 183
Terrorism Threat Assessment Center (TTAC), 116, 179
terrorist attacks of 11 September 2001, 1, 2, 28, 29, 33, 35, 41, 42, 46, 52, 54, 56, 58, 60, 70, 78, 93, 103, 106, 120, 121, 123, 126, 135, 138, 140, 144, 145, 146, 147, 153, 154, 155, 167, 170, 181, 183, 188
Terrorist Threat Integration Center (TTIC), 42, 79, 180
Tet Offensive (1968), 25, *29*
"Third Party" rule, 99
total information awareness, 183, 185
Transitional Executive Authority Act of 1993, 66
Treasury, Department of, 30, *31*, 36
Treverton, Gregory, 147
Trofimoff, George, *142*
Troy, Thomas, 28
Truman, Harry, 21, 22
Turkish invasion of Cyprus in 1974, 26, *29*

Turner, Stansfield, 55, 90, 96
typescripts, 82, 125

U
U-2 aircraft, 24, 89
uncertainty, 4, 6–8, 11, 13, 73, 120, 129, 187
United Kingdom, 60–63, 69, 70, 73
USA PATRIOT Act of 2002, 28, 35, 52, 140, 157, 158, 169, 181
USS *Cole*, 182

V
"vacuum cleaner" approach, 92
VEIL, 102
verbal intelligence, 110–112
Viet Cong, 25, *29*
Vietnam, 23, 25, 26, *29*, 79; French defeat in, *29*; War, 23, 25, 26, *29*, 79, 130
Voice of America, 65

W
Walker, Arthur, *142*
Walker, John, *142*, 143
Walker, Michael, *142*
"Walker Ring," 143
wall of separation between intelligence and law enforcement, 50, 51–52, 57
War of 1812, 19
war on terror, 155, 168, 169
Warner, Michael, 47
warning: strategic 2; tactical 2, 157
Washington, George, 18
weapons of mass destruction (WMD), 42, 53, 152–155, 159, 161; Iraqi, 28, 42, 46, 72–74, 91, 159, 170; proliferation of, 82, 158–159, 179
Whitworth, Jerry, *142*
Working Group on Intelligence Reform of the National Strategy Information Center, report of, 174
World War II, 21, 22, 66, 141, 188
worst-case scenarios, 113

Y
Yardley, Herbert O., 20
Yurchenko, Vitaly, 143

Z
Zhan, Gao, 144

About the Author

Dr. Michael A. Turner is a political scientist who served in the Central Intelligence Agency for fifteen years in analytical and staff positions. He also served on numerous rotational assignments on Capitol Hill and the Departments of State and Defense. Dr. Turner was twice the recipient of the CIA's prestigious Exceptional Performance Award. The author of numerous journal articles and the *Historical Dictionary of United States Intelligence*, he is now working on books examining America's espionage laws as well as on the danger to American civil liberties from legislation on domestic spying.